# French
# Horn
# Discography

RECENT TITLES IN
DISCOGRAPHIES
*Series Editor: Michael Gray*

International Discography of Women Composers
*Aaron I. Cohen, compiler*

Walter Legge: A Discography
*Alan Sanders, compiler*

The Rudy Vallee Discography
*Larry F. Kiner, compiler*

Rockin' the Classics and Classicizin' the Rock:
A Selectively Annotated Discography
*Janell R. Duxbury*

The American 45 and 78 RPM Record Dating Guide, 1940-1959
*William R. Daniels*

The Johnny Cash Discography
*John L. Smith, compiler*

A Discography of Hindustani and Karnatic Music
*Michael S. Kinnear, compiler*

Women in Jazz
*Jan Leder, compiler*

The King Labels: A Discography
*Michel Ruppli, compiler*

Thank You Music Lovers:
A Bio-Discography of Spike Jones and His City Slickers, 1941-1965
*Jack Mirtle, compiler*

John McCormack: A Comprehensive Discography
*Paul W. Worth and Jim Cartwright, compilers*

Count Basie: A Bio-Discography
*Chris Sheridan, compiler*

The Symphonies of Gustav Mahler
*Lewis M. Smoley, compiler*

V-Discs: First Supplement
*Richard S. Sears, compiler*

# French
# Horn
# Discography

*Compiled by*
## Michael Hernon

Discographies, Number 24

GREENWOOD PRESS
New York • Westport, Connecticut • London

LIBRARY OF CONGRESS CATALOGING-IN-PUBLICATION DATA

Hernon, Michael, 1940-
  French horn discography.

  (Discographies, ISSN 0192-334X ; no. 24)
  Includes indexes.
  1. Horn music—Discography. 2. Chamber music—
Discography. 3. Concertos (Horn)—Discography.
I. Title. II. Series.
ML156.4.H7H5  1986      016.7899'12841      86-22817
ISBN 0-313-25434-6 (lib. bdg. : alk. paper)

Library of Congress Catalog Card Number: 86-22817
ISBN: 0-313-25434-6
ISSN: 0192-334X

First published in 1986

Greenwood Press, Inc.
88 Post Road West, Westport, Connecticut 06881

Printed in the United States of America

The paper used in this book complies with the
Permanent Paper Standard issued by the National
Information Standards Organization (Z39.48-1984).

10 9 8 7 6 5 4 3 2 1

IN MEMORY OF
DR. EDWARD JOSEPH PEASE

# Contents

# Preface

This horn discography began as a modest project for use in my own studio. Originally, I was seeking solo horn recordings currently available through the Schwann catalog. The number of entries rapidly exceeded my pre-project expectations, however, and in time, the scope of the discography was expanded to include not only solo horn recordings, but recordings of chamber music in which the horn was found. Further, it was expanded to include other sources for current as well as out-of-print recordings.

Initially, I endeavored to group those ensembles using horn as one of the instruments according to the number of instruments in the ensemble, i.e., sextets, septets, octets, etc., with the quintets being grouped as woodwind or brass quintets. This proved to be too much of a problem, though, especially with the brass quintets. It was not always possible to determine, particularly with the Baroque pieces, if the original instrumentation was being used, or if additional instruments were being added to double certain lines.

Therefore, I have elected to use the following groupings: Solo Horn, the category featuring the single instrument with some form of accompaniment; Two Horns, a category that features two horns with some form of accompaniment; and Multiple Horns, including recordings with three or more horns. The Horn Duos and Horn Trios categories feature the horn in combination with one or two other instruments, while Brass Ensemble comprises recordings of brass ensembles numbering as few as four and continuing upwards. Some recordings in this category clearly feature the brass but include other instruments such as percussion or a keyboard instrument.

Woodwind Ensemble and Horn and Strings are handled similarly and Mixed Ensemble contains recordings where several instrumental families are represented on a more or less equal basis. Other categories include Horn and Voice, where horn, voice and other instruments may be featured. Instrumentation is indicated in the title, where possible, in all

ensemble listings. Following the ten categories of the discography proper are separate indexes to composers, hornists,
and brass, woodwind, and mixed ensembles.

The discography includes, in many instances, recordings
that may not be currently available from the record company
itself, but may be found through various jobbers. Also,
multiple listings do appear where it is clear that one is
dealing with a reissue of the same performance from the same
record company under a different record number, as well as
instances where the same recording is being released under a
different label; this may prove of value to the collector
who is looking for a particular recording. Given the multi-
plicity of reissues and combinations thereof, it was imprac-
tical to attempt to arrange the discography according to
chronology.

The sources used to compile this discography were the
August and November 1984 issues of the Schwann Catalog, the
1985 Schwann Artist Issue, Musical Heritage Society Catalog,
The Horn Call, which is the official journal of the Inter-
national Horn Society, International Trumpet Guild Journal,
The Hornist's Compendium by John R. Brisbin, Horn Biblio-
graphie by Bernhard Bruchle, The Horn by Robin Gregory,
A Teacher's Guide to the Literature of Brass Instruments by
Mary Rasmussen, Trumpet Discography, Volume III, Brass En-
sembles by Alvin Lowrey, Notes, which is the journal of the
Music Library Association, Maleady: Index to Record and
Cassette Reviews, and Myers: Index to Record Reviews.

Because the discography is not limited to what is listed
in the current Schwann Catalog, it provides a kind of his-
torical overview of the horn repertory that has been viewed
as most important or, at least, most marketable. It is
interesting to note that certain compositions have been
recorded by many performers numerous times, while many de-
serving works have received sparing attention.

The format of the discography provides information on the
composer, including life dates when possible, title of composition, performer (when cited), ensemble (when relevant
and cited), record label and number, and up to six review
sources where available. The latter cite the journal, date,
and page, prefixed by a number indicating the quality of the
performance as judged by the reviewer. Four numbers are
used: 1 indicates good to excellent; 2 indicates fair or
average; 3 indicates poor or below average; and 4 indicates
that the review is not conclusive in its opinion. The abbreviations used for record labels and journals are explained
in lists immediately following this preface. The composer,
composer's life dates, and composition title are entered
only once in each chapter instrument grouping, with the recordings by particular hornists and ensembles following.
Under each composition, the hornist/s is entered once.

# PREFACE

Recorded compositions where the hornist/s is not cited will
be entered immediately following the citing of the composition, with the known hornist/s following in alphabetical
order.

Example:

Mozart, W. A. (1756-1791)
     Concerti (4) for Horn
          Classics for Pleasure CFP 148
          Baumann, Hermann
               Tel 64230
                    2-GR 10-79 P. 643
                    1-HFN 8-79 P. 109
               Tel Dec 641272 AW

Here we have three recordings of the Mozart four horn
concerti. The hornist on the Classics for Pleasure label
is unknown. The next entry is a recording of the Mozart
four-horn concerti by Hermann Baumann. Only the hornist,
record label, and reviews are cited. The third entry is
another Baumann recording of the Mozart four-horn concerti.
No reviews were found. As Baumann was already cited in the
previous entry, only the record label and number were
entered.

Care has been taken to correct obvious typographical
errors as they were encountered in the various sources.
If the compiler was unable conclusively to verify an error,
the recording was cited as found.

Finally, some acknowledgments are in order. First, I
wish to thank Shirley Marie Watts, music librarian at Van-
derbilt University, for her kind assistance, and the library
staff at The University of Tennessee at Martin for their
assistance and cooperation.

I wish to thank Professor Phil Miller, Director of Fac-
ulty Research, and The University of Tennessee at Martin
for having provided financial assistance in this project.
I must also thank Dr. Jim Clark, Professor of Math and
Computer Science at The University of Tennessee at Martin,
who freely gave of his time and knowledge of computers and
computer software in assisting me with this project. Lastly
and most importantly, I wish to express my deep appreciation
to my wife, Bonnie, who has spent many hours assisting me
in this project.

# Record Label Abbreviations

This list only includes record labels that are commonly abbreviated and are so found in the discography. Multiple abbreviations for companies, which may be found, normally pertain to different series issued by the same company.

| | |
|---|---|
| AAS | Award Artist Series |
| ARA | Arabesque |
| ARL | RCA |
| AS | American Society |
| Cap | Capitol |
| CAP | Caprice |
| CBC | Chestnut Brass Company |
| CBC SM | Canadian Broadcasting Corporation |
| CCC | Orion |
| CRD | Continental Record Distributors |
| CRDD | Continental Record Distributors |
| CRI | Composers Recordings |
| CRYS | Crystal |
| CSP | Columbia |
| DC | Desto |
| DG | Deutsche Grammophon |
| DGG | Geutsche Grammophon Gesellschaft |

# RECORD LABEL ABBREVIATIONS

| | |
|---|---|
| ERA | Eastman Rochester Archives |
| ERS | Entr'acte Recording Society |
| HMV | His Master's Voice |
| MDG | EMI |
| MHS | Musical Heritage Society |
| MMO | Music Minus One |
| MON | Monitor |
| New W | New World |
| Olymp | Olympic |
| ORS | Orion |
| PLE | Peters |
| PRO | Pro Arte Sinfonia |
| PYE GSGC | Golden Guinea |
| QUIN | Quintessance |
| RAV | Ravenna |
| RCI | Radio Canada International |
| REM | Remington |
| RTV | Ljubljana |
| SPA | Society of Participating Artists |
| SRS | Serenus |
| TEL | Telefunken |
| TV | Turnabout |
| TVS | Turnabout |
| UMBC | University of Minnesota Brass Choir |
| VAN | Vanguard |
| VAR/SARA | Varese/Sarabande |
| VIC | Victrola |
| WGS | Westminister |
| WISA | WISA Grammofon A. B. |

# Periodical Abbreviations

| | |
|---|---|
| AM | Atlantic Monthly |
| AMR | The American Recorder |
| AR | The American Record Guide |
| AU | Audio |
| CR | Consumer Research Bulletin |
| CU | Consumer Reports |
| DI | Disques |
| ET | Etude |
| FF | Fanfare |
| FU | Fugue |
| GR | Gramophone |
| GS | Gramophone Shop Supplement |
| HA | Harper's Magazine |
| HF | High Fidelity |
| HFN | HI-Fi News & Record Review |
| HSR | Hi-Fi/ Stereo Review |
| IN | Instrumentalist |
| JR | Just Records |
| LJ | Library Journal |
| MA | Musical America |

| | |
|---|---|
| MG | Monthly Guide to Recorded Music |
| MH | HI-FI Music at Home |
| MJ | Music Journal |
| ML | Monthly Letter from EMG |
| MM | Music & Musicians |
| MQ | Musical Quarterly |
| MT | Musical Times |
| MUM | Music Magazine |
| NA | The Nation |
| NR | The New Records |
| NRE | New Republic |
| NS | New Statesman & Nation |
| NYT | New York Times |
| ON | Opera News |
| OR | On The Record |
| OV | Ovation |
| PP | Pan Pipes of Sigma Alpha Iota |
| RR | Record Review |
| R&R | Records & Recordings |
| SFC | San Francisco Examiner & Chronicle |
| SR | Saturday Review/World |
| ST | Stereo Review |
| STR | Stradivarius |

# French
# Horn
# Discography

# Solo Horn

Abbott, Alan
    Alla Caccia
        James, Ifor
            PYE GSGC 14087
        Kavalovski, Charles
            MHS 3547
                1-FF 9-77 P. 69
Adler, Samuel (1928-     )
    Sonata for Horn & Piano
        Schaberg, Roy
            Coronet 3039
Agthe, Federico (1790-1873)
    Grand Concerto
        Ceccarossi, Domenico
            Magic Horn DC 191110/2
Akimenko, Fyodor (1876-1945)
    Melody, Op. 16
        Stagliano, James
            Sinequan PLS 8
Albinoni, Tomaso (1671-1750)
    Adagio in G
        Orval, Francis
            Disques Duchesne   DD 6044
Alfven, Hugo (1872-1960)
    Notturno Elegiaco, Op. 5
        Oien, Ingegard
            BIS 171
Amram, David (1930-     )
    Concerto for Horn (1966-68)
        Herrick, Jack
            Soundmark-Denver
Archer, Violet (1913-     )
    Sonata for Horn & Piano (1965)
        Del Vescovo
            Radio Canada International 412
                1-FF 3/4-80 P. 36
Arnold, Malcolm (1921-     )
    Fantasy for Horn, Op. 88 (1966)
        Greer, Lowell
            Coronet LPS 3100
                1-FF 9/10-82 P. 455
                2-NR 9-82 P. 9

Atterberg, Kurt (1887-1974)
    Horn Konsert in a-moll, Op. 28
        Linder, Albert
            Caprice CAP 1144
Babell, William (1690-1723)
    Sonata in G
        Ritzkowsky, Johannes
            Schwann 0 610
Bach/ Baller (1685-1750)
    Jesus Bleibet Meine Freude
        Fensterer, Manfred
            M. Fensterer
Bach, J. S.
    Partita in Bb, S 825
        De Rosa
            Capitol P 8582
                1-GR 11-62 P. 59
                2-HSR 8-62 P. 59
                3-LJ 10-1-62 P. 3430
                3-NYT 5-27-62 P. X17
                3-SR 6-30-62 P. 42
    Suite for Cello BWV 1009
        Ritzkowsky, Johannes
            Schwann 0 610
Bakaleinikov, Vladimir (1885-1953)
    Cavatina
        Chambers, James
            Award Artist Series AAS 704
Banks, Don (1923-    )
    Concerto (1965)
        Tuckwell, Barry
            Argo ZRG-726
                1-GR 8-75 P. 315
                1-HF 6-76 P. 90
                1-ML 8-75 P. 5
                1-NR 2-76 P. 4
                2-SR 1-24-76 P. 53
Barbier, Rene (1890-    )
    Concerto for Horn & Orchestra
        Orval, Francis
            Alpha DMB F275
Bartok/ Eger
    From "For Children" # 17 & # 33
        Eger, Joseph
            Victor LM 2146
                2-AR 4-58 P. 357
                4-AU 1-58 P. 48
                2-CR 2-58 P. 37
                2-HF 1-58 P. 66
                1-LJ 5-15-58 P. 1527
                4-MA 12-1-57 P. 28
Beethoven, L. Van (1770-1827)
    Scherzo from Septet, Op. 20
        Jones, Mason
            MMO 6010
    Sonata, Op. 17
        Barboteu, Georges
            Arion 30 A111

Beethoven, L. Van (Cont'd)
    Sonata, Op. 17 (Cont'd)
        Baumann, Hermann
            Telefunken SAWT 9547
                1-AU 8-70 P. 54
                1-GR 7-70 P. 179
                2-HF 10-70 P. 94
                1-NR 8-70 P. 6
                2-SR 6-27-70 P. 52
                1-ST 12-70 P. 86
        Bloom, Myron
            DG 2531293 PSI
                2-FF 7/8-81 P. 63
                2-GR 3-81 P. 1208
                4-MG 5-81 P. 10
                2-NR 7-81 P. 8
                3-ST 10-81 P. 118
        Brain, Dennis
            Disco Corp. IGI 370
                4-HF 5-81 P. 64
                1-NR 4-81 P. 7
            Seraphim M60040 (MD)
                1-GR 10-66 P. 225
                1-HSR 10-67 P. 159
                1-ML 11-66 P. 7
                1-NR 9-67 P. 13
                1-NYT 8-6-67 P. D17
                1-SR 5-27-67 P. 59
            EMI/HMV  RLS 7701
        Bujanovski, V.
            Melodiya D13175-6
            Melodiya C10-11037-38
        Cazalet, Andre
            Ades 14028 PSI
                1-FF 3/4-83 P. 335
        Ceccarossi, Domenico
            Angelicum- Milano LPA 5937
            MHS 1808
        Civil, Alan
            Decca SXL 6170
            MHS 4500
                1-GR 8-79 P. 347
        Coursier, Gilbert
            London 50033
                2-AR 10-55 P. 30
                2-CR 1-55 P. 104
                2-GR 11-54 P. 252
                2-HF 10-55 P. 86
                3-ML 10-54 P. 10
                1-MR 5-55 P. 179
        Damm, Peter
            Eterna 8 25 990
        Eger, Joseph
            Victor LSC-2420
                1-AR 1-61 P. 390
                1-HF 2-61 P. 66
                2-HSR 2-61 P. 66
                2-NR 12-60 P. 11
                2-SR 11-26-60 P. 54

Beethoven, L. Van (Cont'd)
    Sonata, Op. 17 (Cont'd)
        Fitzpatrick, Horace
           Golden Crest GC 4014
               2-LJ 2-15-60 P. 786
               2-NYT 4-26-59 P. X15
               1-SR 4-25-59 P. 50
        Klanska, Vladimira
           Panton 8111 0046
        Linder, Albert
           BIS 47
               3-FF 7/8-77 P. 104
               1-HFN 12-77 P. 168
               2-R&R 11-77 P. 85
               1-SFC 11-12-78 P. 49
        Molnar, Joseph
           VDE 3001
        Rife, Jean
           Titanic 94
        Schaberg, Roy
           Coronet 3039
        Seifert Gerd
           DGG 272 0015
           Vox SVBX-580
               2-NR 7-69 P. 8
        Stagliano, James
           Boston Records CMS L-200
               2-HF 9/10-53 P. 76
               1-NR 3-53 P. 15
               2-NYT 20-26-52 P. X10
        Tarjani, Ferenc
           Hungaroton 12473
           Qualiton SLPX-11354
               2-GR 3-69 P. 1302
               2-ML 2-69 P. 12
               1-ST 6-72 P. 86
        Tuckwell, Barry
           Decca SXL 6717
           London CS-6938
               2-GR 8-75 P. 342
               1-HF 4-77 P. 118
               1-ML 8-75 P. 7
               2-NR 4-77 P. 115
               1-ST 3-77 P. 149
Bellonci/Maxamilian Josef Leidesdorf
    Sonate pour Pianoforte et Cor, Op. 164
        Pizka, Hans
           Hans Pizka Editions HPE CM 1001
Bentzon, Niels (1919-    )
    Sonata for Horn & Piano, Op. 47 (1947)
        Lansky-Otto, Ib
           BIS LP 204
               2-FF 1/2-84 P. 303
               2-MG 1-84 P. 12
Berge, Sigurd
    Horn Call (1972)
        Belfrage, Bengt
           (Sweden) Fermat F1PS 49

Bernstein, Leonard (1918-    )
     Elegy for Mippy I
               Cerminaro, John
                    CRYS S375
               Eger, Joseph
                    Victor LM 2146
                         2-AR 4-58 P. 357
                         4-AU 1-58 P. 48
                         2-CR 2-58 P. 37
                         2-HF 1-58 P. 66
                         1-LJ 5-15-58 P. 1527
                         4-MA 12-1-57 P. 28
Beversdorf, Thomas (1924-1981)
     Sonata for Horn and Piano, Op. 1 (1945)
               Beversdorf, Thomas
                    Coronet 3009
Blanc, A.
     Sonate pour Cor et Piano, Op. 43
               Pizka, Hans
                    Hans Pizka Edition HPE CM 1001
Borodin/ Baumann
     Serenad
               Baumann, Hermann
                    Firebird K 28C-211
Bozza, Eugene (1905-    )
     En Foret, Op. 40
               Cerminaro, John
                    CRYS S 375
               Farkas, Phil
                    Coronet 1293M
                         1-NR 2-70 P. 7
               Greer, Lowell
                    CRYS S 374
                         4-FF 7/8-83 P. 282
                         2-NR 7-83 P. 3
               James, Ifor
                    PYE GSGC 14140
Bradford-Anderson
     March, in Canon
               Chambers, James
                    Award Artist Series AAS 704
Brahms, Johannes (1833-1897)
     Scherzo from Serenade in D, Op. 11
               Jones, Mason
                    MMO 6010
Braun, Yehezkel
     Sonata (1969)
               Rimon, Meir
                    RCA YJRL 1-0007
Bucchi, Annibale
     Concerto in D (1898)
               Ceccarossi, Domenico
                    Magic Horn DC 191110/2
Bucchi, Valentino (1916-1976)
     3 Lieder
               Ceccarossi, Domenico
                    Magic Horn DC 191110/2

Bujanovski, V.
      Solo Sonata # 1
            Bujanovski, V.
                  Melodiya C10-16969-70
Busser, Henri (1872-1973)
      Cantecor, Op. 77
            Greer, Lowell
                  CRYS S 374
                        4-FF 7/8-83 P. 282
                        2-NR 7-83 P. 3
      La Chasse de Saint Hubert, Op. 99
            Ceccarossi, Domenico
                  RCA SL 20257
            Linder, Albert
                  Fermat FLPS 53
Ceccarossi, Domenico
      Caprices, Ten for Horn
            Ceccarossi, Domenico
                  MHS 3815
                        2-FF 1 & 2-79 P. 33
      Caprices, # 2 & # 6
            Ceccarossi, Domenico
                  Angelicum- Milano LPA 5937
                  MHS 1808
Chabrier, Emmanuel (1841-1894)
      Larghetto for Horn & Orchestra
            Bourgue, Daniel
                  Peters PLE-009
                        1-FF 7/8-78 P. 105
            Jones, Mason
                  CSP 91 A 02033
                  Columbia ML 4629
                        1-AR 3-53 P. 203
                        1-GS 2-53 P. 7
                        1-HF 9/10-53 P. 77
                        1-MA 4-15-53 P. 18
                        1-NR 3-53 P. 4
            Wekre, Froydis Ree
                  CRYS S 377
Chailly, Luciano (1920-     )
      Dittico
            Ceccarossi, Domenico
                  MHS 3961
Charpentier, Jacques
      Pour Diane
            Greer, Lowell
                  CRYS S 374
                        4-FF 7/8-83 P. 282
                        2-NR 7-83 P. 3
Cherubini, Luigi (1760-1842)
      Etude # 2 for Horn & Strings
            Tuckwell, Barry
                  L'Oiseau Lyre OL 227
                        2-AR 2-66 P. 513
                        1-GR 4-65 P. 482
                        1-HF 3-66 P. 95
                        1-HSR 2-66 P. 104
                        1-ML 5-65 P. 10

Cherubini, Luigi (Cont'd)
    Sonatas (2) for Horn & Strings
        Baumann, Hermann
            ARA 8084; 9084
                2-AR 3-82 P. 39
                4-NR 12-81 P. 11
            BASF 25 21889-9
        Bujanovski, V.
            Melodiya D 025809-10
        Ceccarossi, Domenico
            Audio Fidelity FCS 50037
        Greer, Lowell
            Coronet 3122
                1-FF 11/12-83 P. 375
                1-NR 3-84 P. 5
    Sonata # 2 in F for Horn & Strings
        Tuckwell, Barry
            Angel S 36996
                1-GR 8-74 P. 369
                1-HF 7-74 P. 112
                1-ML 7-74 P. 7
                2-NR 6-74 P. 5
                1-ST 8-74 P. 124
        Wekre, Froydis Ree
            CRYS S 377
Chevreuille, Raymond (1901-1976)
    Concerto, Op. 43(1949)
        Carael, Georges
            (Belgian) Decca 143 369
Clerisse, Robert (1899-1973)
    Chant sans Paroles
        Chambers, James
            Award Artists Series AAS 704
Cooke, Arnold (1906-   )
    Rondo in Bb (1950)
        Greer, Lowell
            Coronet LPS 3100
                1-FF 9/10-82 P. 455
                2-NR 9-82 P. 9
Corelli, Arcangelo (1653-1713)
    Sonata in F, Op. 5 # 5
        Rimon, Meir
            RCA YJRL 1-0007
        Schaberg, Roy
            Coronet 1257
    Sonata in d, Op. 5 # 7
        James, Ifor
            PYE GSGC 14140
    Sonata in F, Op. 5 # 10
        Neal, Caswell
            Desto DC 7199
                3-FF 11/12-80 P. 214
Corelli, Arcangelo/ M. Franco
    Sonata, Op. 10 # 5
        Maes, Ernest
            Duchesne DD 6039

Corette, Michel (1709-1795)
   7 Concertos Comiques
      Magnardi, Jacky
         Philips PHC 9012
            1-AR 1-67 P. 400
            4-AU 2-67 P. 50
            1-HF 10-66 P. 169
            1-HSR 10-66 P. 132
            2-NR 3-67 P. 5
            2-NYT 10-2-66 P. D30
   Concerto in C " La Choisy "
      Bourgue, Daniel
         Peters PLE 009
            1-FF 7/8-78 P. 105
      Molnar, Joseph
         Evasion LPE 118
Cortese, Luigi (1899-1976)
   Sonata in Bb (1958)
      Ceccarossi, Domenico
         RCA SL 20257
Cui, Cesar (1835-1918)
   Moment Musical Op. 50 # 1
      Stagliano, James
         Sinequan PLS 8
   Perpetual Motion
      Wekre, Froydis Ree
         CRYS S 126
Czerny, Carl (1791-1857)
   Andante & Polacca
      Hermansson, Soeren
         Thorofon Capella MTH 257
Daetwyler, Jean (1907-     )
   Concerto pour Cor des Alpes
      Molnar, Joseph
         Evasion EB 100-808
Dahl, Ingolf (1912-1970)
   Allegro & Arioso (1942)
      Creech, Robert
         CBC SM 139
Damase, Jean- Michel (1928-     )
   Berceuse, Op. 19
      Wekre, Froydis Ree
         Varese Int. VS 81017
Danzi, Franz (1763-1826)
   Sonata in e, Op. 44
      Ceccarossi, Domenico
         RCA SL 20257
   Sonata Concertante in e
      Hefti, Jakob
         Disco Jecklin 542
   Concerto in E
      Baumann, Hermann
         Teldec 6 3505.7
         Tel 641288
            1-HFN 3-81 P. 95
         Telefunken TK 11540/1-2

Danzi, Franz (Cont'd)
      Concerto in E (Cont'd)
            Baumann, Hermann (Cont'd)
                  Telefunken TK 11540/1-2
                        1-GR 2-74 P. 1575
                        1-R&R 12-73 P. 64
                  Teldec SAT 22516
                        2-HF 2-71 P. 104
                        1-NR 9-70 P. 7
      Sonata in Eb for Horn, Op. 28
            Covert, John
                  Mark Records MC 37272
            Koch, Franz
                  SPA 29
            Tuckwell, Barry
                  Decca SXL 6717
                  London CS 6938
                        2-GR 8-75 P. 342
                        1-HF 4-77 P. 118
                        1-ML 8-75 P. 7
                        2-NR 4-77 P. 15
                        1-ST 3-77 P. 149
      Sonata for Horn, Op. 44
            Koch, Franz
                  SPA 29
David, Gyula (1913-1977)
      Concerto for Horn & Orchestra (1970)
            Tarjani, Ferenc
                  Hungaroton SLPX-11699
                        4-NR 7-75 P.8
Domazlicky, Frantisek (1913-    )
      Concerto for Horn
                  Supraphon 110 1466 G
Dukas, Paul (1865-1935)
      Villanelle for Horn & Piano
            Bourgue, Daniel
                  Peters PLE 009
                        1-FF 7/8-78 P. 105
                  REM 10924
            Brain, Dennis
                  ARA 8071; 9071
                        4-HF 5-81 P. 64
                        1-NR 11-80 P. 8
                  HMV DV 3300 (78rpm)
                  Da Capo IC 047-01 242
                  EMI/HMV RLS 7701
                  BBC REGL 352
                  Seraphim 60040
                        1-GR 10-66 P. 225
                        1-HF 7-67 P. 80
                        1-HSR 10-67 P. 159
                        1-ML 11-66 P. 7
                        1-NR 9-67 P. 13
                        1-NYT 8-6-67 P. D17
            Bujanovski, V.
                  Melodiya D 025809-10
                  Melodiya CM 02363-64
            Ceccarossi, Domenico
                  RCA SL 20257

11

Dukas, Paul (Cont'd)
   Damm, Peter
     Eterna 8 25 990
   Del Vescovo, Pierre
     Erato STU 71286
     Erato STU 71252
   Devemy, Jean
     Pathe X 98067 (78 rpm)
   Friedrich, Adam
     Qualiton SLPX 11672
   Greer, Lowell
     CRYS S 374
       4-FF 7/8-83 P. 282
       2-NR 7-83 P. 3
   Hermansson, Soeren
     Thorofon Capella MTH 257
   Habik, Josef
     Supraph 20003
   James, Ifor
     PYE GSGC 14140
   Kavalovski, Charles
     MHS 3547
       1-FF 9-77 P. 69
   Stagliano, James
     Boston B 212
     Boston 1009
     Sinequan PLS 8
   Thevet, Lucien
     London LD 9206
   Wekre, Froydis Ree
     Varese Int. VS 81017
Durko, Zsolt (1934- )
  Iconogrphy # 2 for Horn & Chamber Ensemble
   Tarjani, Ferenc
     Hungariton SLPX 11607
  Symbols for Horn & Piano (1968-9)
   Tarjani, Ferenc
     Qualiton SLPX 11363
Eklund, Hans (1927- )
  Horn Concerto
   Linder, Albert
     Caprice 1144
Faure, Gabriel (1845-1924)
  Apres un Reve, Op. 7 #1
   Cerminaro, John
     CRYS S 376
   Stagliano, James
     Sinequan PLS 8
   Wekre, Froydis Ree
     Varese Int. VS 81017
Fick, Peter Johann ( ?  -1743)
  Concerto in Eb for Horn & Strings
   Damm, Peter
     Eterna 8 27 203
Finger, Gottfried (1660-1743)
  Sonata in G
   Damm, Peter
     Eterna 8 27 572

Flosman, Oldrich (1925-    )
    Concerto (1970)
        Petr, Milos
                Panton 11 0268
Foerster, Cristoph (1693-1745)
    Concerto in Eb for Horn & Strings
        Friedrich, Adam
                Qualiton SLPX 12118
                        1-FF 5/6-81 P. 171
                        1-NR 2-81 P. 6
        Greer, Lowell
                Coronet 3122
                        1-FF 11/12-83 P. 375
                        1-NR 3-84 P. 5
        Tuckwell, Barry
                Angel S 36996
                        1-GR 8-74 P. 369
                        1-HF 7-74 P. 112
    Concerto for Waldhorn & Orchestra
        Baumann, Hermann
                Teldec AW 6 41932
                        2-CR 9-76 P. 43
                        1-NR 2-76 P. 15
Francaix, Jean (1912-    )
    Canon in Octave
        Farkas, Phil
                Coronet 1293M
                        1-NR 2-70 P. 7
        Hustis, Gregory
                CRYS S 378
        Jones, Mason
                MMO 8084
    Divertimento (1959)
        Greer, Lowell
                Coronet LPS 3100
                        1-FF 9/10-82 P. 455
                        2-NR 9/82 P. 9
        Wekre, Froydis Ree
                Varese Int. VS 81017
Franco, M.
    Divertimento for Horn & Strings
        Maes, Ernest
                Duchesne DD 6039
Franz, Robert (1815-1892)
    Delight of Melancholy, Op. 1 #1
        Yanich, Milan
                Helden HR 109/10
                        2-FF 9/10-80 P. 283
Fricker, Peter (1921-    )
    Sonata, Op. 24
        James, Ifor
                PYE GSGC 14087
Frumerie, Gunnar De (1908-    )
    Concerto for Horn & Orchestra, Op. 70
        Lansky-Otto, Ib
                Caprice CAP 1103

Frumerie, Gunnar De (Cont'd)
    Monologue from Concerto for Horn & Orchestra, Op. 70
        Belfrage, Bengt
           (Sweden) Fermat FLPS 49
Gagnebin, Henri (1886-1977)
    Aubade
        Greer, Lowell
           CRYS S 374
               4-FF 7/8-83 P. 282
               2-NR 7-83 P. 3
Gallay, J. F. (1795-1864)
    Unmeasured Preludes
        Farkas, Phil
           Coronet 1293M
               1-NR 2-70 P. 7
Gershwin, George (1898-1937)
    Prelude # 2
        Eger, Joseph
           Victor LM 2146
               2-AR 4-58 P. 357
               4-AU 1-58 P. 48
               2-CR 2-58 P. 37
               2-HF 1-58 P. 66
               1-LJ 5-15-58 P. 1527
               4-MA 12-1-57 P. 28
Glaser, Werner (1910-    )
    Dialogue for Horn & Organ (1977)
        Linder, Albert
           Fermat FLPS 53
Glazunov, Alexander (1865-1936)
    Reverie, Op. 24
        Brain, Aubrey
           Opal 805
         Farkas, Phil
           Coronet 1293M
               1-NR 2-70 P. 7
        Linder, Albert
           Fermat FLPS 53
    Reverie
        Jones, Mason
           MMO 6010
    Serenade # 2 for Horn & Strings
        Rimon, Meir
           CRYS S 507
               1-AU 12-83 P. 94
               2-CR 9-83 P. 43
               2-NR 7-83 P. 7
Gliere, Reinhold (1875-1956)
    Concerto for Horn, Op. 91
        Klishans, A.
           Melodiya 33C10
        Polekh, Valerie
           Classic Editions 3001
               3-NR 5-54 P. 6
               4-NYT 5-16-54 P. X9
               4-SR 5-29-54 P. 42
    Concerto for Horn, Op. 91 (mvts 2 & 3)
        Schaberg, Roy
           Coronet 1257

Gliere, Reinhold (Cont'd)
    Intermezzo, Op. 35, # 11
        Bloom, Myron
            MMO 8045
        Cerminaro, John
            CRYS S 375
        Farkas, Phil
            Coronet 1293M
                1-NR 2-70 P. 7
        Neal, Caswell
            Desto DC 7199
                3-FF 11/12-80 P. 214
        Stagliano, James
            Sinequan PLS 8
    Nocturne, Op. 35, # 10
        Stagliano, James
            Sinequan PLS 8
Grant, Parks (1910-    )
    Essay for Horn & Organ, Op. 25
        Jones, Mason
            Coronet S 2738
                4-NR 4-73 P. 8
Graziani, Ytzhak
    Variations on a Theme by Haydn
        Rimon, Meir
            CRYS S 506
            Hed Arzi- Ban 14212
Gretchaninov, Alexander (1864-1956)
    Lullaby, Op. 1, # 5
        Stagliano, James
            Sinequan PLS 8
Grieg, Edvard (1843-1907)
    Solveig's Song
        Yanich, Milan
            Helden HR 109/10
                2-FF 9/10-80 P. 283
    A Swan Op. 25, # 2
        Yanich, Milan
            Helden HR 109/10
                2-FF 9/10-80 P. 283
Guion/ Eger-Rosenthal
    Harmonica Player
        Eger, Joseph
            Victor LM 2146
                2-AR 4-58 P. 357
                4-AU 1-58 P. 48
                2-CR 2-58 P. 37
                2-HF 1-58 P. 66
                1-LJ 5-15-58 P. 1527
                4-MA 12-1-57 P. 28
Halpern, Eddie
    The Nigun of Rabbi Ytzhak
        Rimon, Meir
            CRYS S 506
Hamilton, Iain (1922-    )
    Sonata Notturna
        Hill, Douglas
            CRYS S 670

15

Hamilton, Iain (Cont'd)
    Sonata Notturna (Cont'd)
        Tuckwell, Barry
                Argo ZRG-5475
                        1-GR 11-66 P. 268
                        1-ML 11-66 P. 9
    Voyage for Horn & Orchestra (1970)
        Tuckwell, Barry
                CRI SD 280
                        4-AR 5-72 P. 413
                        1-NR 5-72 P. 8
Handel, G. F.  (1685-1759)
    Concerto for Oboe (Arranged for Horn & Organ)
        Ritzkowsky, Johannes
                Schwann 0 610
    Concerto Grosso # 2 In F
        Baumann, Hermann
                Teldec AW 6 41932
                        2-CR 9-76 P. 43
                        1-NR 2-76 P. 15
    Horn & Organ Concerto Grosso 29
        Baumann, Hermann
                Tel 642326
    I See a Huntsman
        Jones, Mason
                MMO 6010
Hartley, Walter S.  (1927-    )
    Sonorities II (1975)
        Smith, Calvin
                CRYS S 371
                        1-NR 6-76 P. 7
Haydn, Franz Joseph (1732-1809)
    Concerto
        Afanasiev, Boris
                Richesse Classique Musidisc RC 864
    Concerto in D
        Baumann, Hermann
                Telefunken SLT 43102
                        1-AU 7-69 P. 56
                        1-LJ 6-1-69 P. 2216
        Penzel, Erich
                Victrola VICS 1324
                        1-HSR 8-68 P. 82
                        1-LJ 6-15-69 P. 2447
        Tuckwell, Barry
                MHS 895
    Concerto # 1 in D
        Baumann, Hermann
                Teldec 6 35057
                Telefunken SAT 22516
                        2-HF 2-71 P. 104
                        1-NR 9-70 P. 7
                Tel 641288
                Tel 642326
                Telefunken TK 11540/1-2
                        1-GR 2-74 P. 1575
                        1-R&R 12-73 P. 64

Haydn, Franz Joseph (Cont'd)
        Concerto # 1 in D (Cont'd)
                Brain, Alfred
                        Capitol P. 8137
                                2-CR 7-51 P. 31
                                2-GS 7-51 P. 3
                                1-HF 9/10-52 P. 61
                                2-ML 8-51 P. 5
                                3-NS 9-8-51 P. 263
                Cecere, Anthony
                        Peters PLE 060
                                2-AR 12-78 P. 29
                                2-FF 11/12-78 P. 71
                Penzel, Erich
                        Quin 7124
                        BASF BAC 3005
                                1-GR 7-74 P. 205
                                1-R&R 6-74 P. 41
                Smith, Martin
                        Turnabout QTVS 34646
                Stolzinger, Ernst
                        Pirouette JAS 19010
                                1-AU 9-67 P. 58
                                4-NR 6-67 P. 8
                Tarjani, Ferenc
                        Fidelio 3317
                        Qualiton SLPX 11513
                                1-GR 10-72 P. 693
                                1-HF 11-72 P. 77
                                1-ML 9-72 P. 6
                                1-NR 3-73 P. 6
                Tuckwell, Barry
                        Angel SZ 37569
                                1-GR 10-79 P. 639
                                3-ML 12-79 P. 7
                                2-NR 11-79 P. 4
                                1-NYT 12-2-79 P. D23
                                1-ST 1-80 P. 95
                        Argo 5498
                                1-GR 5-82 P. 1486
                                1-HFN 6-82 P. 74
                        Decca SPA 393
                        London STS 15546
                Van Woudenberg, Adriaan
                        Mercury SR 90396
                                2-AR 6-55 P. 582
                                2-HF 6-65 P. 70
                                2-HSR 7-65 P. 69
                                1-NR 3-65 P. 7
        Concerto # 2 in D
                Arnold, Karl
                        Murray Hill Stereo 2937
                        Turnabout TV 34031-S
                                1-GR 3-66 P. 456
                                3-HF 5-66 P. 94
                                2-LJ 9-15-66 P. 4083
                                2-ML 3-66 P. 7

Haydn, Franz Joseph (Cont'd)
    Concerto # 2 in D (Cont'd)
        Arnold, Karl (Cont'd)
            Vox DL 480
                2-AR 5-60 P. 279
                4-AU 3-60 P. 48
                1-NR 5-60 P. 7
                2-SR 2-27-60 P. 50
        Baumann, Hermann
            Teldec 6 35057
            Telefunken SLT 43102
                1-AU 7-69 P. 56
                1-LJ 6-1-69 P. 2216
                1-NR 2-69 P. 8
            Telefunken TK 11540/1-2
                1-GR 2-74 P. 1575
                1-R&R 12-73 P. 64
        Brain, Alfred
            Capitol P. 8137
                2-CR 7-51 P. 31
                2-GS 7-51 P. 3
                1-HF 9/10-52 P. 61
                2-ML 8-51 P. 5
                3-NS 9-8-51 P. 263
        Ceccarossi, Domenico
            Audio Fidelity FCS 50 037
        Falout, Joze
            RTV Ljubljana LD 0448
        Lind, Rolf
            DG 198651
            DG Archiv ARC 3151
                1-GR 1-61 P. 383
                2-MA 9-61 P. 38
                2-ML 12-60 P. 9
                1-NR 9-61 P. 2
                1-SR 6-24-61 P. 36
        Penzel, Erich
            Electrola C 047-50 801
            Mace 9039
                1-HF 2-67 P. 88
                2-NR 1-67 P. 5
        Tarjani, Ferenc
            Fidelio 3317
            Qualiton SLPX 11513
                1-GR 10-72 P. 693
                1-HF 11-72 P. 77
                1-ML 9-72 P. 6
                1-NR 3-73 P. 6
        Tuckwell, Barry
            Angel SZ 37569
                1-GR 10-79 P. 639
                3-ML 12-79 P. 7
                2-NR 11-79 P. 4
                1-NYT 12-2-79 P. D23
                1-ST 1-80 P. 95

Haydn, Franz Joseph (Cont'd)
      Concerto # 2 in D (Cont'd)
            Tuckwell, Barry (Cont'd)
                  Argo 5498
                        1-GR 5-82 P. 1486
                        1-HFN 6-82 P. 74
                        1-AR 5-67 P. 781
                        1-GR 11-66 P. 260
                        1-HF 7-67 P. 72
                        1-ML 12-66 P. 7
Haydn, Michael (1737-1806)
      Concerto in D
            Baumann, Hermann
                  Telefunken 6 42418 AW
                        1-FF 11/12-80 P. 214
                        1-NR 2-81 P. 6
            Barboteu, Georges
                  MHS 720
                        1-ML 3-66 P. 7
            Bourgue, Daniel
                  Peters PCE 030
                        1-FF 7/8-78 P. 41
                        1-SFC 6-25-78 P. 61
            Tuckwell, Barry
                  Angel SZ 37569
                        1-GR 10-79 P. 639
                        3-ML 12-79 P. 7
                        2-NR 11-79 P. 4
                        1-NYT 12-2-79 P. D23
                        1-ST 1-80 P. 95
                  Argo ZRG 543
                        1-AR 3-69 P. 562
                        1-GR 12-67 P. 321
                        2-NR 2-69 P. 8
                        1-ST 12-68 P. 134
Heiden, Bernhard (1910-    )
      Sonata for Horn and Piano (1939)
            Cerminaro, John
                  CRYS S 376
            Chambers, James
                  Award Artists Series AAS 704
            Neal, Caswell
                  Desto 7206
                        1-FF 5/6-82 P. 154
                        1-SFC 2-28-82 P. 18
            Kavalovski, Charles
                  MHS 3547
                        1-FF 9-77 P. 69
Heise, Peter Arnold (1830-1879)
      Fantaistyke # 2
            Lansky- Otto, Ib
                  BIS LP 204
                        2-FF 1/2-84 P. 303
                        2-MG 1-84 P. 12
Herberigs, Robert (1886-    )
      "Cyrano de Bergerac" (1912)
            Van Boczstael, J. B. Maurice
                  (Belgian) Decca 173.293

Hermann, Ralph
    Concerto for Horn
        Chambers, James
            Award Artist Series AAS 704
Hermanson, Ake (1923-    )
    Alarme, Op. 11 (1969)
        Lansky- Otto, Ib
            Caprice RIKS 17
Heussenstamm, George
    Etudes
            CRYS S 811
Hindemith, Paul (1895-1963)
    Concerto for Horn & Orchestra (1949)
        Brain, Dennis
            Angel S 35491
                4-AU 5-60 P. 51
                1-HSR 4-60 P. 61
                1-NR 3-60 P. 8
            EMI/HMV RLS 7701
        Bujanovski, V.
            Melodiya CM 02363-64
    Concertino for Horn & Orchestra
        Koch, Franz
            Period 515
                3-AR 2-51 P. 200
                3-GR 3-52 P. 226
                2-GS 1-51 P. 5
                3-ML 12-51 P. 4
                3-SR 12-30-50 P. 46
                2-SR 2-17-51 P. 45
    Sonata for Alto Horn (1943)
        Barrows, John
            Golden Crest GC 7034
                2-NYT 11-9-69 P. D39
        Bujanovski, V.
            Melodiya C 10 16969-70
        Ceccarossi, Domenico
            Angelicum- Milano STA 9044
        Hill, Douglas
            CRYS S 670
        Jones, Mason
            Columbia M 33971
                1-NR 7-76 P. 5
                1-NYT 6-25-76 P. C23
                1-ST 10-76 P. 123
    Sonata for Horn and Piano (1939)
        Bujanovski, V.
            Melodiya D 17355
        Ceccarossi, Domenico
            MHS 3961
            Pentaphon-Roma
        Cerminaro, John
            CRYS S 376
        James, Ifor
            PYE GSGC 14087

Hindemith, Paul (Cont'd)
    Sonata for Horn and Piano (1939) (Cont'd)
        Jones, Mason
                    Columbia M 33971
                            1-NYT 6-25-76 P. C23
                            1-ST 10-76 P. 123
            Lansky-Otto, Ib
                    Caprice Riks 17
            Penzel, Erich
                    Music Heritage OR H290
            Schaberg, Roy
                    Coronet 3039
    Sonatas (2) for Horn and Piano
        Neal, Caswell
                    Desto 7206
Hoddinot, Alyn (1929-    )
    Concerto for Horn, Op. 65
        Tuckwell, Barry
                    Decca SXL 6606
Homilius, Gottfried (1714-1785)
    Komm, Heilger Geist
        Damm, Peter
                    Eterna 8 27 572
    O Heiliger Geist
        Fensterer, Manfred
                    M. Fensterer
Hovhaness, Alan (1911-    )
    Artik, Op. 78 (1949)
        Greer, Lowell
                    Coronet 3122
                            1-FF 11/12-83 P. 375
                            1-NR 3-84 P. 5
        Rimon, Meir
                    CRYS S 507
                            1-AU 12-83 P. 94
                            2-CR 9-83 P. 43
D'Indy, Vincent (1851-1931)
    Andante Cantabile for Horn & Strings
        Bourgue, Daniel
                    Peters PLE 009
                            1-FF 7/8-78 P. 105
Jensen, Adolf (1837-1879)
    Press Thy Cheek Against My Own
        Yanich, Milan
                    Helden HR 109/10
                            2-FF 9/10-80 P. 283
    Row Gently Here, My Gondolier
        Yanich, Milan
                    Helden HR 109/10
                            2-FF 9/10-80 P. 283
Jones, Don
    Allegro for Horn and Piano
        Covert, John
                    Mark Records MC 37272

Jongen, Joseph (1873-1953)
      Lied (1899)
            Greer, Lowell
                  Coronet LPS 3100
                        1-FF 9/10-82 P. 455
                        2-NR 9-82 P. 9
Kalabis, Victor (1923-    )
      Variations for Horn & Piano, Op. 31 (1969)
            Petr, Milos
                  Supraphon 1 19 1053
Kalliwoda, Johann (1801-1866)
      Introduction & Rondo, Op. 51
            Baumann, Hermann
                  ARA 8084; 9084
                        2-AR 3-82 P. 39
                        4-NR 12-81 P. 11
                  BASF 25 21889-9
Koch, Erland Von (1910-    )
      Monologue # 6 (1975)
            Belfrage, Bengt
                  Fermat FLPS 49
            Linder, Albert
                  Fermat FLPS 53
Koechlin, Charles (1867-1950)
      Sonata for Horn and Piano, Op. 70
            Barboteu, Georges
                  Arion 30A 111
Koehler, Siegfried
      Sonata, Op. 32 (1966)
            Damm, Peter
                  Eterna 8 25 990
            Kavalovski, Charles
                  MHS 3547
                        1-FF 9-77 P. 69
Kogan, Lev
      Hassidic Rhapsody
            Rimon, Meir
                  CRYS S 506
      Tfila (Prayer)
            Rimon, Meir
                  CRYS S 506
Korn, Peter (1922-    )
      Concertino for Horn & Strings, Op. 15 (1952)
            Eger, Joseph
                  Westminister 17131
                        1-NR 3-68 P. 3
Kraft, William (1923-    )
      Evening Voluntaries
            Cerminaro, John
                  CRYS S 375
Krebs, Johann Ludwig (1713-1780)
      Wachet Auf
            Damm, Peter
                  Eterna 8 27 572
      Was Mein Gott Will
            Damm, Peter
                  Eterna 8 27 572

Kreisler/ Baumann
    Liebeslied
        Baumann, Hermann
            Firebird K 28C-211
Krek, Uros (1922-   )
    Concerto (1960)
        Falout, Joze
            RTV Ljubljana LD 0448
Krol, Bernhard
    Laudatio for Horn Solo
        Ritzkowsky, Johannes
            Schwann 0 610
    Missa Muta for Horn & Organ, Op. 55
        Damm, Peter
            Eterna 8 27 572
        Ritzkowsky, Johannes
            Schwann 0 610
Kurz, Siegfried (1930-   )
    Horn Konzert (1973)
        Damm, Peter
            Nova 8 85 090
Kvandahl, Johan (1919-   )
    Introduction & Allegro, Op. 30 (1969)
        Greer, Lowell
            Coronet LPS 3100
                1-FF 9/10-82 P. 455
                2-NR 9-82 P. 9
        Oien, Ingegard
            BIS 71
        Wekre, Froydis Ree
            Varese VS 81016
Lang, Istvan (1933-   )
    Concerto Bucolico (1970-1971)
        Tarjani, Ferenc
            Hungaroton SLPX 11784
                1-NR 11-77 P. 5
Larsson, Lars-Erik (1908-   )
    Concertino (1955)
        Lansky-Otto, Ib
            Caprice RIKS 17
Lefebvre, Charles Edouard (1843-1917)
    Romance for Horn & Piano, Op. 30
        Hustis, Gregory
            CRYS S 378
    Romance
        Jones, Mason
            MMO 6010
Levy, Frank (1930-   )
    Suite # 1
        Smith, Calvin
            CRYS S 371
                1-NR 6-76 P. 7
Lundberg
    RVA Staemningar for Solo Horn
        Belfrage, Bengt
            (Sweden) Fermat FLPS 49

Madsen, Trygve (1940-    )
      Sonata, Op. 20
            Wekre, Froydis Ree
                  Varese VS 81016
                        1-AR 10-82 P. 55
                        2-NR 12-82 P. 6
Marais, Marin (1656-1728)
      Le Basque
            Baumann, Hermann
                  Firebird K28C-211
            Brain, Dennis
                  ARA 8071; 9071
                        4-HF 5-81 P. 64
                        1-NR 11-80 P. 8
                  BBC 22175 E
                        3-FF 3/4-81 P. 93
                        1-NR 3-79 P. 10
                  Everest 3432
                        1-NR 3-79 P. 10
Marcello, Benedetto (1686-1739)
      Sonata # 6 (Cello Sonata)
            Linder, Albert
                  Fermat FLPS 53
Marks, Gunther (1897-    )
      Choral Partita fur Horn and Orgel
            Fensterer, Manfred
                  M. Fensterer
Massanet, Jules (1842-1912)
      Elegie, Op. 10
            Neal, Caswell
                  Desto DC 7199
                        3-FF 11/12-80 P. 214
            Yanich, Milan
                  Helden HR 109/10
                        2-FF 9/10-80 P. 283

Mata, Eduardo (1942-    )
      Symphony # 3 for Wind Orchestra & Horn Obbligato
            Zarzo, Vincente
                  (Mexico) RCA MRS 003
Mendelssohn, Felix (1809-1847
      Andante from 5th Symphony, Op. 107
            Jones, Mason
                  MMO 6010
            Lansky-Otto, Ib
                  BIS LP 204
                        2-FF 1/2-84 P. 303
                        2-MG 1-84 P. 12
      Auf Flugeln des Gesanges Op. 34 # 2
            Neal, Caswell
                  Desto DC 7199
                        3-FF 11/12-80 P. 214
      Consolation, Op. 30 # 3
            Yanich, Milan
                  Helden HR 109/10
                        2-FF 9/10-80 P. 283
      Nocturne from Midsummer Night's Dream
            Brain, Dennis
                  EMI/HMV RLS 7701

Mendelssohn/Baumann
 Romance sans Paroles, Op. 38/3
   Baumann, Hermann
    Firebird K28C-211
Mercadante, G. S. (1795-1870)
 Concerto in d
   Baumann, Hermann
    Italia ITL 7002
   Ceccarossi, Domenico
    MHS 3362
 Concerto in F for Horn & Orchestra
   Baumann, Hermann
    Fidelio 3383
   Bourgue, Daniel
    Peters PLE 015
     1-FF 7/8-78 P. 42
     1-SFC 7-30-78 P. 49
 Concerto
   Ceccarossi, Domenico
    Pentaphon MCF 15005
Mouret, Jean (1682-1738)
 Two Divertissements
   Fitzpatrick, Horace
    Golden Crest GC 4014
     2-LJ 2-15-60 P. 786
     2-NYT 4-26-59 P. X15
     1-SR 4-25-59 P. 50
   Molnar, Joseph
    Evasion LPE 118
Mozart, Leopold (1719-1787)
 Concerto in D for Horn & Strings
   Chambers, James
    Award Artists Series AAS 704
   Damm, Peter
    Eterna 8 26 065
   Streitwiesser, Franz Xavier
    Laudate 91 530
   Tuckwell, Barry
    Angel S 36996
     1-GR 8-74 P. 369
     1-HF 7-74 P. 112
     1-ML 7-74 P. 7
     2-NR 6-74 P. 5
     1-ST 8-74 P. 124
Mozart, W. A. (1756-1791)
 Andantino K 374 G
   Baumann, Hermann
    Firebird K28C-211
 Concerti (4) for Horn
    Classics For Pleasure CFP 148
   Barboteu, Georges
    Monitor 2118
     3-AR 6-67 P. 954
     1-NR 6-67 P. 8
     2-NYT 8-6-67 P. D17

Mozart, W. A. (Cont'd)
    Concerti (4) for Horn (Cont'd)
        Baumann, Hermann
            Tel 642360
                    2-GR 10-79 P. 643
                    1-HFN 8-79 P. 109
                    1-R&R 8-79 P. 87
            Tel Dec 641272 AW
            Tele SAWT 9627
                    2-GR 12-74 P. 1137
                    1-HF 7-75 P. 80
                    1-ML 12-74 P. 6
                    1-NR 5-75 P. 7
                    2-ST 7-75 P. 102
        Brain, Dennis
            Angel 35092 (mono)
                    1-HF 4-71 P. 65
                    1-FF 1-78 P. 93
        Bujanovski, V.
            Melodiya 33D 025797-8
        Ceccarossi, Domenico
            MHS 3579/80
            Pentaphon MCF 15003/4
        Chiba, Kaoru
            (Japanese) King SKR 1022
        Civil, Alan
            Angel S 35689
                    2-AR 7-62 P. 873
                    1-GR 11-61 P. 254
                    1-HF 7-62 P. 60
                    1-HSR 8-62 P. 68
                    1-ML 10-61 P. 6
                    2-NR 8-62 P. 6
            Angel RL 32028
                    1-FF 3/4-82 P. 205
            Columbia 33CX 1760
            Philips 6500 325
                    1-AmR 2-74 P. 24
                    1-GR 5-74 P. 2073
                    1-HF 6-73 P. 86
                    1-NR 6-73 P. 5
                    1-R&R 4-74 P. 47
                    1-ST 6-73 P. 120
            RCA LSC 2973
                    2-AR 12-67 P. 306
                    1-GR 9-67 P. 175
                    1-ML 8-67 P. 5
                    2-SR 11-25-67 P. 90
        Damm, Peter
            Eterna 8 26 680
            Eurodisc 88 303 KK
        Del Vescovo, Pierre
            Erato STU 70759
            MHS 1800
                    2-ML 7-73 P.5
        Hauptmann, Norbert
            RCA GRL 30790

Mozart, W. A. (Cont'd)
        Concerti (4) for Horn (Cont'd)
                Hogner, Gunter
                        DG 2531274
                                1-AU 6-81 P. 14
                                1-FF 1/2-81 P. 154
                                1-GR 4-81 P. 1320
                                1-HFN 3-81 P. 89
                                1-NR 1-81 P. 4
                        DG 2740231
                                2-GR 12-80 P. 836
                                2-HFN 11-80 P. 121
                Holtzel, Michael
                        Spectrum SR 101
                Jones, Mason
                        Columbia MS 6785
                                1-HF 12-65 P. 96
                                1-HSR 1-66 P. 82
                                1-NR 12-65 P. 8
                                1-SR 11-27-65 P. 66
                Linder, Albert
                        Vanguard SRV 173-SD
                                1-CR 2-66 P. 27
                                2-HF 12-65 P. 120
                        Vanguard VSD 2092
                                1-AR 7-61 P. 868
                                1-CR 8-61 P. 34
                                1-DI 12-61 P. 431
                                2-HR 1-62 P. 99
                                1-HF 8-61 P. 57
                                1-HSR 8-61 P. 60
                Muhlbacher, Ernst
                        Murray Hill 2937
                        TVS 34188-91
                                2-NR 1-68 P. 7
                        Vox STPL 512630
                                3-AR 12-64 P. 345
                                2-GR 3-65 P. 424
                                3-HF 11-64 P. 92
                                2-ML 1-65 P. 4
                                1-NR 6-64 P. 5
                Penzel, Erich
                        Mercury MG 5 0407
                                1-AH 2-65 P. 134
                                2-HF 11-64 P. 92
                                1-NR 12-64 P. 8
                                2-SR 10-31-64 P. 72
                        Philips Sequenza 6527 106
                                1-AR 10-82 P. 25
                                2-FF 5/6-82 P. 173
                Perrini, Valerie
                        Coronet S 1406
                Petr, Milos
                        Supraphon 1110 2628
                                2-FF 11/12-81 P. 198
                                1-NR 5-81 P. 7

Mozart, W. A. (Cont'd)
    Concerti (4) for Horn (Cont'd)
        Seifert, Gerd
                DG SLPM 139038
                        2-GR 6-69 P. 34
                        2-HF 7-69 P. 88
                        1-ML 6-69 P. 10
                        1-NR 5-69 P. 7
        Stagliano, James
                Boston 401
                        1-HF 6-56 P. 60
                        1-NR 6-56 P. 5
                        2-NYT 7-22-56 P. X8
                        1-SR 4-28-56 P. 58
                Boston BST 1002/1003
                        1-AR 11-58 P. 186
                        2-AU 1-59 P. 67
                        2-HF 12-58 P. 60
                Sinequan Z4RS 1229
        Tuckwell, Barry
                Angel S 36840
                        1-GR 4-72 P. 1716
                        1-HF 10-72 P. 102
                        1-ML 4-72 P. 7
                        1-NR 7-72 P. 7
                London CM 9403
                        1-AM 2-65 P. 134
                        1-AR 2-65 P. 551
                        1-HF 11-64 P. 92
                        1-HSR 1-65 P. 87
                London 41015
                        1-FF 7/8-82 P. 154
                        1-HF 12-82 P. 77
                        1-MUM 11/12-82 P. 30
                        1-SFC 6-6-82 P. 17
    Concerti # 1,# 2, & # 4
        Tarjani, Ferenc
                Fidelio 3324
                Qualiton SLPX 11707
                        1-ML 3-75 P. 5
    Concerti # 1 & # 3
        Tuckwell, Barry
                London CS 6178
                        1-GR 9-60 P. 164
                        1-GR 11-60 P. 276
                        1-HF 10-60 P. 81
                        1-HSR 12-60 P. 80
                London STS 15597
    Concerti # 1 & # 4
        Tuckwell, Barry
                London CS 6403
                        1-AM 2-65 P. 134
                        1-AR 2-65 P. 551
                        1-HF 11-64 P. 92
                        1-HSR 1-65 P. 87

Mozart, W. A.   (Cont'd)
    Concerti #2 & #4
        Brain, Dennis
                    Columbia ML 2088
                            1-AR 2-50 P. 199
                            1-LJ 4-1-50 P. 572
                            1-NA 2-18-50 P. 162
                            1-NR 2-50 P. 4
        Magyari
                    Hungaroton  12354
                            2-AR 10-82 P. 26
                            2-FF 9/10-82 P. 275
                            1-NR 7-82 P. 5
    Concerto #1, K 412
        Ceccarossi, Domenico
                    Campi-Roma SCG 11007
        Gormer, Gerhard
                    Period 544
                            1-AR 4-52 P. 243
                            2-DI #6 4-25-53 P. 265
                            2-GR 8-52 P. 55
                            4-GS 3-52 P. 4
                            2-ML 5-52 P. 6
    Concerto #2, K 417
        Baumann, Hermann
                    Telefunken TK 11540/1-2
                            1-GR 2-74 P. 1575
                            1-R&R 12-73 P. 64
                    Telefunken SLT 43102
                            1-AU 7-69 P. 56
                            1-LJ 6-1-69 P. 2216
                            1-NR 2-69 P. 8
        Bernard
                    Counterpoint 609
                            2-NR 4-64 P. 7
                            2-NYT 2-16-64 P. X12
                            2-SR 2-29-64 P. 54
        Brain, Aubrey
                    Opal 805
        Brain, Dennis
                    EMI/HMV RLS 7701
                    Seraphim 60040
        Farkas, Phil
                    Coronet 1293M
                            1-NR 2-70 P. 7
    Concerto #3, K 447
        Baumann, Hermann
                    Telefunken SLT 43102
                            1-AU 7-69 P. 56
                            1-NR 2-69 P. 8
    Concerto #3, K 447 (1st Movement)
        Brain, A.
                    Victor LM 6130
                            2-HF 12-56 P. 88
                            2-MH 1/2-57 P. 45
                            4-NYT 12-2-56 P. X9

Mozart, W. A. (Cont'd)
    Concerto # 3, K 447 (1st Movement) (Cont'd)
        Cruts, Hurbert
            BASF BAC 3001
                1-GR 7-74 P. 213
                1-R&R 6-74 P. 42
            Harmonia Mundi IC 065 99829
                1-FF 6/6-80 P. 111
                2-ML 4-80 P. 20
        Del Vescovo, Pierre
            Westminister XWN 18833
                1-DI 5/6-57 P. 529-30
                2-HF 8-59 P. 57
                2-HMR 9-59 P. 88
                1-MA 7-59 P. 22
                1-NR 7-59 P. 2
        Eger, Joseph
            Victor LM 2146
                2-AR 4-58 P. 357
                4-AU 1-58 P. 48
                2-CR 2-58
                2-HF 1-58 P. 66
                1-LJ 5-15-58 P. 1527
                4-MA 12-1-57 P. 28
        Friedrich, Adam
            Hungaroton 12264
                2-FF 5/6-82 P. 177
        Jones, Mason
            McIntosh 1016
            WCFM 8
                1-GS 11-51 P. 6
                2-NA 10-20-51 P. 335
                1-NR 2-52 P. 6
                2-NYT 12-9-51 P. X12
                2-SR 10-57-51 P. 58
        Linder, Albert
            VAN T 709/10
        Mansfeld, Klaus
            CMS/ORYX 17
                2-GR 12-68 P. 838
            MHS 1180
        Stefek, Miroslav
            Crossroads 22-16-0035
                1-AU 12-66 P. 40
                2-HF 11-66 P. 119
                3-NR 11-66 P. 7
                2-NYT 9-18-66 P. D20
                3-SR 10-29-66 P. 60
            Supraphon SUA 10709
        Tarjani, Ferenc
            Qualiton SLPX 1219
                2-AR 9-66 P. 46
                2-GR 5-66 P. 557
                1-ML 4-66 P. 6
        Zimolong, Max
            EMI 137 53500/03 M

Mozart, W. A. (Cont'd)
    Concerto # 4 K 495
        Brain, Dennis
            EMI/HMV RLS 7701
        Ceccarossi, Domenico
            Angelicum-Milano LPA 5964
            Campi-Roma SCG 11007
            Audio Fidelity FCS 50 037
        Cecere, Anthony
            Peters PLE 088
        Maes, Ernest
            Disques Duchesnes DD 6062
        Tuckwell, Barry
            Decca SPA 393
        Zwagerman, Jan
            Concert Hall CHS 1073
                2-AU 12-55 P. 45
                2-HF 9-55 P. 61
                1-NYT 8-28-55 P. X12
    Concert Rondo for Horn, K 371
            London STS 15077
        Afanasiev, Boris
            Melodiya 33 D 20259
        Barboteu, Georges
            Erato STU 70516
            MHS 1041
                1-AR 2-71 P. 378
        Berger, Roland
            Decca SXL 6330
            London STS 15077
                1-GR 2-68 P. 430
                1-ML 3-68 P. 4
        Bourgue, Daniel
            Peters PCE 039
        Ceccarossi, Domenico
            Angelicum-Milano LPA 5937
            Campi-Roma SCG 11007
            MHS 1808
            MHS 3579/80
            Pentaphon MCF 15003/04
        Civil, Alan
            Philips 6500 325
                1-HF 6-73 P. 86
                1-NR 6-73 P. 5
                1-ST 6-73 P. 120
        Damm, Peter
            Eterna 8 26 065
        Holtzel, Michael
            Spectrum SR 101; 201
        Lansky-Otto, Ib
            BIS LP 204
                2-FF 1/2-84 P. 303
                2-MG 1-84 P. 12
            MEPRO DK 400 708
        Schaberg, Roy
            Coronet 1257

Mozart, W. A. (Cont'd)
    Concert Rondo for Horn, K 371 (Cont'd)
        Stagliano, James
            Boston Records CMS L200
                2-HF 9/10-53 P. 76
                1-NR 3-53 P. 15
                2-NYT 10-26-52 P. X10
        Tarjani, Ferenc
            Fidelio 3324
            Qualiton SLPX 11707
                1-ML 3-75 P. 5
        Tuckwell, Barry
            Angel S 36840
                1-GR 4-72 P. 1716
                1-HF 10-72 P. 102
                1-ML 4-72 P. 7
                1-NR 7-72 P. 7
                1-ST 10-72 P. 133
    Rondo from Quintet
        Schaberg, Roy
            Coronet 1257
Mueller, Bernhard Eduard
    Gebet, Op. 65a
        Fensterer, Manfred
            M. Fensterer
Musgrave, Thea (1928-    )
    Concerto (1970)
        Tuckwell, Barry
            London HEAD- 8
                1-FF 7/8 P. 117
                1-GR 6-75 P. 46
                2-HFN 6-75 P. 89
                1-MJ 3-76 P. 24
                1-MQ 10-77 P. 576
                1-MT 10-75 P. 886
    Music for Horn & Piano (1967)
        Kavalovski, Charles
            MHS 3547
                1-FF 9-77 P. 69
Muzio, Emanuele (1825-1890)
    Mazurka
        Yanich, Milan
            Helden HR 109/10
                2-FF 9/10-80 P. 283
Nelhybel, Vaclav (1919-    )
    Scherzo Concertante (1963)
        Kavalovski, Charles
            MHS 3547
                1-FF 9-77 P. 69
        Smith, Calvin
            CRYS S 371
                1-NR 6-76 P. 7
Neruda, Jan
    Horn Concerto in Eb
        Streitwiesser, Franz Xavier
            Laudate 91 530

Nielson, Carl (1865-1931)
      Canto Serioso (1928)
                    Chandos ABR 1003
            Brown, William
                    Lyrichord LLST 7155
                            1-GR 11-66 P. 282
                            1-HSR 1-67 P. 86
                            1-NR 6-66 P. 2
                    MHS 1004
            Greer, Lowell
                    Coronet LPS 3100
                            1-FF 9/10-82 P. 455
                            2-NR 9-82 P. 9
            Hermansson, Soeren
                    Thorofon Capella MTH 257
            James, Ifor
                    PYE GSGC 14087
            Lansky-Otto Ib
                    BIS LP 204
                            2-FF 1/2-84 P. 303
                            2-MG 1-84 P. 12
            Linder, Albert
                    WISA LP 587
            Oien, Ingegard
                    BIS 171
Pauer, Jiri (1919-    )
      Concerto (1957)
            Stefek, Miroslav
                    Supraphon SV 8286
Persichetti, Vincent (1915-    )
      Parable VIII
            Hill, Douglas
                    CRYS S 670
      Air de Chasse
            Chambers, James
                    Award Artist Series AAS 704
            Farkas, Phil
                    Coronet 1293M
                            1-NR 2-70 P. 7
            Schaberg, Roy
                    Coronet 1257
Pierne, G.
      Serenade
            Yanich, Milan
                    Helden HR 109/10
                            2-FF 9/10-80 P. 283
Poot, Marcel (1901-    )
      Legend (1958)
            Wekre, Froydis Ree
                    Varese VS 81016
                            1-AR 10-82 P. 55
                            2-NR 12-82 P. 6
      Sarabande (1953)
            Chambers, James
                    Award Artists Series AAS 704

Poulenc, Francis (1893-1963)
    Elegie for Horn & Piano (1957)
        Barrows, John
            Golden Crest GC 7018
                1-HF 4-65 P. 99
                1-HSR 3-66 P. 100
                2-NR 4-65 P. 8
                4-NYT 11-29-64 P. X4
        Ceccarossi, Domenico
            RCA SL 20257
        Cerminaro, John
            CRYS S 375
        Civil, Alan
            Patheo 165 12519 22
            EMI/ Angel EAC 40136
            EMI 2C-165 12519-22
                1-GR 2-81 P. 1098
        Damm, Peter
            Eterna 8 27 572
        Greer, Lowell
            CRYS S 374
                4-FF 7/8-83 P. 282
                2-NR 7-83 P. 3
        Hermansson, Soeren
            Thorofon Capella MTH 257
        James, Ifor
            PYE GSGC 14140
        Stagliano, James
            Sinequan PLS 8
Punto, Giovanni (1746-1803)
    Concerto
        Bujanovski, V.
            Melodiya CM 01913-14
    Concerto in F
        Bujanovski, V.
            MK 33D 022067-68
    Concerti # 5, 6, 10, & 11
        Tuckwell, Barry
            Angel SZ 37781
                1-FF 9/10-81 P. 179
                1-GR 6-81 P. 42
                1-HF 8-81 P. 61
                1-HFN 5-81 P. 83
                1-NR 6-81 P. 7
                1-STR 10-81 P. 131
Purcell, Henry (1659-1695)
    I Attempt from Love's Sickness to Fly
        Jones, Mason
            MMO 6010
Rachmaninoff/ Baumann
    Vocalise, Op. 34/14
        Baumann, Hermann
            Firebird K28C-211
Ramous, Giovanni (1930-    )
    Roll Call for Horn
        Falout, Joze
            RTV Ljubljana LD 0448

Ravanello, Oreste (1871-1938)
    Meditazione per Organo e Corno, Op. 117 # 2
        Fensterer, Manfred
            M. Fensterer
Ravel, Maurice (1875-1937)
    Pavanne
        Abraham, Roger
            MHS 4706
        Jones, Mason
            MMO 6010
Reger, Max (1873-1916)
    Scherzino for Horn & Strings
        Baumann, Hermann
            BASF 25 21889-9
            ARA 8084; 9084
                2-AR 3-82 P. 39
                4-NR 12-81 P. 11
Reichel, Bernhard (1901-    )
    Sonata da Chiesa
        Fensterer, Manfred
            M. Fensterer
Renzi, A.
    Sonata (1954)
        Ceccarossi, Domenico
            MHS 3962 T
Reuter
    Canto Appasionato (1955)
        Damm, Peter
            Eterna 8 25 900
Reynolds, Verne
    Sonata for Horn and Piano
        Covert, John
            Mark Records MC 37272
Rheinberger, Joseph (1839-1901)
    Sonata, Op. 178
        Hill, Douglas
            CRYS S 373
                2-AR 10-81 P. 49
                2-FF 9/10-81 P. 269
        Leonarda 110
Ries, Ferdinand (1784-1838)
    Sonata In F for Horn & Piano, Op. 34
        Hill, Douglas
            CRYS S 373
                2-AR 10-81 P. 49
                2-FF 9/10-81 P. 269
        Hefti, Jakob
            Disco Jecklin 542

        Rife, Jean
            Titanic 94
Rimsky-Korsakov (1844-1908)
    Flight of the Bumble-bee
        Yanich, Milan
            Helden HR 109/10
                2-FF 9/10-80 P. 283

Rooth, Laszlo
    Quiet Monday
        Rimon, Meir
                CRYS S 507
                    1-AU 12-83 P. 94
                    2-CR 9-83 P. 43
                    2-NR 7-83 P. 7
Rosetti, Antonio (1750-1792)
    Concerto in d
        Baumann, Hermann
                Teldec 6 35057
                Telefunken SAT 22516
                    2-HF 2-71 P. 104
                    1-NR 9-70 P. 7
                Tel 641288
                    1-HFN 3-81 P. 95
                Tel 642326
                Telefunken TK 11540/1-2
                    1-GR 2-74 P. 1575
                    1-R&R 12-73 P. 64
                BASF BAC 21189
                    2-GR 11-73 P. 942
                    2-NR 4-74 P. 4
        Penzel, Erich
                Turnabout 34078
                    2-LJ 5-1-67 P. 1817
                    1-SR 1-28-67 P. 66
    Concerto in Eb
        Baumann, Hermann
                Teledec 6 41158
                Teledec 6 35057
                Telefunken TK 11540/1-2
                    1-GR 2-74 P. 1575
                    1-RR 12-73 P. 64
                Telefunken SLT 43102
                    1-AU 7-69 P. 56
                    1-LJ 6-1-69 P. 2216
                    1-NR 2-69 P. 8
        Bujanovski, V.
                Melodiya C 04708
        Rossi, Pasqualino
                Haydn Society 79
                    2-AR 1-54 P. 148
                    1-CR 2-54 P. 35
                    1-HA 2-54 P. 104
                    2-HF 3-54 P. 64
        Suchanek, Stanislav
                Supraphon 11 10 2434
                    2-FF 9/10-81 P. 271
                    1-GR 4-81 P. 1328
                    2-NR 6-81 P. 7
Rosner, Arnold
    Sonata in c for Horn & Piano (1979)
        Garson, Heidi
                Opus One 91

Rossini, Gioacchini (1792-1868)
        Una Voce Poco Fa
                Yanich, Milan
                        Helden HR 109/10
                                2-FF 9/10-80 P. 283
        Prelude, Theme, & Variations for Horn
                Bujanovski, V.
                        Melodiya C10-11037-38
                Cazalet, Andre
                        Ades 14028 PSI
                                1-FF 3/4-83 P. 335
                Ceccarossi, Domenico
                        Angelicum- Milano LPA 5937
                        MHS 1808
                        Musica Mundi VMS 2003
                                2-ML 5-66 P. 4
                Eger, Joseph
                        Vic LM 2146
                                2-AR 4-58 P. 357
                                4-AU 1-58 P. 48
                                2-CR 2-58 P. 37
                                2-HF 1-58 P. 66
                                1-LJ 5-15-58 P. 1527
                                4-MA 12-1-57 P. 28
                Greer, Lowell
                        Coronet LPS 3100
                                1-FF 9/10-82 P. 435
                                2-NR 9-82 P. 9
                Hustis, Gregory
                        CRYS S 378
                James, Ifor
                        PYE GSGC 14140
                Linder, Albert
                        Fermat FLPS 53
                Molnar, Josef
                        VDE 3001
                Neal, Caswell
                        Desto DC 7199
                                3-FF 11/12-80 P. 214
        Le Rende-vous de Chasse
                Baumann, Hermann
                        Firebird K28C-211
                Bujanovski, V.
                        Melodiya D 13770
Rossum, Frederick Van
        Eloquences
                Orval, Francis
                        Polydor Internat. 1980 015
Rota, Nino (1911-    )
        Ballata (1974)
                Ceccarossi, Domenico
                        MHS 3961
Ryba, Jakub Jan (1765-1815)
        Concerto, D# Major
                Suchanek, Stanislav
                        Supraphon 11 10 2434
                                2-FF 9/10-81 P. 271
                                1-GR 4-81 P. 1328
                                2-NR 6-81 P. 7

Saint-Saens, Camille (1835-1921)
  Le Cygne
          Baumann, Hermann
                  Firebird K28C-211
          Bujanovski, V.
                  Melodiya D 13019-20
  Morceau de Concert, Op. 94
          Baumann, Hermann
                  Firebird K28C-211
          Bourgue, Daniel
                  Peters PLE 009
                          1-FF 7/8-78 P. 105
          Jones, Mason
                  Columbia MS 6791
          Lansky- Otto, Ib.
                  MEPRO DK 400 708
          Orval, Francis
                  Turnabout QTV 34723
          Schaberg, Roy
                  Coronet 1257
          Wekre, Froydis Ree
                  CRYS S 377

  Romance
          Falout, Joze
                  RTV Ljubljana LD 0448
          Jones, Mason
                  MMO 6010
  Romance, Op. 36
          Baumann, Hermann
                  Firebird K28C-211
          Cerminaro, John
                  CRYS S 375
          Clevenger, Dale
                  MMO 8049
          Greer, Lowell
                  CRYS S 374
                          4-FF 7/8-83 P. 282
                          2-NR 7-83 P. 3
          Neal, Caswell
                  Desto DC 7199
                          3-FF 11/12-80 P. 214
          Orval, Francis
                  Turnabout QTV 34723
          Schaberg, Roy
                  Coronet 1257
          Wekre, Froydis Ree
                  Varese Int. VS 81017
  Romance, Op. 67
          Civil, Alan
                  HMV 7 EP 7182 (45 RPM)
          Coursier, Gilbert
                  Calliope CAL 1819
          Rimon, Meir
                  CRYS S 507
                          1-AU 12-83 P. 94
                          2-CR 9-83 P. 43
                          2-NR 7-83 P. 7

Saint-Saens, Camille (Cont'd)
     Romance, Op. 67 (Cont'd)
          Tuckwell, Barry
               Decca SXL 6717
               London CS 6938
                    2-GR 8-75 P. 342
                    1-HF 4-77 P. 118
                    1-ML 8-75 P. 7
                    2-NR 4-77 P. 15
                    1-ST 3-77 P. 149
Savagnone, Giuseppe (1903-    )
     Concerto (1969)
          Ceccarossi, Domenico
               MHS 3362
               Pentaphon MCF 15005
Schickle, Peter (1935-    )
     Pentangle - 5 Songs for Horn & Orchestra
          Albrecht, Kenneth
               Louisville Orchestra LS - 76-8
                    2-NR 8-80 P. 5
Schmid
     Im Tiefstem Walde (1920) ?
          Greer, Lowell
               Coronet LPS 3100
                    1-FF 9/10-82 P. 455
                    2-NR 9-82 P. 9
          Neal, Caswell
               Desto DC 7199
                    3-FF 11/12-80 P. 214
Schmidt, William (1926-    )
     Sonata for Horn
          Smith, Calvin
               WIM 14
                    1-IN 7/8-78 P. 78
Schoeck, Othmar (1886-1957)
     Concerto in d for Horn & Strings, Op. 65
          Afanasiev, Boris
               Westminister WGS 8338
                    1-NR 5-77 P. 5
          Baumann, Hermann
               ARA 8092; 9092
                    2-NR 1-83 P. 4
               BASF 20834
                    1-GR 6-73 P. 62
                    1-HF 5-74 P. 104
                    2-HFN 11-73 P. 2331
                    2-NR 11-73 P. 4
                    1-R&R 6-73 P. 56
          Brejza, Jozef
               Horn Mace MCM 9047
                    2-NR 12-66 P. 8
Schubert, Franz (1797-1828)
     Die Forelle, D550
          Eger, Joseph
               Victor LM 2146
     My Peace Thou Art D 766
          Yanich, Milan
               Helden HR 109/10
                    2-FF 9/10-80 P. 283

Schubert, Franz (Cont'd)
        Serenade D 957 # 4
                Yanich, Milan
                        Helden HR 109/10
                                2-FF 9/10-80 P. 283
        Standchen D 957 # 4
                Eger, Joseph
                        Victor LM 2146
Schumann, Robert (1810-1856)
        Adagio & Allegro for Horn, Op. 70
                Afanasiev, Boris
                        Melodiya 33D 20259
                Angus, David
                        Vox SVBX 5111
                Barboteu, Georges
                        Arion 30 A 111
                Baumann, Hermann
                        ARA 8084; 9084
                                2-AR 3-82 P. 39
                                4-NR 12-81 P. 11
                        BASF 25 21889-9
                Bloom, Myron
                        MMO 8048
                Bourgue, Daniel
                        Peters PLE 015
                                1-FF 7/8-78 P. 42
                                1-SFC 7-30-78 P. 49
                Brain, Dennis
                        Seraphim 60040
                                1-GR 10-66 P. 225
                                1-HF 7-67 P. 80
                                1-HSR 10-67 P. 159
                                1-ML 11-66 P. 7
                                1-NR 9-67 P. 13
                                1-NYT 8-6-67 PD17
                Bujanovski, V.
                        Melodiya C10 11037-38
                        Melodiya D 13175-6
                Cazalet, Andre
                        Ades 14028 PSI
                                1-FF 3/4-83 P. 335
                Ceccarossi, Domenico
                        Angelicum-Milano LPA 5937
                        MHS 1808
                Damm, Peter
                        Eterna 8 26 881
                Farkas, Phil
                        Coronet 1293 M
                                1-NR 2-70 P. 7
                Friedrich, Adam
                        Qualiton SLPX 11672
                                1-GR 5-75 P. 1191
                Hefti, Jakob
                        Disco Jecklin 542
                Klanska, Vladimira
                        Panton 8111 0046

Schumann, Robert (Cont'd)
    Adagio & Allegro for Horn, Op. 70 (Cont'd)
        Lansky- Otto, Ib
            BIS LP 204
                2-FF 1/2-84 P. 303
                2-MG 1-84 P. 12
        Leloir, Edmond
            London STS 15373
            London LL 302 D
                1-AU 10-59 P. 84
                1-HF 11-59 P. 88
                2-HF 8-58 P. 47
                1-HMR 9-58 P. 89
                1-HMR 12-59 P. 103
        Linder, Albert
            BIS LP 47
        Molnar, Joseph
            Evasion LPE 118
        Rimon, Meir
            RCA YJRL 1-0007
        Sanders, Neill
            L'Oiseau Lyre SOL 314
        Stagliano, James
            Boston Records CMS L 200
                2-HF 9/10-53 P. 76
                1-NR 3-53 P. 15
                2-NYT 10-26-52 P. X10
        Tarjani, Ferenc
            Qualiton SLPX 11354
                2-GR 3-69 P. 1302
                1-ST 6-72 P. 86
        Tuckwell, Barry
            Decca SXL 6717
            London 6938
                2-GR 8-75 P. 342
                1-HF 4-77 P. 118
                1-ML 8-75 P. 7
                2-NR 4-77 P. 15 1-ST 3-77
        Wekre, Froydis Ree
            CRYS S 377
    Dedication, Op. 25 # 1
        Yanich, Milan
            Helden HR 109/10
                2-FF 9/10-80 P. 283
    Evening Song
        Bujanovski, V.
            Melodiya C 10-11037-38
            Melodiya D 13175-6
Scriabin, Alexander (1872-1915)
    Romance in a minor (1897)
        Afanasiev, Boris
            Melodiya 33D 20259
        Barrows, John
            Golden Crest GC 7018
                1-HF 4-65 P. 99
                1-HSR 3-66 P. 100
                2-NR 4-65 P. 8
                4-NYT 11-29-64 P. X24

Scriabin, Alexander (Cont'd)
        Baumann, Hermann
           Firebird K28C-211
        Cerminaro, John
           CRYS S 375
        Clevenger, Dale
           MMO 8048
        Greer, Lowell
           Coronet LPS 3100
               1-FF 9/10-82 P. 455
               2-NR 9-82 P. 9
        Stagliano, James
           Sinequan PLS 8
Searle, Humphrey (1915-   )
    Aubade, Op. 28
        Tuckwell, Barry
           Argo ZRG 726
               1-GR 8-75 P. 315
               1-HF 6-76 P. 90
               1-ML 8-75 P. 5
               1-NR 2-76 P. 4
               1-SR 1-24-76 P. 53
Shebalin, Vissarion (1902-1963)
    Concertino
        Afanasiev, Boris
           Melodiya 015389-90
Sikorski, Kazimierz (1895-   )
    Concerto (1948)
        Golnik, Edwin
           (Polish) Muza L 0208
Sinigaglia, Leone (1868-1944)
    Song & Humoresque, Op. 28
        Wekre, Froydis Ree
           CRYS S 126
               1-AR 5-81 P. 36
               1-CR 6-81 P. 43
               1-FF 1/2-81 P. 225
               4-NR 2-81 P. 7
Slavicky, Klement (1910-   )
    Caprices for Horn & Piano (1967)
        Petr, Milos
           Supraphon 1 19 0943
Soproni, Jozsef (1930-   )
    Sonata for Horn & Piano (1976)
        Tarjani, Ferenc
           Hungaroton SLPX 12061
               4-FF 3/4-80 P. 158
               4-NR 3-80 P. 8
Sperger
    Concerto in D
        Streitwiesser, Franz Xavier
           Laudate 91 530
Sperger, Johann (1750-1812)
    Concerto in Eb for Orchestra
        Damm, Peter
           Eterna 8 27 203

Stamitz, Carl (1745-1801)
    Concerto in E
        Baumann, Hermann
            Telefunken 6 42418 AW
                1-FF 11/12-80 P. 214
                1-NR 2-81 P. 6
Steinmetz
    Concerto in D for Horn & Orchestra
        Stagliano, James
            Kapp KCL 9053
Stevens, Halsey (1906-   )
    Sonata for Horn & Piano (1953)
        Decker, James
            ERS 6505
                2-R&R 12-78 P. 98
        Leuba, Christopher
            CRYS S 372
                1-NR 9-77 P. 5
Stradella, Alessandro (1644-1682)
    Kirchen Arie
        Jones, Mason
            MMO 6010
Strauss, Franz (1822-1905)
    Concerto in c for Horn, Op. 8
        Bourgue, Daniel
            Peters PLE 015
                2-FF 7/8-78 P. 42
        Tuckwell, Barry
            London CS 6519
                1-GR 5-67 P. 583
                1-HF 7-68 P. 89
                1-HSR 7-68 P. 88
                1-ML 5-67 P. 6
                1-NR 7-68 P. 5
                1-NYT 6-23-68 P. D24
    Fantasie, Op. 2
        Bourgue, Daniel
            Disques REM 10914
    Fantasie, Op. 6
        Pizka, Hans
            Hans Pizka Edition HPE CM 1001
    Nocturno for Horn & Piano, Op. 7
        Bourgue, Daniel
            Disques REM 10914
        Cerminaro, John
            CRYS S 376
        Jeurissen, Hermann
            Dabringhaus Und Grimm MD-GG 1063
    Theme, & Variations, Op. 13
        Bourgue, Daniel
            Disques REM 10914
        Hustis, Gregory
            CRYS S 378
        Jeurissen, Hermann
            Dabringhaus Und Grimm MD-GG 1063
        Molnar, Josef
            Evasion LPE 118

Strauss, Johann
    Dolci Pianti
        Baumann, Hermann
            Firebird K28C-211
Strauss, Richard (1864-1949)
    Andante for Horn & Piano (1888)
        Bourgue, Daniel
            Disques REM 10914
        Bujanovski, V.
            CIO 16969-70
        Cazalet, Andre
            Ades 14028 PSI
                1-FF 3/4-83 P. 335
        Greer, Lowell
            Coronet LPS 3100
                1-FF 9/10-82 P. 455
                2-NR 9-82 P. 9
        Hefti, Jakob
            Disco Jecklin 542
        Hill, Douglas
            CRYS S 373
                2-AR 10-81 P. 49
                2-FF 9/10-81 P. 269
                1-NR 7-81 P. 5
                1-SFC 4-12-81 P. 21
        Rimon, Meir
            RCA YJRL 1 0007
        Tarjani, Ferenc
            Hungaroton 12473
    Concerto # 1, Op. 11
        Bloom, Myron
            CBS MP 39056
            Epic 3841
                1-AR 11-62 P. 190
                1-HF 11-62 P. 102
                1-HSR 1-63 P. 83
                2-NR 1-63 P. 7
            Odyssey Y 32889
                2-HF 12-74 P. 119
        Bourgue, Daniel
            Decca 7154
        Brain, Dennis
            Angel 35496
                1-AM 12-57 P. 187
                1-AR 12-57 P. 162
                1-GR 11-57 P. 220
                1-HF 10-57 P. 102
                1-MA 11-1-57 P. 26
                1-NR 10-57 P. 9
            Columbia ML 4775
                1-AR 1-54 P. 166
                1-HF 4-54 P. 61-62
                4-NR 1-54 P. 9
                4-NYT 6-20-54 P. X8
            EMI/HMV RLS 7701
        Ceccarossi,Domenico
            Magic Horn DC 191110/1

Strauss, Richard (Cont'd)
    Concerto # 1, Op. 11 (Cont'd)
        Damm, Peter
            Angel S 37004
                2-AR 12-76 P. 42
                1-HF 11-76 P. 128
                1-NR 11-76 P. 5
            Eterna 8 25 883
        Jones, Mason
            Columbia M 32233
                1-HF 8-75 P. 100
                1-NR 6-75 P. 3
        Lohan, Heinz
            Urania 7108
                1-AR 6-54 P. 330
                2-HF 10-54 P. 68
                2-LJ 12-1-54 P. 2338
                2-MA 3-54 P. 19
                1-NR 5-54 P. 7
                2-NYT 5-23-54 P. X6
        Tuckwell, Barry
            London CS 6519
                1-GR 5-67 P. 583
                1-HF 7-68 P. 89
                1-HSR 7-68 P. 88
                1-ML 5-67 P. 6
                1-NR 7-68 P. 5
        Tylsar
            Supraphon 1110 2808
                2-FF 1/2-82 P. 186
                2-GR 5-82 P. 1494
                2-HF 8-82 P. 62
                1-MG 6-82 P. 9
                3-NR 3-82 P. 5
    Concerto # 2
        Barboteu, Georges
            MHS 975
                2-AR 12-69 P. 302
        Bourgue, Daniel
            Decca 7154
        Brain, Dennis
            Angel 35496
                1-AM 12-57 P. 187
                1-AR 12-57 P. 162
                1-GR 11-57 P. 220
                1-HF 10-57 P. 102
                1-MA 11-1-57 P. 26
                1-NR 10-57 P. 9
            EMI/HMV RLS 7701
        Ceccarossi, Domenico
            Majic Horn DC 191110/1
        Damm, Peter
            Angel S 37004
                2-AR 12-76 P. 42
                1-HF 11-76 P. 128
                1-NR 11-76 P. 5
            Eterna 8 25 883

Strauss, Richard (Cont'd)
    Concerto # 2 (Cont'd)
        Hauptmann, Norbert
            DG 2530439
                3-GR 6-74 P. 60
                1-HF 9-74 P. 103
                1-ML 6-74 P. 5
                1-NR 9-74 P. 5
                1-ST 10-74 P. 138
        Lansky- Otto, Ib
            Caprice CAP 1103
        Tuckwell, Barry
            Decca SPA 393
            London CS 6519
                1-GR 5-67 P. 583
                1-HF 7-68 P. 89
                1-HSR 7-68 P. 88
                1-ML 5-67 P. 6
                1-NR 7-68 P. 5
        Tylsar
            Supraphon 1110 2808
                2-FF 1/2-82 P. 186
                2-GR 5-82 P. 1494
                2-HF 8-82 P. 62
                1-MG 6-82 P. 9
                3-NR 3-82 P. 5
    Wiegenlied, Op. 41
        Bourgue, Daniel
            Disques REM 10914
Sydeman, William (1928-    )
    Concerto For Horn & Orchestra (1976)
        Tarjani, Ferenc
            Hungaroton 12129
Sylvan, Sixten (1914-    )
    Sonata for Horn & Piano, Op. 7 (1963)
        Linder, Albert
            WISA LP 587
Tchaikowsky, P. (1840-1893)
    Autumn Song
        Stagliano, James
            Sinequan PLS 8
Telemann, Georg Philip (1681-1767)
    Concerto for Horn & Strings
        Maes, Ernest
            Duchesne DD 6039
    Concerto in D for Horn & Orchestra
        Baumann, Hermann
            Teldec AW 6 41932
                2-CR 9-76 P. 43
                1-NR 2-76 P. 15
        Barboteu, Georges
            MHS 822
         Berv, Arthur
            Westminister MCA 1422
                2-FF 5/6-81 P. 170
                1-NR 12-80 P. 6.
        Bourgue, Daniel
            Peters PLE 026
                2-FF 11-12-78 P. 127

Telemann, Georg Philip (Cont'd)
    Concerto in D for Horn & Orchestra (Cont'd)
            Damm, Peter
                Eterna 8 26 065
            Greer, Lowell
                Coronet LPS 3122
                    1-FF 11/12-83 P. 375
                    1-NR 3-84 P. 5
            Jones, Mason
                RCA LSC 3057
                    2-AR 2-69 P. 445
                    1-CR 7-69 P. 19
                    3-HF 3-69 P. 109
                    4-NR 2-69 P. 4
                    2-NYT 6-1-69 P. D26
                    2-ST 4-69 P. 106
            Klecha/Machata/Kunth/Roth
                Da Camera Magna SM 91039
                    3-FF 1/2-80 P. 155
                    3-FF 5/6-80 P. 164
            Penzel, Erich
                Nonesuch 71148
                    1-HSR 10-67 P. 162
                    1-NR 3-67 P. 6
                    4-NYT 7-30-67 P. D21
            Tuckwell, Barry
                Angel S 36996
                    1-GR 8-74 P. 369
                    1-HF 7-74 P. 112
                    1-ML 7-74 P. 7
                    2-NR 6-74 P. 5
                    1-ST 8-74 P. 124
Teyber, Anton (1754-1822)
    Concerto in Eb
            Baumann, Hermann
                Telefunken 6 42418 AW
                    1-FF 11/12-80 P. 214
                    1-NR 2-81 P. 6
Thomas
    Rondo, Gavotte
            Yanich, Milan
                Helden HR 109/10
                    2-FF 9/10-80 P. 283
Tomasi, Henri (1901-1971)
    Chant Corse (1932)
            Bujanovski, V.
                Melodiya D 13019 20
    Chant Corse (1932)
            Wekre, Froydis Ree
                CRYS S 377
    Danse Profane (1960)
            Wekre, Froydis Ree
                CRYS S 377
Tufts, Paul (1924-    )
    Sonata for Horn & Piano (1975)
            Leuba, Christopher
                CRYS S 372
                    1-NR 9-77 P. 5

Verral, John (1908-    )
    Sonata for Horn & Piano (1941)
        Leuba, Christopher
           CRYS S 372
               1-NR 9-77 P. 5
Vignery, Jane (1913-    )
    Sonata, Op. 7
        Wekre, Froydis Ree
           Varese Vs 81016
               1-AR 10-82 P. 55
               2-NR 12-82 P. 6
Vivaldi, Antonio (1678-1741)
    Concerto for Violin # 24 (Tr. for Horn & Organ)
        Orval, Francis
           Disques Duchesne DD 6044
Viviani, Giovanni B. (1638-1692)
    Sonata Prima
        Damm, Peter
           Eterna 8 27 572
Vuillermoz, Edouard (1868-1939)
    Etude
        Stagliano, James
           Sinequan PLS 8
Wagner, Richard
    Siegfried's Horn Call
        Brain, Dennis
           EMI/HMV RLS 7701
        Belfrage, Bengt
           (Sweden) Fermat FLPS 49
Weber, Alain (1930-    )
    Concertino in F
        Ceccarossi, Domenico
           Majic Horn DC 191110/1
Weber, Carl Maria Von (1786-1826)
    Concertino for Horn in e, Op. 45
        Barboteu, Georges
           MHS 1045 T
               2-ML 12-70 P. 16
               2-ST 12-70 P. 106
        Baumann, Hermann
           ARA 8092; 9092
               1-HFN 7-80 P. 114
               1-R&R 7-80 P. 64
               1-SFC 10-24-82 P. 15
           BASF 20834
               1-GR 6-73 P. 62
               2-NR 11-73 P. 4
        Bourgue, Daniel
           PLE 015
               1-FF 7/8-78 P. 43
        Orval, Francis
           Turnabout TVS 34488
               1-HF 11-73 P. 126
               2-NR 11-73 P. 4

Weber, Carl Maria Von (Cont'd)
    Concertino for Horn in e, Op. 45 (Cont'd)
        Tuckwell, Barry
            Angel S 36996
                1-GR 8-74 P. 369
                1-HF 7-74 P. 112
                1-ML 7-74 P. 7
                2-NR 6-74 P. 5
                1-ST 8-74 P. 124
Weismann, Julius (1879-1950)
    Concertino in Eb for Horn & Orchestra, Op. 118
        Baumann, Hermann
            ARA 8084; 9084
                2-AR 3-82 P. 39
                4-NR 12-81 P. 11
            BASF 25 21889-9
Wilder, Alec (1907-1980)
    Sonata # 1 for Horn & Piano
        Schaberg, Roy
            Coronet 3039
    Sonata # 1 & 2 for Horn
        Barrows, John
            Golden Crest GC 7002
                1-AU 4-60 P. 66
                1-NR 5-60 P. 80
                2-SR 3-26-60 P. 48
    Sonata # 3 for Horn & Piano
        Barrows, John
            Golden Crest GC 7034
                2-NYT 11-9-69 P. D39
    Suite for Horn & Piano
        Barrows, John
            Golden Crest GC 7002
                1-AU 4-60 P. 66
                1-NR 5-60 P. 80
                1-SR 3-26-60 P. 48
Zorman, Moshe
    Moods
            Rimon, Meir
            CRYS S 507
                1-AU 12-83 P. 94
                2-CR 9-83 P. 43
                2-NR 7-83 P. 43
                2-NR 7-83 P. 7

# Two Horns

Anonymous
        Duets, Hunting Horns
                        Supraphon 111 0614
                                1-GR 4-74 P. 1862
                                1-HFN 3-74 P. 119
                                1-NR 8-72 P. 15
                                1-RR 2-74 P. 29
Barsanti, Francesco (1690-1772)
        Concerto in D for 2 Horns & Orchestra, Op. 3 #4
                Stagliano/Berv
                        KAPP 3388
                        KAPP 9053
                                1-CR 2-61 P. 34
                                2-HF 2-61 P. 77
                                1-NR 5-61 P. 6
                                1-SR 1-28-61 P. 46

        Concerto for 2 Horns & Orchestra
                Stagliano/Berv
                        MCA Westminister 1422
                                2-FF 5/6-81 P. 170
                                1-NR 12-80 P. 6

Bodinus, Sebastian
        Symphony In F for 2 Horns & Orchestra (1747)
                        Da Camara Magna SM 90149
                                2-FF 9/10-81 P. 83
Feldmayer, Johann Georg (1756-1828)
        Concerto for 2 Horns in F
                Schroeder/Koster
                        MHS 4356
                                1-AR 12-81 P. 40
                                2-CR 1-82 P. 43
Fiala, Joseph (1748-1816)
        Concerto # 1 In Eb for 2 Horns
                Tylsar/Tylsar
                        Supraphon 1 10 2176
                                2-ML 12-78 P. 8
                                1-NR 10-78 P. 4
                Schroeder/Koster
                        MHS 4356
                                1-AR 12-81 P. 40
                                2-CR 1-82 P. 43

Handel, G. F.   (1685-1759)
    Concerto # 1 in Bb
        James/Randall/Burden/Buck
                Philips 6882 004
    Concerto # 2 in F
        Stegner/Baccelli/Steidle
                Archiv Privilege 2547013
    Concerto for 2 Horns in F
        Stagliano/Berv
                KAPP 3388
                KAPP 9053
                    1-CR 2-61 P. 34
                    2-HF 2-61 P. 77
                    1-NR 5-61 P. 6
                    1-SR 1-28-61 P. 46
                MCA Westminister 1422
                    2-FF 5/6-81 P. 170
                    1-NR 12-80 P. 6
        Grafe/Auerbach
                Eterna 8 26 809
    Concerti # 2 & # 3 for 2 Horns in F
        James/Randall
                Philips 6882 004
        Neudecker/Stegner
                Deutsche Grammophon Archiv ARC 3146
                    2-GR 12-62 P. 290
                    2-HF 11-63 P. 94
                    2-HSR 11-63 P. 76
    Largo for 2 Horns & Strings
        Dunn/Buffington
                American Society AS 1002
                    1-AR 5-60 P. 700
                    2-HF 9-60 P. 79
                    2-HSR 5-60 P. 70
Haydn, Franz Joseph (1732-1809)
    Concerto for 2 Horns in Eb
        Barboteu/Coursier
                MHS 533
                    2-AR 5-64 P. 850
                    2-HF 6-64 P. 74
                    1-ML 4-72 P. 17
                    1-ML 3-68 P. 8
                Erato EFM 8055
                (Japan) Columbis OS 3443
        Bourgue/Orval
                Peters PCE 030
                    1-FF 7/8-78 P. 41
                    1-SFC 6-25-78 P. 61
        Hoeltzel/Jeurissen
                (Ger.) MDG EMI Electrola 1039
        Tylsar/Tylsar
                Supraphon 110 1200
                    2-GR 9-73 P. 496
                    1-ML 8-73 P. 7
                    2-NR 1-74 P. 7
                    1-ST 1-74 P. 109

Heiden, Bernhard
        Canons for Two Horns
                Smith/Zsembery
                        CRYS S 371
                                1-NR 6-76 P. 7
Kielland, Olav (1901-    )
        Concerto Grosso Norvegese for 2 Horns
                        CRI 160
                                1-HF 8-62 P. 80
                                2-HSR 8-62 P. 68
                                2-MA 6-62 P. 27
                                1-MQ 7-62 P. 411
Maw, Nicholas (1935-    )
        Sonata for 2 Horns & Strings (1966)
                Civil/Harper
                        Argo ZRG 676
                                1-GR 7-71 P. 186
                                1-ML 7-71 P. 3
Mozart, Leopold (1719-1787)
        Concerto in Eb for 2 Horns & Strings (1752)
                Baumann/Cakar
                        Acanta 40 22 433
                                1-FF 11/12-83 P. 270
                        BASF KBF 21195
                                2-ST 1-74 P. 113
                        BASF 20 22433-3
Mozart, W. A. (1756-1791)
        Divertimento in D, K320b=K334
                        Qualiton HLP MN 1017
                                2-AR 5-65 P. 862
                        DG LPM 39008
                                2-GR 11-66 P. 262
                                2-HF 5-66 P. 96
                                3-ML 11-66 P. 4
                                1-NR 8-66 P. 2
                                2-SR 7-30-66 P. 58

                Berger/Berger
                        Westminister W 9069
                        Westminister 52-76
                                3-AR 6-54 P. 326
                                2-HF 9-54 P. 57
                                2-NYT 8-8-54 P. X6
                                2-SR 6-26-54 P. 52
                (12) Duets for Horn K487
                        Philips 6747 136
                                1-HF 7-76 P. 82
                                1-NR 5-76 P. 11
                                4-NYT 8-8-76 P. D13
                                1-ST 6-76 P. 165

                Cerny/Beranek
                        Supraphon 111 1671-2
                                1-NR 11-75 P. 8
                                1-ST 1-76 P. 100
                Leuba/Binstock
                        Audiophile AP-70
                                1-HF 4-61 P. 108
                                1-HSR 5-61 P. 70
                                2-SR 1-28-61 P. 44

Mozart, W. A. (Cont'd)
    (12) Duets for Horn K487 (Cont'd)
        Leuba/Binstock (Cont'd)
            Audiophile APS 110
                4-NR 5-72 P. 5
        Orval/Janssens
            Disques Duchesne DD 6010
        Soeteman/Peeters
            Philips 6747136
                1-HF 7-76 P. 82
                1-NR 5-76 P. 11
                4-NYT 8-8-76 P. D13
                1-ST 6-76 P. 105
        Tarjani (Plays Both Parts)
            Qualiton SLPX 11354
                2-GR 3-69 P. 1302
                1-ST 6-72 P. 86
Musgrave, Thea (1928-    )
    Night Music for 2 Horns (1969)
        Chidell/Tuckwell
            Argo ZRG 702
                2-GR 5-73 P. 2051
                1-HF 11-74 P. 97
                1-ML 5-73 P. 4
                1-NR 10-74 P. 3
Pokorny, Francis Xavier(1728-1794)
    Concerto for 2 Horns in F
        Baumann/Kohler
            Acanta 40 22 433
                1-FF 11/12-83 P. 270
            BASF 20 22433-3
            BASF BAC 21191/4
                2-GR 12-73 P. 1212
                2-NR 4-74 P. 4
Rasmussen, P.
    Instruktive Duetten
        Linder/Lansky-Otto
            WISA LP 587
Reicha, Joseph (1752-1795)
    Concerto Concertante for 2 Horns in Eb, Op. 5
        Damm/Vincze
            Eterna 8 27 203
        Tylsar/Tylsar
            Supraphon 110 2176
                2-ML 12-78 P. 8
                1-NR 10-78 P. 4
                1-RR 10-78 P. 70
Rosetti,  Antonio (1750-1792)
    Concerto in Eb for 2 Horns
        Baumann/Van Woudenberg
            Teldec SMT 1211
        Bujanovski/Shalyt
            Melodiya D 022067-68
        Sorensen/Sorensen
            Haydn Society HS 9052
                2-HF 5-59 P. 60
                3-LJ 6-15-59 P. 2053

Rosetti, Antonio  (Cont'd)
      Concerto in Eb for 2 Horns (Cont'd)
            Tylsar/Tylsar
                  Supraphon 11-2176
                        2-ML 12-78 P. 8
                        1-NR 10-78 P. 4
                        1-RR 10-78 P. 70
Sammartini, Giovanni Battista (1701-1775)
      Sonata in G for 2 Horns & Strings
            Dover HCR 5247
                        1-NR 12-65 P. 7
            Period SPL 731 A
                        1-AP 7-57 P. 161
                        1-AU 4-58 P. 44
                        1-HA 4-58 P. 100
                        2-HF 8-57 P. 55
                        1-MA 3-58 P. 30
                        1-MQ 7-58 P. 409
      Symphony in A for 2 Horns & Strings
            Dover HCR 5247
                        1-NR 12-65 P. 7
      Symphony for 2 Horns & Strings
            Period SPL 731 A
                        1-AR 7-57 P. 161
                        1-AU 4-58 P. 44
                        1-HA 4-58 P. 100
                        2-HF 8-57 P. 55
                        1-MA 3-58 P. 30
                        1-MQ 7-58 P. 409
Schuller, Gunther (1925-    )
      Duets for Unaccompanied Horns (1 & 3)
            Smith/Zsembery
                  CRYS S 371
                        1-NR 6-76 P. 7
Telemann, Georg Philipp (1681-1767)
      Concerto a 7 for 2 Horns, Strings & Continuo
            MHS 3156
      Concerto in Bb for 2 Horns, Strings & Continuo
            RCA/Erato NUM 750043
                        2-FF 3/4-83 P. 276
                        1-GR 6-82 P. 42
      Concerto in D for 2 Horns
            Bujanovski/  ?
                  Melodiya C10-09489-90
      Concerto in Eb for 2 Horns & Strings
            Barboteu/Coursier
                  Nonesuch 71066
                        2-AR 11-65 P. 256
                        2-HF 1-66 P. 95
                        1-NR 10-65 P. 4
            Bourgue/Fournier
                  Peters PLE 026
                        2-FF 11/12-78 P. 127
            Bujanovski/ ?
                  Melodiya C10-09489-90
            Creech/Kent
                  CBC SM 136

Telemann, Georg Philipp (Cont'd)
    Concerto in Eb for 2 Horns & Strings (Cont'd)
      Freund/Berger
          Audio Fidelity 50077
        Friedrich/Brunner
          Hungaroton SLPX 12118
              1-FF 5/6-81 P. 171
              1-NR 2-81 P. 6
        Lexutt/Alfing
          Harmonia Mundi 065 99674
              1-FF 11/12-78 P. 128
              1-ML 9-78 P. 6
        Tylsar/Tylsar
          Supraphon 110 1200
              2-GR 9-73 P. 496
              1-ML 8-73 P. 7
              2-NR 1-74 P. 7
              1-ST 1-74 P. 109
    Concerto in F for 2 Horns & Strings
          Telefunken SAWT 9483
              2-AR 6-67 P. 910
              2-GR 7-67 P. 68
              1-ML 8-67 P. 6
    Minuet in F for 2 Cornes des Chasse
      Alfing/Alfing
          DGG 198430
              1-HSR 10-68 P. 136
              1-ML 7-68 P. 16
    Musique de Table (Complete)
      Baumann/Van Woudenberg
          Telefunken 635298
    Overture (Suite) in F
      Schroeder/Koster
          MHS 4356
              1-AR 12-81 P. 40
              2-CR 1-82 P. 43
    Suite for 2 Horns, 2 Violins & Continuo in F
      Bourgue/Fournier
          PLE 026
              2-FF 11/12-78 P. 127
        Friedrich/Brunner
          Hungaroton SLPX 12118
              1-FF 5/6-81 P. 171
              1-NR 2-81 P. 6
      Stagliano/Berv
        KAPP 9053
             1-CR 2-61 P. 34
             2-HF 2-61 P. 77
        MCA Westminister 1422
             2-FF 5/6-81 P. 170
             1-NR 12-80 P. 6
    Tylsar/Tylsar
        Panton 11 0585
    Freund/Sungler
        MHS 0759

Telemann, Georg Philipp (Cont'd)
    Tafelmusik III (Concerto Grosso in Eb)
        Freund/Sungler
            MHS 641/642
        Penzel/Baccelli
            Archiv Privilege 2547 006
Vivaldi, Antonio (1678-1741)
    Concerto for 2 Horns
        Baumann/Van Woudenberg
            Telefunken SAWT 9499
                1-GR 3-67 P. 474
                1-ML 4-67 P.
                1-NR 6-67 P. 5

        Baumann/  ?
            Teldec 641158
        Tylsar/Tylsar
            Supraphon 110 1200
                2-GR 9-73 P. 496
                1-ML 8-73 P. 7
                2-NR 1-74 P. 7
                1-ST 1-74 P. 109
    Concerto for 2 Horns (P320)
        Klamand/Schmitz
            Claves D 602
        Spach/Roth
            Murray Hill S 2937
            Turnabout 34078
                2-LJ 5-1-67 P. 1817
                1-SR 1-28-67 P. 66
    Concerto for 2 Horns (P321)
        Brown/David
            Argo ZRG 840
                2-GR 4-78 P. 1732
                2-ML 4-78 P. 7

        Brown/Hill
            Philips 6514379
        Guerin/Delwande
            Nonesuch 71018E
                3-AR 11-64 P. 219
                4-GR 7-65 P. 61
                2-HF 10-64 P. 154
                2-ML 6-65 P. 6
                2-NR 7-65 P. 7
        Baumann/Van Woudenberg
            Teldec SMT 1211
    2 Concerti for 2 Horns (P320, P321)
            DG ARC 2533044
        Barboteu/Coursier
            Nonesuch 71091
                1-HF 2-66 P. 96
                3-NR 3-66 P. 5
                2-NYT 12-19-65 P. X28
        Ceccarossi/Marchi
            Angel45030
                1-AR 2-59 P. 416
                1-GR 10-58 P. 204

Vivaldi, Antonio (Cont'd
        Ceccarossi/Marchi (Cont'd)
            Angel 45030 (Cont'd)
                1-HF 1-59 P. 62
                1-NR 1-59 P. 9
                4-SR 12-27-58 P. 36
Wilder, Alec (1907-1980)
    (22) Duets (3, 15, 17, & 19 Only)
        Smith/Zsembery
            CRYS S 371
                1-NR 6-76 P. 7
Witt, Friedrich (1770-1837)
    Concerto in Eb for 2 Horns
        Koster/Schroeder
            MHS 4356 W
                1-AR 12-81 P. 40
                2-CR 1-82 P. 43

# Multiple Horns

Anonymous
    Four Short Pieces (4 Horns)
        Leuba/Binstock/Barrington/Wirth/Brouk
                Concert Disc CS 243
                        4-AR 7-64 P. 1042
Artot, Jean
    Trio (3 Horns)
        Bujanovski/ ? / ?
                Melodiya C10 05397-8
Bach, Johann Sebastian  (1685-1750)
    Andante from "Jesu Meine Freude" (4 Horns)
        Seiffert/McDonald/Park/Shaw
                Mark Ed. Recordings Ens.
                Series MES 29088
    Bouree II, English Suite # 2 (4 Horns)
        Seiffert/McDonald/Park/Shaw
                Mark Ed. Recordings Ens.
                Series MES 29088
    Fugue XI, WTC, Vol. I (4 Horns)
        Seiffert/McDonald/Park/Shaw
                Mark Ed. Recordings Ens.
                Series MES 29088
    Gigue from Suite for Harpsichord (4 Horns)
        Seiffert/McDonald/Park/Shaw
                Mark Ed. Recordings Ens.
                Series MES 29088
    Sarabande, English Suite #2 (4 Horns)
        Seiffert/McDonald/Park/Shaw
                Mark Ed. Recordings Ens.
                Series MES 29088
    Two Chorales (4 Horns)
        Leuba/Binstock/Barrington/Wirth/Brouk
                Concert Disc CS 243
                        4-AR 7-64 P. 1042
Boismortier, Joseph  (1691-1755)
    Sonata (4 Horns)
        Seiffert/McDonald/Park/Shaw
                Mark Ed. Recordings Ens.
                Series MES 29088

Bruckner, Anton (1824-1896)
     Drei Stuecke Fuer Hornquartett
          Gottfried/Greutter/Fuchs/Reiter
               Profil 120 622
Bujanovski, V.
     Dedication to Rimsky-Korsakov for 6 Horns
               Melodiya C10 05397-8
Cantin, Jules (1874-1956)
     Noces di chasseur
               Orfeo S 034821 A
Dauprat, Louis Francois (1781-1868)
     Grand Trios, Op. 4 (3 Horns)
               Grieve/Lott/Meek
                    Avant AV 1013
     Sextets (6) for Horns, Op. 10
               Leuba, Christopher
                    Coronet LPS 3045
                         1-NR 1-80 P. 5
     Trio (3 Horns)
               Bujanovski/ ? / ?
                    Melodiya C10 05397-8
Deisenroth, Friedrich
     Hunting Music (4 Horns)
                    Orfeo S 034821 A
     Hunting Suite for 4 Horns
               Baar/Berger/Hogner/Fischer/Gabler
                    MHS 1224T
Garcia
     Variation on a 5 Note Theme
                    Capitol SP 8525
                    Seraphim S 60095
Heiden, Bernhard (1910-    )
     Variation for Solo Tuba & 9 Horns
                    Golden Crest GC 4147
                         1-AR 5-77 P. 23
Hill, Douglas (1946-    )
     Abstraction for Solo & 8 Horns
                    CRYS S 670
Hindemith, Paul (1895-1963)
     Sonata for 4 Horns (1952)
                    Westminister WGS 8322
                         1-NR 10-76 P. 7
               Bujanovski/Yevstignejev/Shalyt/Ivanov
                    Melodiya CM 01953-4
               Leuba/Binstock/Barrington/Wirth/Brouk
                    Concert Disc CS 243
                         4-AR 7-64 P. 1042
                         1-HF 8-64 P. 88
                         1-NR 6-64 P. 6
               Gottfried/Greutter/Fuchs/Reiter
                    Profil 120 622
Hyde
     Color Contrasts
                    Capitol SP 8525
                    Seraphim S 60095
                         1-NR 5-69 P. 5

Johnson, Roger (1941-    )
    Suite for 6 Horns
                Angel S 36036
                        1-HF 8-70 P. 98
                        1-NR 7-70 P. 7
                        1-ST 9-70 P. 122
Kraft
    Games - Collage # 1
                Angel S 36036
Kubin, Rudolph (1909-1973)
    Sinfonia Concertante for 4 Horns & Strings (1937)
                (Czech) Panton 01 0259
Lassus (1532-1594)
    Echo Song
                Capitol SP 8525
                Seraphim S 60095
                        1-NR 5-69 P. 5

    Madrigal
                Angel S 36036
Liadov/Bujanovski
    Two Pieces for 8 Horns
                Melodiya C10 05937
Lo Presti, Ronald
    Suite for 8 Horns
                Capitol SP 8525
                Seraphim S 60095
                        1-NR 5-69 P. 5
Leutgen, W. A. (ca. 1850)
    Quartett fuer vier Waldhoerner (Op. 19)
            Gottfried/Greutter/Fuchs/Reiter
                Profil 120 622
Mendelssohn, Felix (1809-1847)
    Tarantella
                Capitol SP 8525
                Seraphim S 60095
                        1-NR 5-69 P. 5
Mityushin, Alexander
    Concertino for 4 Horns
            Leuba/Binstock/Barrington/Wirth/Brouk
                Concert Disc CS 243
                        4-AR 7-64 P. 1042
                        1-HF 8-64 P. 88
                        1-NR 6-64 P. 6
Mozart, Leopold (1719-1787)
    Sinfonia da Caccia (4 Horns)
            Baumann/ ?
                BASF KBF Z 1195
                        1-ST 1-74 P. 113
Nelhybel, Vaclav (1919-    )
    Quartet for Horns (1957)
                Seraphim 12007
Palestrina, Giovanni (1525-1594)
    O che Splendor
                Angel S 36036

    Stabat Mater
                Capitol SP 8525
                Seraphim S 60095
                        1-NR 5-69 P. 5

Pauer, Jiri
    Slepici Serenada (3 Horns)
            Tylsar/Tylsar/Beranek
                Panton 8111 0045
Raskin
    Morning Revisited
                Capitol SP 8525
                Seraphim S 60095
                    1-NR 5-69 P. 5
Reicha, Anton Joseph (1770-1836)
    (17) Rejcha Horn Trios, Op. 24
            Tylsar/Hrdina/Tylsar
                Supraphon 111 2617
                    2-FF 3/4-81 P. 179
                    1-NR 3-81 P. 7
    Six Trios for Horn in E, Op. 82
            Stefek/Kubat/Cir
                Supraphon A 19035
    (8) Trios, Op. 82
            Lockwood/Chernin/Whitmore
                MHS 3500
Rossini
    Fanfare de Chasse
                Angel S 36036
                    1-HF 8-70 P. 98
                    1-NR 7-70 P. 7
                    1-ST 9-70 P. 122
    Rendevous de Chasse
                Orfeo S 034821 A
Schuller, Gunther
    Lines and Contrasts for 16 Horns
                Angel S 36036
                    1-HF 8-70 P. 98
                    1-NR 7-70 P. 7
                    1-ST 9-70 P. 122
Schumann, Robert (1810-1856)
    Konzertstuck in F for 4 Horns & Orchestra, Op. 8
                Vox C 9071
            Barboteu/Berges/Coursier/Dubar
                Nonesuch 71044
                    2-GR 8-65 P. 107
                    1-HF 7-65 P. 68
                    1-HSR 9-65 P. 90
                    1-ML 4-65 P. 5
                    1-NR 5-65 P. 4
                    1-NYT 8-1-64 P. X17
            Baumann/Cakar/Meyendorf/Ritzkowsky/Lepetit
                Arabesque APA 8092
                    1-HFN 7-80 P. 114
                    1-RR 7-80 P. 64
                    1-SFC 10-24-82 P. 15
                BASF 20834
                    1-GR 6-73 P. 62
                    3-ML 8-73 P. 7
                    2-NR 11-73 P. 4

Schumann, Robert (Cont'd)
      Konzertstuck in F for 4 Horns & Orchestra, Op. 8
      (Cont'd)
              Clevenger/Oldberg/Howell/Scheweikert
                  DG 2530 939
                        1-GR 4-78 P. 1731
                        1-ML 4-78 P. 4
                        1-RR 12-78 p. 43
                  DG 2709 075
                        1-FF 7/8-78 P. 83
                        1-NR 7-78 P. 2
                        1-NYT 4-9-78 P. D22
                        1-ST 9-78 P. 124
              Damm/Maerker/Pilz/Boehner
                  Eterna 9 25 296
                  Philips 6780 754
              Decker/Lott/Hude/Markowitz
                  Columbia ML 5107
                        1-AR 9-56 P. 2
                        1-CR 10-56 P. 35
                        1-HF 12-56 P. 96
                        2-LJ 9-1-56 P. 1888
                        1-MH 7/8-56 P. 31
                        1-SR 9-29-56 P. 44
              Gormer/Krumbein/Huhne/Himmer
                  Vox PLP 7740
                        1-AR 9-53 P. 19
                        2-GS 1-53 P. 8
                        4-NR 5-54 P. 6
              Orval/Tommasini/Desprez/Janssens
                  Vox QSVBX 5145
                        2-HF 7-78 P. 77
                        2-NR 6-78 P. 6
              Seiffert/Hauptmann/Kohler/Klier
                  Angel SZ 37655
                        2-AR 4-80 P. 43
                        3-FF 5/6-80 P. 147
                        1-GR 12-79 P. 1018
                        1-ML 2-80 P. 3
                        2-NR 4-80 P. 4
                        1-ST 5-80 P. 92
              Shapiro/Afanasiev/Starozhilov/Krivnetsky
                  Monitor 2023
                        2-HF 1-59 P. 60
                        3-HMR 3-59 P. 70
                        2-SR 10-25-58 P. 50
              Tylsar/Tylsar/Hrdina/Suchaanek
                  Panton 110 585
                        1-GR 6-78 P. 62
                        1-HFN 5-78 P. 141
                        1-RR 5-78 P. 37
Shaw, Lowell
      Fripperies for 4 Horns ( #2, 4, 5, 7, 8, 9, 12)
              Seiffert/McDonald/Park/Shaw
              Mark Ed. Recordings Ens.
              Series MES 29088

Stravinsky, Igor (1882-1971)
    Four Russian Choruses (Arranged for 4 Horns)
            Decker/Lott/Hude/Markowitz
            Columbia ML 5107
                    1-AR 9-56 P. 2
                    1-CR 10-56 P. 35
                    1-HF 12-56 P. 96
                    2-LJ 9-1-56 P. 1888
                    1-MH 7/8-56 P. 31
                    1-SR 9-29-56 P. 44
Tchaikovsky, P. I. (1840-1893)
    Pizzicato Ostinato from Symphony # 4 (4 Horns)
            Seiffert/McDonald/Park/Shaw
            Mark Ed. Recordings Ens.
            Series MES 29088
Telemann, Georg Philipp (1681-1767)
    Concerto for 3 Horns
            Stagliano/Berv/Buffington
            Kapp 3388
    Concerto for 3 Horns in D
            Bujanovski/ ? / ?
            Melodiya C10 09489-90
            Stagliano/Berv/Buffington
            Kapp 9053
                    1-CR 2-61 P. 34
                    2-HF 2-61 P. 77
                    1-NR 5-61 P. 6
                    1-SR 1-28-61 P. 46
            Westminister MCA 1422
                    2-FF 5/6-81 P. 170
                    1-NR 12-80 P. 6
    Suite in F for 3 Horns
            Stagliano/Berv/Buffington
            Kapp 3388
Tippett, Michael (1905-    )
    Sonata for 4 Horns (1955)
            Tuckwell/ ?
            Argo ZRG 535
Traditional
    Christmas Music
            Stolat 0120
Tscherepnin, Nikolai (1873-1945)
    Six Pieces for 4 Horns
            Van Woudenberg/Schepel/Soeteman/Steinmann
            (German) RCA RL 30321 AW
    The Hunt (4 Horns)
            Leuba/Binstock/Barrington/Wirth/Brouk
            Concert Disc CS 243
                    4-AR 7-64 P. 1042
                    1-HF 8-64 P. 88
                    1-NR 6-64 P. 6
Wagner (1813-1883)
    Fantasy (5 Horns)
            Bujanovski/Yevstignejev/Shalyt/Ivanov/Glukhov
            Melodiya CM 10 05397-8


63

Weber, Friedrich Dionys (1766-1828)
      Quartet, 4 Horns, # 3
                  Supraphon 111 0164
                        1-GR  4-74 P. 1862
                        1-HFN 3-74 P. 119
                        1-NR  8-72 P. 15
                        1-RR  2-74 P. 29

# Horn Duos

Bach, J. S. (1685-1750)
    Partita in Bb, S. 825 (Horn & Guitar)
        De Rosa, Vincent
            Capitol P. 8582
                1-GR 11-62 P. 258
                2-HSR 8-62 P. 59
                3-LJ 10-1-62 P. 3430
                3-NYT 5-27-62 P. X17
                3-SR 6-30-62 P. 42
Dauprat, Louis Francois (1781-1868)
    Air Ecossaise Varie for Horn & Harp
        Barboteu, Georges
            Erato STU 70643
    Sonata for Harp with Horn Accompaniment
        Barboteu, Georges
            Erato STU 70643
Duvernoy, Frederic (1765-1838)
    Nocturne (Horn & Harp)
        Barboteu, Georges
            Erato STU 70643
Harrison, Lou (1917-    )
    Main Bersama-Sama for Gamelan & French Horn
        Hartman, Scott
            CRI S 455
                1-ARG 3-82 P. 21
                1-FF 3/4-82 P. 161
                1-HF 3-82 P. 58
                1-NR 1-82 P. 6
                1-OV 1-82 P. 31
Haydn, Michael (1737-1806)
    Adagio & Allegro Molto for Horn, Alto Trombone &
    Orchestra
        Baumann, Hermann
            Telefunken Cassette 4 42 419
            Avant AV 1013
    Concerto for Horn & Trombone in D
        Bujanovski, V.
            Melodiya CM 16649-50
Isoz, Etienne (1905-    )
    Divertissement for Horn & Harp
        Molnar, Josef
            VDE 3001

Makovecky, Jan
    Duo Concertant # 1 for Horn & Viola
        Linder, Albert
            Fermat FLPS 53
Mumma, Gordon
    Hornpipe for Horn (dbl reed mouthpiece)
    & Cybersonic Console
            Mainstream MS 5010
                4-HF 4-73 P. 100
                4-ST 4-73 P. 128
Olsen, Sparre (1903-    )
    Aubade, Op. 57 # 3 (Horn & Flute)
        Oien, Ingegard
            BIS LP 171
                1-FF 9/10-81 P. 277
                2-GR 8-81 P. 317
                1-NR 2-81 P. 7
Schickele, Peter (1935-    )
    Concert for Horn & Hardart, S. 27
        Froelich, Ralph
            Vanguard VSD 79195
                1-AR 2-66 P. 508
                1-AU 4-66 P. 57
                4-GR 12-66 P. 328
                3-HF 2-66 P. 101
                1-HSR 3-66 P. 73
Wolff, Christian
    Duet II (Horn & Piano)
        Hillyer, Howard
            Mainstream 5015
                1-HF 5-64 P. 64
                4-MA 3-64 P. 51
                4-NYT 1-26-64 P. X18
                4-SR 3-28-64 P. 61
Yannay, Yehuda (1937-    )
    The Hidden Melody (Cello & Horn)
        Benjamin, Barry
            Advance Recordings F GR 275

# Horn Trios

```
Banks, Don (1923-    )
     Trio (Hn/Vln/Pf)
          Tuckwell, Barry
               Argo ZRG 5475
                    1-GR 11-66 P. 268
                    1-ML 11-66 P. 9
                    1-NR 2-67 P. 6
Berkeley, Lennox (1903-    )
     Trio for Horn, Violin & Piano, Op. 19
          Brain, Dennis
               Seraphim 60073
                    1-AU 10-68 P. 98
                    1-GR 12-65 P. 312
                    2-HF 10-68 P. 140
                    1-HSR 9-68 P. 102
                    1-NR 9-68 P. 8
          Cap G 7175
                    1-AR 12-59 P. 265
                    1-GR 2-53 P. 399
                    2-ML 2-55 P. 10
                    1-NYT 9-13-59 P. X21
          Hermansson
               Thorofon Capella MTH 257
Beyer, Frederick
     Conversations for Brass Trio
     (Tpt/Hn/Trb)
          Robinson, William
               Golden Crest CRS 4081
Brahms, Johannes (1833-1897)
     Trio in Eb, Op. 40 for Horn, Violin & piano
          Barrows, John
               Mercury MG 50210; SR 90210
                    2-HF 10-60 P. 74
                    1-HSR 9-60 P. 74
                    1-NR 10-60 P. 4
          Baumann, Hermann
               BASF MPS 25 21184-3
```

Brahms, Johannes (Cont'd)
    Trio in Eb, Op. 40 for Horn, Violin & Piano (Cont'd)
       Bloom, Myron
           Columbia ML 8643
           Columbia MS 6243
               1-CR 9-61 P. 34
               1-HF 9-61 P. 85
               1-HSR 9-61 P. 69
               1-MA 10-61 P. 36
               2-NR 7-61 P. 7
           Columbia MS 7266
               3-NR-69 P. 9
       Brain, Aubrey
           OPAL 805
           Pathe-Odeon PCOLH 41
               1-AM 1-64 P. 111
               1-GR 6-59 P. 27
               1-ML 4-59 P. 9
           Seraphim IC 6044
               1-HA 12-69 P. 46
               1-HF 10-69 P. 82
               4-NYT 8-31-69 P. D17
               1-SR 9-27-69 P. 61
               1-ST 11-69 P. 112
       Brain, Dennis
           Perennial 2007
           BBC REB 175
               1-GR 7-74 P. 225
               2-RR 8-74 P. 44
           Everest 3432
               1-NR 3-79 P. 10
       Ceccarossi, Domenico
           Angelicum Milano STA 9044
       Civil, Alan
           Angel 36472
               3-AM 7-68 P. 105
               2-GR 3-68 P. 489
               3-HF 5-68 P. 76
               2-HSR 7-68 P. 76
               3-LJ 10-1-68 P. 3536
               2-ML 3-68 P. 10
           Angel RL 32132
           (France) EMI 2C 181 03710/1
           (England) HMV ASD 2354
       Damm, Peter
           Eterna 8 26 231
       Devemy, Jean
           Mercury MG 15015
               3-AR 12-50 P. 135
               3-GR 3-53 P. 257
               2-GS 10-50 P. 3
               3-LJ 3-15-51 P. 540
               2-NR 9-51 P. 4
               3-SR 1-20-51 P. 37
       Del Vescovo, Pierre
           Erato STU 71159

Brahms, Johannes (Cont'd)
      Trio in Eb, Op. 40 for Horn, Violin & Piano (Cont'd)
            Eger, Joseph
                  RCA LM 2420
                        1-AR 1-61 P. 390
                        1-HF 2-61 P. 66
                        2-HSR 2-61 P. 66
                        2-NR 12-60 P. 11
                        2-SR 11-26-60 P. 54
            Friedrich
                  Hungaroton SLPX 11 672
                        2-GR 5-75 P. 1991
                        1-ML 5-75 P. 6
            Grigorev
                  2 Monitor 2158/9
                        1-ARG 11-78 P. 19
                        2-AU 5-79 P. 104
                        2-HF 7-79 P. 140
                        1-NR 10-78 P. 5
                        1-ST 12-78 P. 156
            Hauptman, Norbert
                  DG 2532 097
            Hogner
                  London 410114-1
            James, Ifor
                  PYE GSGC 14132
            Jones, Mason
                  Columbia ML 4892
                        1-AR 10-54 P. 64
                        1-HF 11-54 P. 50
                        1-NR 10-54 P. 10
            Klanska-Bouchalova, Vlad
                  Panton 8111 0046
            Klein, Fred
                  Renaissance 13
                        2-NR 11-50 P. 6
                        2-SR 1-20-51 P. 37
            Koch
                  Westminister 51-46
                        2-AR 9-52 P. 23
                        2-CR 9-54 P. 44
                        2-GR 10-54 P. 203
                        1-GS 8-52 P. 2
                        2-HF 11/12-52 P. 52
                        3-LJ 6-15-53 P. 1100
            Kopp, Gunter
                  Electrola WDLP 549
            Orval, Francis
                  Phillips 9500 161
                        1-AR 4-77 P. 15
                        3-GR 1-77 P. 1159
                        1-HF 4-77 P. 94
                        3-ML 1-77 P. 6
                        3-NR 2-77 P. 8
            Penzel, Erich
                  Vox SVBX 578
                        2-ML 6-67 P. 7
                        2-HF 12-66 P. 86

Brahms, Johannes (Cont'd)
    Trio in Eb, Op. 40 for Horn, Violin & Piano (Cont'd)
        Sanders
            L'Oiseau Lyre SOL 314
                1-SFC 6-14-74 P. 29
        Seifert
            DG SLPM 139398
                2-AR 9-69 P. 47
                1-GR 8-69 P. 313
                1-GR 1-69 P. 1014
                1-NR 11-69 P. 5
                1-NYT 10-19-69 P. D34
                1-SR 12-27-69 P. 56
        Shapero, Yakov
            Bruno 14010
                2-MH 6-58 P. 31
        Shapiro, Jacob
            Monitor S 2066 E
            Westminister XWN 18181
                1-AR 10-56 P. 26
                1-HF 12-56 P. 76
                2-LJ 12-1-56 P. 2836
                1-MH 11/12-56 P. 45
                2-SR 12-8-56 P. 40
        Stagliano, James
            Boston Records B 209
                1-AU 8-56 P. 30
                1-HF 6-56 P. 54
                1-MH 7/8-56 P. 30
        Stefek, Miraslav
            Supraphon SUA ST 11 105 16
        Tarjani, Ferenc
            Hungaroton 12473
        Tuckwell, Barry
            London 6628
                1-GR 5-69 P. 1572
                1-HF 11-69 P. 93
                1-ML 5-69 P. 7
                1-ST 12-69 P. 108
        Tylsar
            Supraphon 111 2251 52
                2-ML 6-79 P. 8
                1-NR 12-79 P. 7
        Vogelsang, Frederick
            Lance Productions NYC FV3B
                2-HF 6-69 P. 86
Chavez, Carlos (1899-1978)
    Soli IV (1964)
        Zarzo, Vincente
            Odyssey Y 31534
                2-HF 1-73 P. 82
Crusell, Bernhard (1755-1838)
    Sinfonia Concertante (Hn/Cl/Bsn)
        Linder, Albert
            Caprice CAP 1144

Danzi, Franz (1763-1826)
      Trio in F (Hn/Bsn/Vln)
            Tuckwell, Barry
                  RCI 405
                        4-FF 7/8-81 P. 48
Devienne
      Trio in F (Hn/Cl/Bsn)
                  Eichendorff Wind Quintet
                  Baroque (Canada) 2869
                        2-NR 12-67 P. 10
Doppler
      Nocturne, Op. 19 (Fl/Hn/Pf)
                  BIS 128
      Souvenir du Rigi, Op. 34 (Fl/Hn/Pf)
                  BIS 128
Duvernoy, Frederic
      Trio # 1 (Hn/Vl/Pf)
            Friedrich
                  Hungaroton SLPX 11 672
Godfrey, Daniel S. (1949-    )
      Trio (Hn/Cl/Vla) (1976)
            Hundemer
                  Orion ORS 79340
                        1-NR 11-79 P. 5
Hambraeus, Bengt (1928-    )
      Transit II for Horn, Trombone,
      & Electric Guitar
            Lansky-Otto, Ib
                  (Swedish) Artist ALP 102
Haydn, Franz Joseph (1732-1809)
      Divertimento a Tre (Hn/Vln/Vc)
            Koch
                  Haydn Society HSLP 1044
                        1-GR 10-53 P. 144
                        1-GS 3-52 P. 3
                        2-HF SUMMER '52 P. 54
                        1-ML 5-53 P. 3
            Linder, Albert
                  Amadeo AVRS 6222
                        3-AR 3-63 P. 556
                        4-NR 8-63 P. 7
                        1-NYT 8-4-63 P. X11
                  Mace MXX 9087
            Neudecker
                  MHS 1961
            Hamilton, William
                  Sonar SD 130
            Rife, Jean
                  Titanic 94
Herzogenberg, Heinrich (1843-1900)
      Trio for Oboe, Horn & Piano, Op. 61
            Tuckwell, Barry
                  Claves D 803
                        1-CR 1-82 P. 43
                        1-FF 5/6-82 P. 56
                        1-HFN 6-80 P. 107
                        1-ML 4-80 P. 7
                        1-RR 4-80 P. 88

Hughes, M.
     Divertimento (Tpt/Hn/Trb)
          Robinson, William
               Golden Crest CRS 4081
Huston, Scott (1916-    )
     Idioms (Hn/Cl/Vln) (1968)
          Little
               Music Now CFS 3037
                    1-NR 10-74 P. 8
Jeppesen, Knud (1892-1974)
     Lille Trio in D
     (Hn/Fl/Pf) ("La Primavera")
          Oien, Ingegard
               BIS LP 171
                    1-FF 9/10-81 P. 277
                    2-GR 8-81 P. 317
                    1-NR 2-81 P. 7
Kellaway, Roger (1939-    )
     Sonoro and Dance of the Ocean Breeze
     (Hn/Bass Hn/Pf)
          Wekre, Froydis Ree
               CRYS S 126
Keller, Homer (1915-    )
     Interplay for Flute, Horn & Percussion
               Advent 11
Knight, Morris (1933-    )
     Cassation for Trumpet, Horn & Trombone
          Robinson, William
               Golden Crest CRS 4081
Moylan, William
     Trio for Flute, Horn & Piano (1981)
          Wakefield, David
               Opus One 74
Nelhybel, Vaclav (1919-    )
     Brass Trio
               Soloists/Orchestra Sinfonica Di Roma
               SRS 12006
                    2-HF 9-65 P. 94
                    1-NR 8-65 P. 15
Poulenc, Francis (1899-1963)
     Sonata for Trumpet, Horn & Trombone
               Philip Jones Brass Ensemble
               ARGO ZRG 731
                    4-GR 6-73 P. 62
                    1-ML 6-73 P. 4
                    1-NR 10-73 P. 13
                    1-ST 1-74 P. 118
          Barboteu, Georges
               Ars Nova Brass Quartet
               MHS 3753 H
          Berv, Arthur
               Stradivari STR 605 A
                    1-NYT 12-16-51 P. X10
                    4-SR 2-23-52 P. 69
          Birdwell, Edward
               American Brass Quintet
               4-Desto 6474/7
                    1-ST 3-70 P. 120
72

Poulenc, Francis (Cont'd)
    Sonata for Trumpet, Horn & Trombone (Cont'd)
        Cerminaro, John
            CRYS S 367
        Civil, Alan
            EMI 2C 165 12579-22
                1-GR 2-81 P. 1098

        Schneider, Vincent
            Brass Arts Quintet
            Grenadilla GS 1027
Presser, William (1916-      )
    Prelude, Fugue & Postlude (Tpt/Hn/Trb)
        Robinson, William
            Golden Crest CRS 4081
Reicha, Anton (1770-1836)
    Twelve Trios for 2 Horns & Bassoon
        Lockwood/Chernin
            MHS 3500
Reinecke, Carl (1824-1910)
    Trio in a, Op. 88 # 3 (Hn/Ob/Pf)
        Johannesen, Fred
            Varese/Sarabande 81003
                1-FF 3/4-78 P. 35
    Trio in a, Op. 188 (Hn/Ob/Pf)
        Tuckwell, Barry
            Claves D 803
                1-CR 1-82 P. 43
                1-FF 5/6-82 P. 56
                1-ML 4-80 P. 7
    Trio for Horn, Clarinet & Piano, Op. 274
        Smith, Calvin
            WIMR 20
                1-FF 9/10-81 P. 167
                1-NR 8-81 P. 9
Running, A.
    Aria & Allegro
        Barnett, George
            Chestnut Brass Company
                Chestnut Brass Company 3 0001
Schuller, Gunther (1925-      )
    Trio for Horn, Oboe & Viola (1948)
        Bakkegard
            CRI S 423
                1-FF 11/12-80 P. 222
                1-NR 10-80 P. 6
Telemann, G. P. (1681-1767)
    Concerto a, 3 in F for Horn, Recorder & Continuo
        Nonesuch 71065
                1-AR 9-65 P. 71
                1-NR 9-65 P. 7
        Baumann, Hermann
            Intercord 944-09 K
Wilder, Alec (1907-1980)
    Sonata for Horn, Tuba & Piano (1972)
        Barrows, John
            Golden Crest GC 7018

Wilder, Alec (Cont'd)
    Sonata for Horn, Tuba & Piano (1963) (Cont'd)
       Barrows, John (Cont'd)
              1-HF 4-65 P. 99
              1-HSR 3-66 P. 100
              2-NR 4-65 P. 8
  ·  Suite # 2 for Horn, Tuba & Piano (1972)
       Barrows, John
          Golden Crest GC 4147

# Horn and Strings

Amon, Johannes Andreas (1763-1825)
        Quartet in F for Horn & Strings (Hn/Vn/Vc)
                Baumann, Hermann
                        BASF BAC 21189-4
                                2-GR 11-73 P. 942
                                2-NR 4-74 P. 4
                        HNH 4033
                                1-FF 9/10-79 P. 177
                                1-NR 8-79 P. 8
                                1-ST 9-79 P. 96
                Linder, Albert
                        BIS 47
                                3-FF 7/8-78 P. 104
                                1-HFN 12-77 P. 168
                                2-R&R 11-77 P. 85
                                1-SFC 11-12-78 P. 49
Baer, Jonathan (1655-1700)
        Concerto in Bb for Post Horn, Hunting Horn,
        Strings & Continuo
                Neudecker, Gustav
                        DGG Archiv 198473
Beethoven, L. Van (1770-1827)
        Sextet in Eb, Op. 81b (2 Hn/2 Vn/Va/Vc)
                Bujanovski/Shalyt
                        Melodiya CM 02949-50
                Leuba/Binstock
                    Lenox String Quartet
                        Audiophile AP-70
                                1-HF 4-61 P. 108
                                1-HSR 5-61 P. 70
                                2-SR 1-28-61 P. 44
                        Audiophile APS 110
                                4-NR 5-72 P. 5
                Linder/Ruetten
                        Amadeo AVRS 6222
                                3-AR 3-63 P. 556
                                4-NR 8-63 P. 7
                                1-NYT 8-4-63 P. X11
                Penzel/Haucke
                    Endres Quartet
                        Vox SVBX 579
                                2-LJ 4-1-70 P. 1348

Beethoven, L. Van (Cont'd)
      Sextet in Eb, Op. 81b (2 Ha/2 Vn/Va/Vc) (Cont'd)
            Sanders/  ?
                  HMV ASD 2671
            Seifert/Klier
                  DGG 272 0015
                  Philips SAL 3709
            Speth/Rawyler
                  Pascal String Quartet
                  Concert Hall CHS 1216
                        2-GS 4-53 P. 2
                        2-HF 11/12-53 P. 67
            Tombock/Altmann
                  Vienna Octet (Members)
                  Decca SXL 6464
                  Vienna Octet (Members)
                  London CS 6674
                        1-GR 11-70 P. 811
                        2-HF 11-71 P. 92
                        2-ML 11-70 P. 8
                        1-NR 10-71 P. 8
                        1-ST 12-71 P. 83
Bentzon, Jorgen (1897-1951)
      Symphonic Trio for 3 Instrumental Groups
                  Odeon Moak 10
Boccherini, Luigi
      (2) Concertos in C for Violoncello, 2 Horns & Strings
            Baumann/Van Woudenberg
                  Telefunken AWT 9473
                        2-CR 9-66 P. 26
                        1-HF 8-66 P. 80
                        1-NR 6-66 P. 4
Boehner, Johann Ludwig (1787-1860)
      Sechs Variation fuer Horn, 2 Violins, Viola & Cello,
      Op. 24
            Machata, Siegfried
                  RBM 3038
Heiden, Bernhard (1910-    )
      Quintet for Horn & String Quartet (1952)
            Jones, Mason
                  Gasparo GS 207
                        2-AR 4-81 P. 30
                        2-FF 11/12-80 P. 140
                        1-IN 7-81 P. 29
                        1-NR 8-80 P. 10
            Leuba, Christopher
                  Olymp 102
                        1-NR 2-72 P. 6
                        1-ST 2-73 P. 112
Hoffmeister, Franz (1754-1812)
      Quintet in Eb for Horn & String Quartet
            Nalli, Guelfo
                  (Argentine) CBS Estereo 5488
Mozart, L. (1719-1787)
      Sinfonia da Camera (Hn/Vn/2 Vla/Cont)
            Baumann, Hermann
                  Concerto Amsterdam
                  BASF KBF 21195

Mozart, L.   (Cont'd)
    Sinfonia di Caccia (Hn/Vn/2 Vla/Cont)
        Baumann, Hermann
            Concerto Amsterdam
                HNH 4033
                    1-FF 9/10-79 P. 177
                    1-NR 8-79 P. 8
                    1-ST 9-79 P. 96
Mozart, W. A. (1756-1791)
    Divertimento # 7 in D, K. 173a=205
        Klein/Rottensteiner
            MHS 609
                2-AR 8-65 P. 1172
                2-HF 12-65 P. 98
    Divertimento # 10 in F, K. K. 247
        Klein/Rottensteiner
            MHS 609
                2-AR 8-65 P. 1172
                2-HF 12-65 P. 98
        Kotulan/Peter
            Philips 6500 538
                1-NR 4-74 P. 2
                1-NYT 1-27-74 P. D24
    Divertimento # 11 in D, K. 251
        Kotulan/Peter
            Philips 6500 538
                1-NR 4-74 P. 2
                1-NYT 1-27-74 P. D24
    Divertimento # 15 in Bb, K. 287
    (2 Hn/2 Vn/Va/Vc)
        Koch/Hoffman
            Vienna Baroque Ensemble
                Erato EFM 8045
        Seifert/Klier
            Philips SA L 3710
    Quintet for Horn & Strings in Eb, K386c=407
            DG 2530 012
                GR 4-71 P. 1639
        Barrows, John
            Allegro Elite 62
                3-GS 10-50 P. 6
                3-JR 7/8-50 P. 23
                2-NA 9-23-50 P. 275
            Concert Disc CS 204
                1-NYT 4-19-59 P. X15
            Orion 7281
                2-AU 12-72 P. 87
                4-NR 10-72 P. 6
        Baumann, Hermann
            Telefunken 641009
                2-NR 1-69 P. 6
                1-ST 1-69 P. 104
            Telefunken 642173
                1-FF 3/4-80 P. 125
                2-HF 5-80 P. 76
                1-ML 4-78 P. 8
            Teldec SMT 1211

Mozart, W. A. (Cont'd)
     Quintet for Horn & Strings in Eb (Cont'd)
          Bourgue, Daniel
               (French) Decca 7233
          Brain, Dennis
               Everest 3432
                    1-NR 3-79 P. 10
               BBC 22175 E (Mono)
          Brown
               Phillips 9500772
          Ceccarossi, Domenico
               MHS 3579-80
               Angelicum Milano LPA 5965
               Pentaphon MCF 15003-4
          Cerny
               Supraphon 111 1671-2
                    1-NR 11-75 P. 8
                    1-ST 1-76 P. 100
          Damm, Peter
               Eterna 8 26 758
          de Rosa, Ottavio
               Stradivari 601
                    2-AR 7-51 P. 387
                    2-SR 4-28-51 P. 48
                    4-SR 7-14-51 P. 48
          Del Vescovo, Pierre
               MHS 557
                    2-AR 12-64 P. 346
          Huber, Sebastian
               Vox SVBX 548
                    3-AR 5-66 P. 864
                    2-NYT 4-3-66 P. X16
               Turnabout 34035
                    1-GR 6-66 P. 30
                    1-HSR 12-66 P. 94
                    2-ML 6-66 P. 7
                    2-NR 9-66 P. 6
               Vox DL 1000
                    1-AR 10-64 P. 142
                    1-GR 3-65 P. 430
                    1-NR 11-65 P. 7
                    2-SR 2-27-65 P. 60
          James, Ifor
               PYE GSGC 14132
          Jones, Mason
               Gasparo GS 207 D
                    1-CR 9-801-CR 9-80 P. 43
                    3-FF 11/12-80 P. 140
                    2-NR 8-80 P. 10
          Klier, Manfred
               Phillips 6747 383
          Lexutt, Walter
               EMC IC 065-99 695
          Linder, Albert
               Amadeo AVRS 6222
                    3-AR 3-63 P. 556
                    2-HSR 1-64 P. 80
                    4-NR 8-63 P. 7

Mozart, W. A. (Cont'd)
     Quintet for Horn & Strings in Eb (Cont'd)
          Linder, Albert (Cont'd)
               Mace MXX 9087
          Magnardi, Jacky
               ORYX 5XL C3
               Telefunken 5635017
               Telefunken SLAT 25097
                    2-GR 3-73 P. 1705
                    1-HF 12-74 P. 93
                    1-ML 3-73 P. 9
                    1-ML 4-74 P. 14
                    1-NR 10-74 P. 7
          Nalli, Guelfo
               Phillips, 65 99 226
          Neudecker, Gustav
               MHS 1961
          Pandolfi
               Turnabout 37018
                    1-FF 9/10-82 P. 284
                    1-OV 7-82 P. 28
               Desto DC 7208
                    3-FF 9/10-82 P. 286
          Penzel, Erich
               CMS/ORYX EXP 43
                    2-GR 10-70 P. 615
          Seifert, Gerd
               Phillips 6503066
          Speth, Werner
               Mon S 2114
                    1-AR 4-67 P. 662
                    1-NR 3-67 P. 9
               Concert Hall CHS 1188
                    2-AR 9-53 P. 21
                    1-GS 8-53 P. 5
                    1-NR 6-54 P. 9
                    2-NYT 8-9-53 P. X7
                    1-SR 8-29 53 P. 57
          Stagliano, James
               Boston 201
                    1-NYT 5-31-53 P. X6
          Tarjani, Ferenc
               Hungaroton SLPX 11828
                    2-FF 7/8-78 P. 58
     Sextet in F, K.522 (2Hn/2 Vn/Va/Vc)
          DGG C 922
          Westminister 53-15
                    2-AR 11-54 P. 101
                    1-GR 5-55 P. 527
                    2-HF 12-54 P. 67
                    2-NR 12-54 P. 9
                    1-NYT 11-7-54 P. X12
                    1-SR 10-30-54 P. 74

Mozart, W. A. (Cont'd)
    Sextet in F, K.222 (2 Hn/2 Vn/Va/Vc) (Cont'd)
        Vienna Mozart Ensemble
           London STS 15301
                1-AU 11-75 P. 96
                1-GR 2-71 P. 1316
                1-ML 2-71 P. 3
                1-NR 7-75 P. 2
        Berger/Koller

           Westminister W9035
                1-AR 12-63 P. 324
        Seifert/Klier
           Philips 6503 066
          Amadeus Quartet
           DG 2531 253
        Spach/Roth
           TV 34134-5
                1-GR 5-68 P. 592
                1-LJ 6-15-68 P. 2464
                1-ML 6-68 P. 4
        Stoesser/Irmscher
           Vox PLP 9780
                1-AR 8-56 P. 196
                2-GR 12-56 P. 250
                1-HF 10-56 P. 94
                2-ML 12-56 P. 3
                2-NR 8-56 P. 6
Reicha, Anton
    Quintet in E for Horn & String Quartet
        Hamilton, William
           Sonar SD 130
    Quintet for Horn & Strings
        Machata, Siegfried
           RBM 3038
Rust, Friedrich Wilhelm (1739-1796)
    Quartet for Viola (Va/Vc/2 Hn)
        Stagliano/Shapiro
           Boston Records 201
                1-NYT 5-31-53 P. X6
Stich, Johann Wenzel (1746-1803)
    Quartet in F for Horn & Strings (Hn/Vn/Va/Vc)
        Neudecker, Gustav
           MHS 1961
         Stagliano, James
           Boston Records B 209
                1-HF 6-56 P. 54
                1-MH 7/8-56 P. 30
    Quartet in F, Op. 2, # 1 (Hn/Vn/Va/Vc)
        Linder, Albert
           MACE MXX 9087
           Amadeo AVRS 6222
                3-AR 3-63 P. 556
                4-NR 8-63 P. 7
                1-NYT 8-64-63 P. X11
    Quartet in F, Op. 18, # 1 (Hn/Vn/Va/Vc)
        Hamilton, William
           Sonar, SD 130

Telemann, Georg Philipp (1681-1767)
    Concerto for 2 Violins & 2 Natural Horns
        Fischer/Rohrer
                Vienna Concentus Musicus
                        Telefunken SAWT 9483
                            1-ML 8-67 P. 6
    Concerto Grosso in D for Horn, Violin, Strings
    & 2 Horns
        Bourgue
                Peters PLE 026
                        1-FF 11/12-78 P. 127
    Suite in D for Hunting Horns & Orchestra
                MHS 822
    Suite in F for 2 Horns, 2 Violins & Cont
        Bourgue/Fournier
                Peters PLE 026
                        1-FF 11/12-78 P. 127
        Friedrich/Brunner
                Hungaroton 12118
                      1-FF 5/6-81 P. 171
                      1-NR 2-81 P. 6
        Stagliano/Berv
                Kapp 9053
                      1-CR 2-61 P. 34
                      2-HF 2-61 P. 77
                      1-NR 5-61 P. 6
                      1-SR 1-28-61 P. 46

# Horn and Voice

Bach, W. F. (1710-1784)
    Aria Zerbrecht Zerreist
    Ihr Schnoeden Bande (Sop/Hn/Pf)
        Linder, Albert
            Fermat FLPS 53
Berlioz, Hector (1803-1869)
    Le Jeune Patre Breton
    (Sop/Hn Obligato/Pf)
            Philips 6500 009
                2-GR 6-70 P. 62
                2-HF 2-71 P. 74
                2-ML 5-70 P. 11
                1-NR 2-71 P. 10
                3-SR 12-26-70 P. 42
Brahms, Johannes (1833-1897)
    (4) Gesange, Op. 17
        Tarjani/Kiss
            Hungaroton SLPX 11691
                1-HF 8-76 P. 83
                2-NR 6-76 P. 12
Britten, Benjamin (1913-1976)
    The Burning Fiery Furnace, Op. 77
        Sanders
            London OSA 1163
                1-GR 12-67 P. 337
                1-HF 8-68 P. 78
                1-HSR 9-68 P. 84
                1-ML 12-67 P. 11
                1-NR 8-68 P. 7
    Canticle III, Op. 55
    (Still Falls The Rain)
        Civil
            (Eng) CBS 79316
        Tuckwell, Barry
            Argo ZRG 5277
                1-HF 4-71 P. 116
                1-NR 2-71 P. 19
            London OS 25332
                1-AR 1-63 P. 361
                1-GR 1-62 P. 360
                1-HF 12-62 P. 70
                4-HSR 3-63 P. 68

Britten, Benjamin (Cont'd)
    Curlew River, Op. 71
        Sanders
            London A 4156
                1-AM 8-66 P. 113
                1-AR 7-66 P. 1034
                4-AU 8-66 P. 86
                1-CR 9-66 P. 26
                1-GR 1-66 P. 348
    Nocturne, Op. 60
    (Tenor/Fl/E Hn/Cl/Hn/Bsn/Hp/Perc/Strings)
        Tuckwell, Barry
            London CS 6179
                1-AR 10-60 P. 122
                1-AU 9-60 P. 51
                1-GR 5-60 P. 585
                1-HSR 9-60 P. 76
                4-MA 8-60 P. 34
                2-ML 4-60 P. 13
    Serenade for Tenor, Horn & Strings, Op. 31
        Brain
            London 5358
        Brain, Dennis
            London LLP 994
                1-CR 7-54 P. 21
                1-GR 11-54 P. 261
                1-ML 7-54 P. 12
                3-NA 10-23-54 P. 372
                1-NR 11-54 P. 12
                1-NYT 10-24-54 P. X9
            Decca Eclipse ECM 814
        Busch
            Classics For Pleasure CFP 40250
        Bujanovski, Vitali
            Melodiya CM 03880
        Civil, Alan
            Angel S 36788
                1-GR 3-71 P. 1496
                2-HF 9-71 P. 88
                1-LJ 9-15-71 P. 2752
                2-ML 4-71 P. 13
                1-NR 9-71 P. 11
                2-ST 10-71 P. 90
        Clevenger, Dale
            DG 2531 199
                2-FF 7/8-80 P. 66
                1-GR 1-80 P. 1182
                2-HF 8-80 P. 70
                1-ML 3-80 P. 14
                1-NR 8-80 P. 2
                2-NYT 6-15-80 P. D31
        Froelich, Ralph
            Decca DL 10132
                2-AR 12-66 P. 320
                2-HF 12-66 P. 85
                2-HSR 4-67 P. 75
                2-NR 11-66 P. 6

Britten, Benjamin (Cont'd)
    Serenade for Tenor,Horn & Strings, Op. 31 (Cont'd)
        Froelich, Ralph (Cont'd)
                Var/Sara 81057
                        1-ARG 6-79 P. 16
                        1-ARG 4-82 P. 3
                        1-FF 5/6-80 P. 43
            Stagliano, James
                Boston 205
                        2-AR 11-53 P. 100
                        1-GS 10-53 P. 4
                        2-HF 1/2-54 P. 54
                        1-MQ 4-54 P. 284
            Tuckwell, Barry
                London CS 6398
                        2-AU 2-65 P. 50
                        1-GR 9-64 P. 140
                        1-HF 11-64 P. 102
                        1-HSR 1-65 P. 84
                London OS 26161
                        1-GR 9-70 P. 474
                        1-HF 6-71 P. 98
                        1-ML 9-70 P. 14
Bujanovski, V.
    Evening Songs (with Soprano)
            Bujanovski, Vitali
                Melodiya C 10-16969-70
Druckman, Jacob (1928-    )
    Dark Upon the Harp
    (Brass Quintet & Mezzo-Soprano + Perc)
            Froelich, Ralph
                CRI 167
                        1-LJ 4-1-64 P. 1585
                        1-MQ 1-64 P. 115
                        1-NR 7-63 P. 4
                        4-NYT 5-12-63 P. X10
Farbermann, Harold
    Evolution (Sop/Hn/Perc)
            Portch, Al
                Mercury SR 80015
            Pottle, Ralph
                Cambridge CRS 1805
                        1-AR 11-65 P. 239
                        1-HF 12-65 P. 92
                        2-HSR 2-66 P. 92
                        4-NR 10-65 P. 15
Fine, Vivian (1913-    )
    Paean (Choral ensemble/brass ensemble/tenor speaker)
                CRI S 260
                        1-NR 8-71 P. 6
Franco, Johan (1908-    )
    As the Prophets Foretold (Chorus/Soloists/Carillon &
    Brass)
            Birdwell, Ed
                CRI S 222

Goodman, Joseph
    4 Songs on Poems of Juan Jiminez (Hn/Voice)
        Kappy, David
            CRYS S 257
Grantham, Donald (1947-    )
    La Noche en la Isla (Baritone/Hn/Pf)
            CRI S 458
Henze, Hans Werner (1926-    )
    Versuch uber Schweine
            DG SLPM 139456
                    1-HF 8-70 P. 90
                    4-NR 8-70 P. 7
                    1-ST 9-70 P. 114
Hiller, Lejare (1924-    )
    Computer Cantata (1963)
        Tyler, Basil
            CRI SD 310
Jersild, J./Bujanovski
    3 Norwegian Folk Songs (Soprano/Hn)
        Bujanovski, V.
            Melodiya D 025233-34
Myslivecek, Josef
    Aria in Dis for Soprano, Horn & Strings
        Tylsar, Zdenek
            Panton 110 229 H
Plog, Anthony (1947-    )
    Four Sierra Scenes for Soprano & Brass Quintet (1972)
        Henderson, Robert
            CRYS S 205
Putsche, Thomas (1929-    )
    The Cat & the Moon (3 voices + mixed ensemble)
        Ondracek, Paul
            CRI SD 245
Rusconi, G.
    Cantata "Per I Semi Non Macinati"
    (Hn/Voice/Chorus/Orch)
        Ceccarossi, Domenico
            MHS 3362
Sacco, Peter (1928-    )
    3 Psalms for Brass Quintet & Tenor Voice (1966)
            Avant AV 1005
                    1-NR 7-73 P. 12
Schubert, Franz (1797-1828)
    Auf dem Strom (Soprano/Hn/Pf)
        Brain, Dennis
            Perennial 2007
        Bloom, Myron
            Columbia MS 6243
                    1-CR 9-61 P. 34
                    1-HF 9-61 P. 85
                    1-HSR 9-61 P. 69
                    3-MA 10-61 P. 36
                    1-NR 7-61 P. 7
        Damm
            Eterna 8 26 219
            MHS 3915
                    1-CR 6-79 P. 43
                    1-FF 9/10-79 P. 134

Schubert, Franz (Cont'd)
     Auf dem Strom (Soprano/Hn/Pf) (Cont'd)
          Linder, Albert
               BIS LP 47
                    1-FF 7/8-78 P. 104
          Sanders, Neill
               L'Oiseau Lyre SOL 314
          Smith, Calvin
               CRYS S 371
                    3-NR 6-76 P. 7
          Stagliano, James
               Boston 200
                    2-HF 9/10-53 P. 76
                    1-NR 3-53 P. 15
                    2-NYT 10-26-52 P. X10
          Studebaker, Julia
               Peters, Int. PLE 123
                    1-NYT 10-28-79 P. 024
                    1-ST 2-80 P. 136
     Nachtgesang im Walde D913 (Men's Choir & 4 Hn)
               Die Volks Platte SMVP 8043
     Songs (Tenor/Hn/Pf)
          Damm, Peter
               MHS 3915 H
Schuman, William (1910-    )
     The Young Dead Soldiers (Soprano/Hn/Choral Ensemble)
          CRI S 439
                    1-FF 11/12-81 P. 236
                    1-HF 11-81 P. 96
                    1-NR 8-81 P. 10
                    1-ST 8-81 P. 97
Shafer, Murray
     Minnelieder for Mezzo-Soprano & Woodwind Quintet
          Rittich, Eugene
               CBC SM 218
Shapey, Ralph (1921-    )
     Incantations for Soprano & 10 Instruments (1961)
          CRI SD 232
Starer, Robert (1924-    )
     Anna Margarita's Will (Soprano/Fl/Vc/Hn/Pf)
          Ingraham, Paul
               CRI S 453
                    1-FF 1/2-82 P. 181
                    1-NR 1-82 P. 6
Stravinski, Igor (1882-1971)
     Four Russian Choruses (Women's Voices/4 Horns)
          Nonesuch H 1133
                    1-AU 2-67 P. 48
                    1-HF 12-66 P. 106
                    1-HSR 1-67 P. 96
                    1-NR 12-66 P. 13
                    1-NYT 11-6-66 P. D28
Tredici, David Del
     Syzygy for Soprano, Horn, Chimes & Chamber Orch (1966)
          Columbia MS 7281
                    4-HF 11-69 P. 120
                    1-NR 10-69 P. 4
                    1-ST 12-69 P. 126

Tredici, David Del (Cont'd)
      Syzygy for Soprano, Horn, Chimes &
      Chamber Orchestra (1966)    (Cont'd)
                     CRI SD 492
                           1-FF 3/4-84 P. 237
                           2-NR 3-84 P. 12
Ussachevsky, Vladimir (1911-    )
      Missa Brevis (1971-72)
      (Sop/Chorus/3 Tpt/3 Hn/3 Trb/Ta)
                     CRI SD 297
Witkin, Beatrice (1916-    )
      Prose Poem for Contralto, Horn, Cello & Percussion
                     Opus One 10

# Brass Ensemble

Abreu, Jose
        Tico Tico
                                Philip Jones Brass Ensemble
                                Argo ZRG 895
                                        2-FF 5/6-80
                                        1-GR 1-79 P. 1334
Adam/Schlabach
        Cantique de Noel
                La Bar, Arthur
                                Annapolis Brass Quintet
                                Richardson Records RRS-5
Addison, John (1920-    )
        Divertimento for Brass, Op. 9 (2 Tpt/Hn/Trb)
                                Philip Jones Brass Ensemble
                                Argo ZRG 813
                                        1-GR 12-75 P. 1066
                                        1-ML 12-75 P. 6
                                        1-NR 8-76 P. 6
Adler, Samuel (1928-    )
        5 Movements for Brass Quintet
                Neilson, Diana
                                Chicago Chamber Brass
                                Pro Arte Sinfonia S 616
Adson, John
        2 Ayres for Cornetts & Sagbuts (2 Tpt/Hn/Trb/Bar)
                                Eastern Brass Quintet
                                Klavier KS 536
                                        1-AU 12-75 P. 106
                                        1-NR 5-75 P. 8
        2 Ayres for Cornetts & Sagbuts
        (7 Tpt/2 Hn/4 Trb/Bar/Tba)
                Andrus/Haines
                                Georgia State College Brass Ensemble
                                Golden Crest GC S 4083
        2 Ayres for Cornetts & Sagbuts
                Ingraham, Paul
                                New York Brass Quintet
                                RCA AGL 1 3968
                                        1-HF 9-67 P. 98B
                                        4-NR 7-67 P. 9

Adson, John (Cont'd)
    2 Ayres for Cornetts & Sagbuts (Cont'd)
        Meek/Keaney
            Voisin Brass Ensemble
            Unicorn 1003
                1-AR 2-55 P. 202
                1-ET 3-55 P. 18
                2-HF 3-55 P. 64-VII
                1-LJ 5-15-55 P. 1205
                11-MA 3-55 P. 22
                2-NR 4-55 P. 6
        Soper, Kenneth
            New York Brass Quintet
            Golden Crest CRS4148
                1-AR 3-77 P. 40
        Tillotson, Brooks
            Chamber Brass Players
            Classic Editions CE 1039
    3 Courtly Masquing Ayres
            Guy Touvron Brass Quintet
            MHS 4168
        Katzen
            Empire Brass Quintet
            Digitech DIGI 102
                1-ST 7-80 P. 86
    4 Courtly Masquing Ayres
            Paris Brass Quintet
            PLE 084
                2-FF 9/10-79 P. 181
Agricola
    Oublier Veul
            Philip Jones Brass Ensemble
            Argo ZRG 823
                1-GR 6-76 P. 61
                2-ML 5-76 P. 7
                1-NR 10-77 P. 7
Aichinger, Gregor (1564-1628)
    Jubilate Deo
            New York Brass Society
            WIM 3
                1-NR 5-72 P. 5
        Soper, Kenneth
            New York Brass Choir
            Golden Crest CRS 4148
                1-AR 3-77 P. 40
Albinoni, Tomaso (1671-1750)
    Adagio
            Canadian Brass Quintet
            CBS 1M 39035
    Suite in a
            Budapest Brass Quintet
            Hungaroton SLPX 12486
                1-FF 3/4-84 P. 322
                2-NR 3-84 P. 6
    Suite en Sol
        Ohanian, David
            Empire Brass Quintet
            Sine Qua Non SA 2014

Albinoni, Tomaso (Cont'd)
        Suite en La
                Osborne, Larry
                        Vintage Brass Ensemble
                        Ohlone Band Album CR 8242
Albrici
        Sonata
                        Berlin Philharmonic Brass Ensemble
                        DG 2532 066
                                1-FF 7/8-82 P. 268
                                1-FF 1/2-83 P. 336
                                1-NR 2-83 P. 4
                        Berlin Philharmonic Brass Ensemble
                        DG 2741 011
                                1-FF 1/2-83 P. 336
                                1-GR 11-82 P. 591
                                3-HF 11-83 P. 76
                                1-MG 7-82 P. 10
Allanbrook
        Invitation to the Sideshow
                Guy, Marc
                        Annapolis Brass Quintet
                        CRYS S 213
                                1-FF 9/10-83 P. 327
                                4-NR 8-83 P. 3
Alwyn, William (1905-    )
        Fanfare for a Joyous Occasion
        (3 Tpt/4 Hn/3 Trb/ Ta/Perc)
                        Locke Brass Consort
                        Unicorn UN 1-72012
                                1-FF 7/8-79 P. 133
                                2-GR 5-78 P. 1889
Amram, David Werner (1930-    )
        Fanfare
                Goldstein, Arthur
                        Grenadilla GS 1040
                                2-FF 7/8-80 P. 187
                                2-NR 7-78 P. 7
Amy, Gilbert (1936-    )
        Relais for Five Brass Instruments
                Wakefield, David
                        American Brass Quintet
                        CRYS S 214
Anderson, Leroy (1908-1975)
        Bugler's Holiday
                Soper, Kenneth
                        New York Brass Choir
                        Golden Crest CRS 4148
                                1-AR 3-77 P. 40
        Suite of Carols
        (4 Tpt/4 Hn/3 Trb/B Trb/Bar/Ta)
                Berger/Watson
                        Kansas University Brass Choir
                        Audio House AH 21473
Andresen
        Music from Royal Court of King Christian IV
                Hansen, Henning
                        Royal Danish Brass
                        Rondo Grammofon RLP 8303

Andresen (Con't)
        Suite Danica
                Hansen, Henning
                        Royal Danish Brass
                        Rondo Grammofon RLP 8303
Andrix, George (1932-    )
        Sequences for Brass Quintet (1971)
                Hackleman, Ralph
                        Tidewater Brass Quintet
                        Golden Crest GC 4174
Anonymous
        L'Amour de Moy
                        Ars Nova Brass Quintet
                        MHS 1446 Z
                                1-GR 1-72 P. 1233
        French Suite # 8
        de la Bibliotheque de Cassel
                        Ensemble de Cuivres
                        Societe Francaise du Son SXL 20093
                                2-AU 4-66 P. 59
                                1-NR 2-66 P. 6
        General Burgoyne's March
                Smith, Calvin
                        Annapolis Brass Quintet
                        Richardson Records RRS-3
        Just A Closer Walk With Thee
                Page, Graeme
                        Canadian Brass Quintet
                        Umbrella 05862
        Partie in G
                        Ars Nova Brass Quintet
                        MHS 4244W
        Partita # 6 in Bb
                        Ars Nova Brass Quintet
                        MHS 4244W
        16th Century Carmina
                Anderson, Paul
                        Iowa Brass Quintet
                        University of Iowa Press 29001
                                2-HF 7-77 P. 118
                                1-NR 2-77 P. 7
        Resonet in Laudibus
                Snyder, Kurt
                        Las Vegas Brass Quintet
                        Ashland Records AR 7118
        Sonata from Die Bankelsangerlieder
                        Ars Nova Brass Quintet
                        MHS 4244 W
                                1-GR 5-80 P. 1689
                        Pacific Brass Quintet
                        Avant AV 1004
                                2-NR 6-72 P. 8
                        Philip Jones Brass Ensemble
                        Argo ZRG 898
                                1-FF 1/2-80 P. 173
                                1-FU 5-80 P. 46
                                1-GR 8-79 P. 348
                                1-ML 5-79 P. 9

Anonymous (Cont'd)
    Sonata from Die Bankelsangerlieder (Cont'd)
                American Brass Quintet
                Folkways FMS 33652
                        2-AU 7-68 P. 46
                        4-NR 9-67 P. 6
            Meek/Keaney
                Voisin Brass Ensemble
                Unicorn 1003
                        1-AR 2-55 P. 202
                        1-ET 3-55 P. 18
                        2-HF 3-55 P. 64-VII
                        1-LJ 5-15-55 P. 1205
                        11-MA 3-55 P. 22
                        2-NR 4-55 P. 6
            Ingraham, Paul
                New York Brass Quintet
                RCA AGL 1 3968
                        1-HF 9-67 P. 98B
                        4-NR 7-67 P. 9
            Soper, Kenneth
                New York Brass Choir
                Golden Crest CRS 4148
                        1-AR 3-77 P. 40
            Tillotson, Brooks
                Chamber Brass Players
                Classic Editions CE 1039
            Ward, Charles
                Metropolitan Brass Quintet
                CRYS S 208
                        2-NR 5-78 P. 5
    Veni, Veni, Emmanuel
            Snyder, Kurt
                Las Vegas Brass Quintet
                Ashland Records AR 7118
Arban, Jean Baptiste
    Etude Characteristique
    (# 13 from 14 Characteristic Studies)
            James, Ifor
                Philip Jones Brass Ensemble
                Argo ZRG 852
                        1-GR 7-77 P. 201
                        1-HF 5-78 P. 116
                        1-ML 8-77 P. 6
                        1-NR 7-78 P. 7
Arnold, Malcolm (1921-    )
    Quintet, Op. 73 (1961)
                Concord S 1001
                Berlin Brass Quintet
                CRYS S 201
                        1-CR 3-75 P. 36
                        1-NR 1-75 P. 6
                Canadian Brass Quintet
                Moss Music Group MMG 1123
                        3-NR 3-81 P. 7

92

Arnold, Malcolm (Cont'd)
 Quintet, Op. 73 (1961) (Cont'd)
    Eastern Classical Brass Quintet
     Klavier KS 561
      2-FF 7/8-79 P. 131
    Swedish Brass Quintet
     BIS 248
   Baker, Julian
     Halle Brass Consort
     PYE Golden Guinea GSGC 14114
   Covert, John
     Ithaca Brass Quintet
     Mark Ed. Records MEC 32558
   James, Ifor
     Philip Jones Brass Ensemble
     Argo ZRG 655
      1-GR 11-70 P. 812
      4-HF 11-71 P. 118
      1-NR 9-71 P. 6
      1-ML 11-70 P. 9
   Lloyd, Frank
     Decca SB 313
      1-GR 9-74 P. 488
   Page, Graeme
     Canadian Brass Quintet
     CBC: SM 239
   Strieby, Lawrence
     St. Louis Brass Quintet
     CRYS S 215
   Talamantes, Nona
     Mount Royal Brass Quintet
     McGill University 77004
      1-FF 5/6-82 P. 292
 Symphony for Brass Instruments, Op. 123
    Philip Jones Brass Ensemble
    Argo ZRG 906
     4-FF 1/2-81 P. 801
     1-GR 11-79 P. 801
     1-ML 12-79 P. 7
Aston, Hugh (1480-1522)
 Hornpipe
    Philip Jones Brass Ensemble
    Argo ZRG 717
     1-GR 11-74 P. 910
     2-ML 11-74 P. 5
Aubin, Tony (1907-  )
 Vitrail (Fanfare)
 (3 Tpt/4 Hn/3 Trb/Ta/Perc)
    Baldwin-Wallace College Brass Choir
    Mark Ed. Records MES 32565
Bach, Carl Philipp Emanuel (1714-1788)
 March
    Philip Jones Brass Ensemble
    Argo ZRG 898
     1-FF 1/2-80 P. 173
     1-FU 5-80 P. 46
     1-GR 8-79 P. 348
     1-ML 5-79 P. 9

Bach, Carl P. E. (Cont'd)
        March (Cont'd)
                        Philip Jones Brass Ensemble
                        London CS 7242
                                2-FF 7/8-82 P. 268
Bach, Jan (1937-      )
        Laudes (1971)
                Ingraham, Paul
                        New York Brass Quintet
                        CRYS S 210
                                1-AR 9-80 P. 50
                                1-FF 5/6-80 P. 129
                                1-NR 5-80 P. 8
Bach, J. S. (1685-1750)
        Air pour les Trompettes
                        Canadian Brass Quintet
                        Vanguard VSD 71253
                                2-CR 5-79 P. 43
                                1-FF 7/8-79 P. 132
                                1-NR 3-79 P. 9
                Page, Graeme
                        Canadian Brass Quintet
                        Boot BMC 3003
                Pyle, Ralph
                        Los Angeles Brass Quintet
                        CRYS S 602
                                2-NR 10-68 P. 5
                Strieby, Lawrence
                        St. Louis Brass Quintet
                        CRYS S 212
                                2-FF 7/8-83 P. 283
        Air on G String
                Page, Graeme
                        Canadian Brass Quintet
                        RCA ARV 1 4574
                                2-FF 7/8-83 P. 284
                                4-NR 6-83 P. 6
        Brandenburg Suite
                Page, Graeme
                        Canadian Brass Quintet
                        RCA ARC 1 4574
                                2-FF 7/8-83 P. 284
                                4-NR 6-83 P. 6
        Canzona in d
                        New York Brass Society
                        WIM 3
                                1-NR 5-72 P. 5
        Chorale, Trio & Fugue after Jesu Meine Freude S227
                        Ars Nova Brass Quintet
                        MHS 3635
        Christ Lag In Todesbanden
                        American Brass Quintet
                        BASF KMB 20812
                                1-NR 2-74 P. 6
        3 Christmas Pieces
                Snyder, Kurt
                        Las Vegas Brass Quintet
                        Ashland Records AR 7118

Bach, J. S. (Cont'd)
    Contrapunctus I
                Eastern Brass Quintet
              Klavier KS 536
                    1-AU 12-75 P. 106
                    1-NR 5-75 P. 8
          Barnett, George
              Chestnut Brass Company
              Chestnut Brass Company 3 0001 9
          Meek/Keaney
              Voisin Brass Ensemble
              Unicorn 1003
                    1-AR 2-55 P. 202
                    1-ET 3-55 P. 18
                    2-HF 3-55 P. 64-VII
                    1-LJ 5-15-55 P. 1205
                    11-MA 3-55 P. 22
                    2-NR 4-55 P. 6
          Talamantes, Nona
              Mount Royal Brass Quintet
              McGill University 77004
                    1-FF 5/6-82 P. 292
    Contrapunctus III
    (7 Tpt/2 Hn/4 Trb/Bar/Ta)
          Andrus/Haines
              Georgia State College Brass Ensemble
              Golden Crest GC S 4083
    Contrapunctus III
          Happe, Richard
              American Brass Quintet
              Folkways FM 3651
                    4-NR 12-65 P. 8
    Contrapunctus IV
          Osborne, Larry
              Vintage Brass Ensemble
              Ohlone Band Album CR 8242
    Contrapunctus VII
          Smith, Calvin
              Annapolis Brass Quintet
              CRYS S 206
                    2-NR 11-76 P. 7
          Wakefield, David
              American Brass Quintet
              CRYS S 214
    Contrapunctus IX
                  Canadian Brass Quintet
                Moss Music Group MMG 1123
                    3-NR 3-81 P. 7
                Eastern Brass Quintet
              Klavier KS 536
                    1-AU 12-75 P. 106
                    1-NR 5-75 P. 8
                Eastern Classical Brass Quintet
              Klavier KS 561
                    2-FF 7/8-79 P. 131
          Ohanian, David
              Empire Brass Quintet
              Sine Qua Non SA 2014

Bach, J. S. (Cont'd)
      Contrapunctus IX (Cont'd)
            Page, Graeme
                  Canadian Brass Quintet
                  CBC:   SM 239
            Page, Graeme
                  Canadian Brass Quintet
                  Moss Music Group MMG 1139
            van Driessche, Andre
                  Theo Mertens Brass Ensemble
                  Eufoda 1029
      Contrapunctus I & IX
            Ingraham, Paul
                  New York Brass Quintet
                  RCA AGL 1 3968
                        1-HF 9-67 P. 98B
                        4-NR 7-67 P. 9
      Contrapunctus III & IX
            Anderson, Paul
                  Iowa Brass Quintet
                  University of Iowa Press 29001
                        2-HF 7-77 P. 118
                        1-NR 2-77 P. 7
            Wakefield, David
                  American Brass Quintet
                  Delos DMS 3003
                        1-NR 3-80 P. 7
                        1-NYT 5-18-80 P. D32
                        1-ST 7-80 P. 84
      Fantasie
                  Eastern Brass Quintet
                  Klavier KS 536
                        1-AU 12-75 P. 106
                        1-NR 5-75 P. 8
            Page, Graeme
                  Canadian Brass Quintet
                  CBC:   SM 203
      Fantasie in C
                  Canadian Brass Quintet
                  Vanguard VSD 71254
                        4-FF 7/8-80 P. 186
                        2-NR 7-80 P. 6
            Ohanian, David
                  Empire Brass Quintet
                  Sine Qua Non SA 2014
            Page, Graeme
                  Canadian Brass Quintet
                  Boot BMC 3001
            Pyle, Ralph
                  Los Angeles Brass Quintet
                  CRYS S 602
                        2-NR 10-68 P. 5
      Fantasie in G, S. 572
            Lantz/Davis/Hadfield/Gullickson
                  University of Minnesota Brass Choir
                  UMBC 002

Bach, J. S. (Cont'd)
    Fuga IV
        Smith, Calvin
            Annapolis Brass Quintet
            2 CRYS S 202
                1-CR 3-75 P. 36
                1-NR 1-75 P. 6
    Fugue in g
            Canadian Brass Quintet
            Vanguard VSD 71254
                4-FF 7/8-80 P. 186
                2-NR 7-80 P. 6
        Page, Graeme
            Canadian Brass Quintet
            Boot BMC 3001
    Fugue in g, S. 578
        Halloin, Beth
            Chicago Chamber Brass
            Pro Arte Sinfonia S05616
                1-AR 3-84 P. 62
                1-FF 3/4-84 P. 324
        Page, Graeme
            Canadian Brass Quintet
            ARL 1 3554
                2-AR 11-80 P. 39
                1-CR 8-80 P. 43
                1-FF 7/8-80 P. 186
                1-NR 7-80 P. 6
                2-NYT 5-18-80 P. D32
            Canadian Brass Quintet
            ARL 1 3554
                2-AR 11-80 P. 39
                1-CR 8-80 P. 43
                1-FF 7/8-80 P. 186
                1-NR 7-80 P. 6
                2-NYT 5-18-80 P. D32
    Jesu Meine Freude
            Canadian Brass Quintet
            CBS IM 39035
    Jesu Meine Freude (3 Harmonizations)
        Tillotson, Brooks
            Chamber Brass Players
            Golden Crest CR 4008
                4-HF 12-57 P. 94
                2-LJ 1-1-58 P. 70
    Jesu, Joy of Man's Desiring
            Eastern Brass Quintet
            Klavier KS 536
                1-AU 12-75 P. 106
                1-NR 5-75 P. 8
        Page, Graeme
            Canadian Brass Quintet
            Moss Music Group MMG 1123
                3-NR 3-81 P. 7
            Canadian Brass Quintet
            Moss Music Group MMG 1139

Bach, J. S.  (Cont'd)
        Little Fugue in g
                Page, Graeme
                        Canadian Brass Quintet
                        Umbrella 05862
        Menuetto & Courante, S. 1107
                        Philip Jones Brass Ensemble
                        Argo ZRG 898
                                1-FF 1/2-80 P. 173
                                1-FU 5-80 P. 46
                                1-GR 8-79 P. 348
                                2-ML 5-79 P. 9
        Nun Danket Alle Gott (fr. Cantata 79)
                        Philip Jones Brass Ensemble
                        Argo ZRG 898
                                1-FF 1/2-80 P. 173
                                1-FU 5-80 P. 46
                                1-GR 8-79 P. 348
                                1-ML 5-79 P. 9
                        Philip Jones Brass Ensemble
                        London CS 7242
                                2-FF 7/8-82 P. 268
        Passacaglia & Fugue In c, S. 582
                Page, Graeme
                        Canadian Brass Quintet
                        ARL 1 3554
                                2-AR 11-80 P. 39
                                1-CR 8-80 P. 43
                                1-FF 7/8-80 P. 186
                                1-NR 7-80 P. 6
                                2-NYT 5-18-80 P. D32
        Postillion's Aria & Fugue
                        Philip Jones Brass Ensemble
                        Argo ZRG 898
                                1-FF 1/2-80 P. 173
                                1-FU 5-80 P. 46
                                1-GR 8-79 P. 348
                                1-ML 5-79 P. 9
        Prelude & Fugue in e
                Pyle, Ralph
                        Los Angeles Brass Quintet
                        CRYS S 602
                                2-NR 10-68 P. 5
        Prelude & Fugue in g
                Pacific Brass Quintet
                Avant AV 1004
                                2-NR 6-72 P. 8
        Prelude & Fugue on a Bach Theme
                Page, Graeme
                        Canadian Brass Quintet
                        RCA ARC 1-4574
                                2-FF 7/8-83 P. 284
                                4-NR 6-83 P. 6
        Rounds & Dances
                Becknell, Nancy
                        Wisconsin Brass Quintet
                        University of Wisconsin UW 103

Bach, J. S.  (Cont'd)
    Sarabande & Minuet
                    Eastern Brass Quintet
                        Klavier KS 536
                            1-AU 12-75 P. 106
                            1-NR 5-75 P. 8
            Cowden, Hugh
                        Chicago Symphony Brass Ensemble
                        Audiophile AP 21
    Sheep May Safely Graze
            Page, Graeme
                        Canadian Brass Quintet
                        ARL 1 3554
                            2-AR 11-80 P. 39
                            1-CR 8-80 P. 43
                            1-FF 7/8-80 P. 186
                            1-NR 7-80 P. 6
                            2-NYT 5-18-80 P. D32
    Singet Dem Hernn
                        Canadian Brass Quintet
                        CBS IM 39035
    Toccata & Fugue in d, S. 565
                        Atlanta Brass Ensemble
                        Crystal Clear CCS 7010
                            2-AR 11-79 P. 31
                            3-NR 6-80 P. 14
                            2-ST 2-80 P. 141
            Page, Graeme
                        Canadian Brass Quintet
                        ARL 1 3554
                            2-AR 11-80 P. 39
                            1-CR 8-80 P. 43
                            1-FF 7/8-80 P. 186
                            1-NR 7-80 P. 6
                            2-NYT 5-18-80 P. D32
                        Canadian Brass Quintet
                        RCA ARL 1 4733
                        Canadian Brass Quintet
                        Umbrella 05862
    Wachet Auf
            Page, Graeme
                        Canadian Brass Quintet
                        ARL 1 3554
                            2-AR 11-80 P. 39
                            1-CR 8-80 P. 43
                            1-FF 7/8-80 P. 186
                            1-NR 7-80 P. 6
                            2-NYT 5-18-80 P. D32
Balada, Leonardo (1923-    )
    Mosaico (1970)
                        American Brass Quintet
                        Serenus SRS 12041
                            1-NR 9-72 P. 6
Balbastre, Claude (1727-1799)
    Noel With Variations
            Snyder, Kurt
                        Las Vegas Brass Quintet
                        Ashland Records AR 7118

Banchieri, Adriano (1567-1634)
        Fantasia
                        Philip Jones Brass Ensemble
                        Argo ZRG 717
                                1-GR 11-74 P. 910
                                2-ML 11-74 P. 5
        2 Fantasias
                        Music Hall Brass Ensemble
                        Monogram 817
                                1-AR 7-54 P. 348
                                1-HF 12-54 P. 77
                                1-MA 12-15-54 P. 24
                                2-NYT 7-25-54 P. X6
                                2-SR 6-26-54 P. 52
        Udite, Ecco le Trombe
                        Philip Jones Brass Ensemble
                        London CS 7221
                                2-FF 11/12-81 P. 296
                                2-NR 1-82 P. 7
                                4-ST 5-82 P. 81
Barber, Samuel (1910-1981)
        Mutations from Bach
        (3 Tpt/4 Hn/3 Trb/Ta)
                        Locke Brass Consort
                        Unicorn RHS 339
                                1-GR 6-76 P. 58
Barboteu, Georges (1924-    )
        Astral (Brass Quintet & Metronome)
                        Ars Nova Brass Quintet
                        MHS 1446 Z
                                1-GR 1-72 P. 1233
        Chansonnerie
                Barboteu, Georges
                        Ars Nova Brass Quintet
                        MHS 3753 H
        Divertissement
                Barboteu, Georges
                        Ars Nova Brass Quintet
                        MHS 3753 H
Bartok/Mattern
        Folk Song Suite
                Boen, Jonathan
                        Chicago Brass Quintet
                        CRYS S 211
                                1-FF 11/12-82 P. 305
                                1-NR 11-82 P. 6
Bartok, Bela (1881-1945)
        For Children
                Pyle, Ralph
                        Los Angeles Brass Quintet
                        CRYS S 102
Bazelon, Irwin (1922-    )
        Brass Quintet (1963)
                Birdwell, Edward
                        American Brass Quintet
                        CRI SD 327
                                1-NR 1-75 P. 7

Beethoven, L. Van (1770-1827)
      Drie Contradansen
            van Aeken, Alex
                  Theo Mertens Chamber Brass Quintet
                  Eufoda 1082
      String Quartet, Op. 18 # 2
      (4th Movement)
            Cowden, Hugh
                  Chicago Symphony Brass Ensemble
                  Audiophile AP 21
            Neilson, Diana
                  Chicago Chamber Brass
                  Pro. S 616
Bennet, Richard Rodney (1936-     )
      Commedia IV for Brass (1973)
                  Philip Jones Brass Ensemble
                  Argo ZRG 813
                        1-GR 12-75 P. 1066
                        1-ML 12-75 P. 6
                        1-NR 8-76 P. 6
      Fanfare for Brass Quintet
            James, Ifor
                  Philip Jones Brass Ensemble
                  Argo ZRG 851
                        1-GR 7-77 P. 201
                        1-HF 5-78 P. 116
                        1-ML 8-77 P. 6
                        1-NR 7-78 P. 7
Berezowski, Nicolai (1900-1953)
      Brass Suite, Op. 24
      (2 Tpt/2 Hn/2 Trb/Ta) (1938)
            Keaney/McConathy
                  Voisin Brass Ensemble
                  Unicorn 1031
                        1-AR 11-56 P. 40
                        4-HA 1-57 P. 96
                        1-HF 12-56 P. 104
                        1-MH 11/12-56 P. 49
Berger, Arthur (1912-     )
      Canzon Octavi Modi
                  Berlin Philharmonic Brass Ensemble
                  DG 2532 066
                        1-FF 7/8-82 P. 268
                        1-FF 1/2-83 P. 336
                        1-NR 2-83 P. 4
                  Berlin Philharmonic Brass Ensemble
                  DG 2741 011
                        1-FF 1/2-83 P. 336
                        1-GR 11-82 P. 591
                        3-HF 11-83 P. 76
                        1-MG 7-82 P. 10
            Covert, John
                  Ithaca Brass Quintet
                  Golden Crest GC 4114
Bergsma, William (1921-     )
      Suite for Brass Quartet (1945)
                  American Brass Quintet
                  DC 6474/6477

Berlioz, Hector (1803-1869)
        March to the Scaffold
                    Locke Brass Consort
                    CRDD 1102
                            1-FF 5/6-83 P. 269
                            1-GR 3-83 P. 1059
                            1-MG 4-83 P. 6
                            2-NR 6-83 P. 6
Bernstein, Leonard (1918-      )
        Fanfare for Bima (Tpt/Hn/Trb/Ta)
                    Johns, Michael
                            Cambridge Brass Quintet
                            CRYS S 204
                                    2-HF 7-77 P. 118
                                    1-NR 11-76 P. 7
        West Side Story
                            Empire Brass Quintet
                            Digitech DIGI 104
Bertali, Antonio (1605-1669)
        2 Sonatas
                    Wakefield, David
                            American Brass Quintet
                            CRYS S 214
Blank, Allan (1925-      )
        Aphoristic Studies
                            Iowa Brass Quintet
                            Trilogy/Composers Theatre
                            Series CTS 1001
                                    1-NR 8-73 P. 6
        Involution
                            Iowa Brass Quintet
                            Trilogy/Composers Theatre
                            Series CTS 1001
                                    1-NR 8-73 P. 6
Blanton
        3 Christmas Pieces
                    Snyder, Kurt
                            Las Vegas Brass Quintet
                            Ashland Records AR 7118
Bliss
        Salute
                            Atlanta Brass Ensemble
                            Crystal Clear CCS 7010
                                    2-AR 11-79 P. 31
                                    1-NR 6-80 P. 14
                                    2-ST 2-80 P. 141
Boda, John
        Prelude-Scherzo-Prelude
                    Gelston/Terry
                            Georgia State College Brass Ensemble
                            Golden Crest GC S 4084
Bogar
        3 Movements for Brass Quartet
                            Hungarian Brass Ensemble
                            Hungaroton SLPX 11811
                                    2-AR 8-77 P. 39
                                    3-FF 9-77 P. 63

Bonelli, A. (Ca. 1600)
    Toccata
            Meek/Keaney
                    Voisin Brass Ensemble
                    Unicorn 1003
                            1-AR 2-55 P. 202
                            1-ET 3-55 P. 18
                            2-HF 3-55 P. 64-VII
                            1-LJ 5-15-55 P. 1205
                            11-MA 3-55 P. 22
                            2-NR 4-55 P. 6
    Toccata (Athalanta)
            Jones/Miller
                    Philadelphia Brass Ensemble
                    Columbia MS 6684
                            4-GR 5-67 P. 584
                            1-HF 5-67 P. 92
                            1-ML 4-67 P. 4
Boyce/Cable
    Suite
            Page, Graeme
                    Canadian Brass Quintet
                    RCA ARC 1 4574
                            2-FF 7/8-83 P. 284
                            4-NR 6-83 P. 6
Bozza, Eugene (1905-    )
    Overture for a Ceremony
                    Locke Brass Consort
                    Unicorn UN 1-72012
                            1-FF 7/8-79 P. 133
                            2-GR 5-78 P. 1889
    Sonatine (1951)
                    Budapest Brass Quintet
                    Hungaroton SLPX 12496
                            1-FF 3/4-84 P. 322
                            2-NR 3-84 P. 6
                    Cambridge Brass Quintet
                    CRYS S 204
                    Philip Jones Brass Ensemble
                    Argo ZRG 731
                            4-GR 6-73 P. 62
                            1-ML 6-73 P. 4
                            1-NR 10-73 P. 13
                            1-ST 1-74 P. 118
                    Swedish Brass Quintet
                    BIS 248
            Anderson, Paul
                    Iowa Brass Quintet
                    University of Iowa Press 29001
                            2-HF 7-77 P. 118
                            1-NR 2-77 P. 7
            Johns, Michael
                    Cambridge Brass Quintet
                    CRYS S 204
                            2-HF 7-77 P. 118
                            1-NR 11-76 P. 7

Bozza, Eugene (Cont'd)
      Sonatine (1951) (Cont'd)
            Schmitt, Frederick
                  New York Brass Quintet
                  Golden Crest GC S 4023
                        1-AU 5-60 P. 53
                        4-NR 4-60 P. 7
                        4-NYT 4-3-60 P. X10
Brade, W. (1560-1630)
      2 Festive Dances
            Katzen
                  Empire Brass Quintet
                  Digitech DIGI 102
                        1-ST 7-80 P. 86
            Jones/Miller
                  Philadelphia Brass Ensemble
                  Columbia MS 6684
                        4-GR 5-67 P. 584
                        1-HF 5-67 P. 92
                        1-ML 4-67 P. 4
      2 Pieces
            Soper, Kenneth
                  New York Brass Quintet
                  Golden Crest CRS 4148
                        1-AR 3-77 P. 40
      Galliard
                  Philip Jones Brass Ensemble
                  Argo ZRG 717
                        1-GR 11-74 P. 910
                        2-ML 11-74 P. 5
Brahms, Johannes (1883-1897)
      Es ist ein Ros' entsprungen
                  Baldwin-Wallace College Brass Choir
                  Mark Ed. Records MES 32565
                  Kansas University Brass Choir
                  Audio House AH 21473
      Las dich nur nichts
                  Atlanta Brass Ensemble
                  Crystal Clear CCS 7010
                        2-AR 11-79 P. 31
                        3-NR 6-80 P. 14
                        2-ST 2-80 P. 141
      (3) Motets
                  New York Brass Society
                  WIM # 3
                        1-NR 5-72 P. 5
Brant, Henry (1913-    )
      Millenium II
      (10 Tpt/8 Hn/10 Trb/2 Ta/Perc)
                  Lehigh Ensemble
                  Lehigh University 1103
      Millenium IV
            Nadaf, George
                  Modern Brass Ensemble
                  Advance Records FGR 2
                        4-AR 5-65 P. 816
                        2-NYT 9-20-64 P. X17

Brehm, Alvin (1925-    )
     Quintet for Brass (1967)
          Birdwell, Edward
                    American Brass Quintet
                    Nonesuch H 71222
                         4-AR 6-69 P. 941
                         1-HF 7-69 P. 98
                         4-NR 7-69 P. 7
                         1-ST 9-69 P. 120
               Karasick
                    New York Brass Ensemble
                    CRI S 192 (78)
Brown, Rayner (1912-    )
     Brass Quintet # 2
                    Pacific Brass Quintet
                    Avant AV 1004
     Concertino for Harp & Brass
                    Los Angeles Brass Quintet
                    CRYS S 602
                         2-NR 10-68 P. 5
     3 Diverse Movements
                    Iowa Brass Quintet
                    Trilogy/Composers Theatre
                    Series CTS 1001
                         1-NR 8-73 P. 6
     Fantasy-Fugue for Brass
     (6 Tpt/4 Hn/4 Trb/Ta)   (1971)
                    L. A. Philharmonic Brass Ensemble
                    and L. A. Brass Society Quintet
                    Avant 1005
                         1-NR 7-73 P. 12
Brubeck, Dave
     Blue Rondo a la Turc
               van Aeken, Alex
                    Theo Mertens Chamber Brass Quintet
                    Eufoda 1082
Bubalo, Rudolf (1927-    )
     3 Pieces for Brass Quintet (1959)
               Waas, Roy
                    Cleveland Brass Quintet
                    CRI 183
                         1-HF 2-65 P. 95
                         2-LJ 3-1-65 P. 1105
                         4-MA 11-64 P. 47
                         1-NR 7-64 P. 14
                         1-NYT 11-8-64 P. X24
                         2-SR 11-28-64 P. 58
     5 Pieces for Brass Quintet & Percussion (1964)
                    Baldwin-Wallace College Faculty
                    Advent USR 5004
                         1-CR 9-72 P. 36
                         1-NR 11-82 P. 5
               Solis, Richard
                    Cleveland Orchestra Members
                    CRYS S 533
                         1-FF 11/12-82 P. 117
                         1-NR 11-82 P. 5

Buonamente, Giovanni Battista (    -1643)
    Sonata (2 Tpt/2 Hn/Trb/Bar/Ta)
            Andrus/Haines
                Georgia State College Brass Ensemble
                Golden Crest GC S 4083
    Sonata
                Locke Brass Consort
                Unicorn UN 1-72012
                    1-FF 7/8-79 P. 133
                    2-GR 5-78 P. 1889
            Meek/Keaney
                Voisin Brass Ensemble
                Unicorn 1003
                    1-AR 2-55 P. 202
                    1-ET 3-55 P. 18
                    2-HF 3-55 P. 64-VII
                    1-LJ 5-15-55 P. 1205
                    11-MA 3-55 P. 22
                    2-NR 4-55 P. 6
Buxtehude, Dietrich (1637-1707)
    Fanfare & Chorus (4 Tpt/2 Hn/Bar/Trb)
                Locke Brass Consort
                Unicorn RHS 339
                    1-GR 6-76 P. 58
    Fanfare & Chorus
                Vienna State Opera Brass Ensemble
                Westminister XWN 18931
                    4-AU 12-60 P. 67
Byrd, William (1543-1623)
    Alleluia, Alleluia
            Ohanian, David
                Empire Brass Quintet
                Sine Qua Non SA 2014
    Earle of Oxford's Marche
                Philip Jones Brass Ensemble
                Argo ZRG 823
                    1-GR 6-76 P. 61
                    2-ML 5-76 P. 7
                    1-NR 10-77 P. 7
            Neilson, Diana
                Chicago Chamber Brass
                Pro Arte Sinfonia S 616
    La Volta
            Snyder, Kurt
                Las Vegas Brass Quintet
                Ashland Records AR 7118
    The Battell
                Philip Jones Brass Ensemble
                London CS 7221
                    2-FF 11/12-81 P. 296
                    2-NR 1-82 P. 7
                    4-ST 5-82 P. 81
Cabezon, Antonio De (1510-1566)
    Susana unjur
            Guy, Marc
                Annapolis Brass Quintet
                CRYS S 213
                    1-FF 9/10-83 P. 327

Cabezon, Antonio De (Cont'd)
    (2) Variations
        Guy, Marc
            Annapolis Brass Quintet
            CRYS S 213
                1-FF 9/10-83 P. 327
                4-NR 8-83 P. 3
Cable
    Songs of Newfoundland
        Page, Graeme
            Canadian Brass Quintet
            Umbrella 05862
Cabus, P.(1923-    )
    Varieties (1971)
        La Bar, Arthur
            Annapolis Brass Quintet
            CRYS S 207
                2-AR 6-79 P. 41
                2-CR 9-79 P. 43
                1-NR 5-79 P. 7
Calvert, Morley (1928-    )
    Chanson Melancolique
            Canadian Brass Quintet
            Vanguard VSD 71254
                4-FF 7/8-80 P. 186
                2-NR 7-80 P. 6
        Page, Graeme
            Canadian Brass Quintet
            Boot BMC 3001
    Montenegian Hills Suite
            Baldwin-Wallace College Brass Choir
            Mark Ed. Records MES 32565
            Eastern Classical Brass Quintet
            Klavier KS 561
                2-FF 7/8-79 P. 131
        Gainsforth, Nona
            Mount Royal Brass Quintet
            McGill University 80012
        Goldstein, Arthur
            Grenadilla GS 1040
                2-FF 7/8-80 P. 187
                2-NR 7-78 P. 7
Campo, Frank (1927-    )
    Madrigals for Brass Quintet
        Pyle, Ralph
            Los Angeles Brass Quintet
            CRYS S 821
                1-NR 7-71 P. 12
    3 Madrigals for Brass Quintet, Op. 38
            Canadian Brass Quintet
            CBC SM 203
Capuzzi
    Rondo
        van Aeken, Alex
            Theo Mertens Chamber Brass Quintet
            Eufoda 1082

Carr, Gordon
    Dialogue for Trumpet & Brass
                Locke Brass Consort
                    Unicorn UN 1-72012
                        1-FF 7/8-79 P. 133
                        2-GR 5-78 P. 1889
    Prism for Brass
                Locke Brass Consort
                    Unicorn RHS 339
                        1-GR 6-76 P. 58
Carr (Fetter)
    Trumpets of Victory
            Smith, Calvin
                Annapolis Brass Quintet
                Richardson Records RRS-3
Carter, Elliott (1908-    )
    A Fantasy about Purcell's
    'Fantasia upon one note'
                American Brass Quintet
                  Odyssey Y 34137
                        2-NR 1-77 P. 9
                        1-SR 11-13-76
                        1-HF 5-77 P. 81
Chabrier, Emmanuel (1841-1894)
    Bouree Fantasque
                Philip Jones Brass Ensemble
                London LDR 71094-1
Chance, Nancy Laird (1931-    )
    Chance-Ritual Sounds for Brass & Percussion (1975)
                Apple Brass Quintet + 3 Percussion
                Opus One 69
                    2-FF 9/10-82 P. 460
Chase, Allen
    Fugue for Brass Sextet
    (2 Tpt/Hn/Bar/Trb/Ta)
            Goldstein, Arthur
                Brass Guild
                Grenadilla GS 1040
Cheetham, John (1939-    )
    Scherzo
                    Eastern Classical Brass Quintet
                    Klavier KS 561
                        2-FF 7/8-79 P. 131
                    Los Angeles Brass Quintet
                    CRYS S 602
                        2-NR 10-68 P. 5
                    Tidewater Brass Quintet
                    Golden Crest CRS 4205
                        1-NR 10-81 P. 5
            van Driessche, Andre
                Theo Mertens Brass Ensemble
                Eufoda 1029
Cherubini, Luigi (1760-1842)
    Marche # 2
            Leroy, C.
                Ades 14 032
                    1-FF 5/6-83 P. 268

Cherubini, Luigi (Cont'd)
    (8) Marches for Brass Ensemble
    (Tpt/3 Hn/Trb)
                  Ars Nova Brass Quintet
                  MHS 4244
                      1-GR 5-80 P. 1689
    Pas redouble # 4
        Leroy, C.
                  Ades 14 032
                      1-FF 5/6-83 P. 268
    Sonata # 2
        van Driessche, Andre
                  Theo Mertens Brass Ensemble
                  Eufoda 1029
Childs, Barney (1926-    )
    Vars sur une Chanson de Canotier
    for Brass Quintet (1963)
        Battey, David
                  Dallas Brass Quintet
                  CRYS S 203
                      1-AR 6-79 P. 41
                      1-FF 7/8-79 P. 130
                      2-NR 5-79 P. 7
Civil, Allan (1929-    )
    Taratango
                  Philip Jones Brass Ensemble
                  HNH 4037
                      1-HF 2-78 P. 100
                      2-ST 5-78 P. 110
Clarke, Jeremiah (1673-1707)
    Prince of Denmark's March
        Page, Graeme
                  Canadian Brass Quintet
                  RCA ARL 1 4733
                  Canadian Brass Quintet
                  RCA ARC 1 4574
                      2-FF 7/8-83 P. 284
                      4-NR 6-83 P. 6
Cooper, John (Coperario) (1575-1626)
    Al Primo Giorno
        Wakefield, David
                  American Brass Quintet
                  Delos DMS 3003
                      1-NR 3-80 P. 7
                      1-NYT 5-18-80 P. D32
                      1-ST 7-80 P. 84
    Fancie a 5
        Wakefield, David
                  American Brass Quintet
                  Delos DMS 3003
                      1-NR 3-80 P. 7
                      1-NYT 5-18-80 P. D32
                      1-ST 7-80 P. 84

Copland, Aaron (1900-    )
        Fanfare for the Common Man
        (3 Tpt/4 Hn/3 Trb/Ta/Perc)
                        Atlanta Brass Ensemble
                        Crystal Clear CCS 7010
                            2-AR 11-79 P. 31
                            3-NR 6-80 P. 14
                            2-ST 2-80 P. 141
        Fanfare for the Common Man
                        Baldwin-Wallace College Brass Choir
                        Mark Ed. Records MES 32565
Couperin, Francois (1668-1773)
        Chaconne
                        Atlanta Brass Ensemble
                        Crystal Clear CCS 7011
                            2-AR 11-79 P. 31
                            1-NR 6-80 P. 14
        2 Pieces
                        Eastern Brass Quintet
                        Klavier KS 536
                            1-AU 12-75 P. 106
                            1-NR 5-75 P. 8
Crosley
        Days Before Yesterday
                Page, Graeme
                        Canadian Brass Quintet
                        Boot BMC 3004
                        Canadian Brass Quintet
                        CBC:    RCI 403
Custer, Arthur (1923-    )
        Concerto for Brass Quintet
                        New York Brass Quintet
                        Sorenns SRS 12031
                            2-NR 7-72 P. 8
        3 Pieces for 6 Brass Instruments
        (2 Tpt/2 Hn/2 Trb)
                Birdwell/ ?
                        Serenus SRS 12024
                            1-NR 3-70 P. 14
Dahl, Ingolf (1912-1970)
        Music for Brass Instruments (1944)
                        American Brass Quintet
                        BASF KMB 20812
                            1-NR 2-74 P. 6
                        American Brass Quintet
                        4 Desto DC 6474/7
                            1-ST 3-70 P. 120
                Smith, Calvin
                        Annapolis Brass Quintet
                        CRYS S 202
                            1-CR 3-75 P. 36
                            1-NR 1-75 P. 6
        Music for Brass Instruments
                        Canadian Brass Quintet
                        Vanguard VSD 71253
                            2-CR 5-79 P. 43
                            1-FF 7/8-79 P. 132
                            1-NR 3-79 P. 9
                        110

Dahl, Ingolf (Cont'd)
      Music for Brass Instruments (Cont'd)
                  Fine Arts Brass Quintet
                  CRYS S 205
            Hagen/Hatfield/Thelander/Gullickson
                  University of Minnesota Brass Choir
                  UMBC:  001
            Gainsforth, Nona
                  Mount Royal Brass Quintet
                  McGill University 80012
            Henderson, Robert
                  Fine Arts Brass Quintet
                  CRYS S 205
                        2-CR 3-81 P. 43
                        2-NR 3-81 P. 7
            Keaney/McConathy
                  Voisin Brass Ensemble
                  Unicorn 1031
                        1-AR 11-56 P. 40
                        4-HA 1-57 P. 96
                        1-HF 12-56 P. 104
                        1-MH 11/12-56 P. 49
            Page, Graeme
                  Canadian Brass Quintet
                  Boot BMC 3003
            Smith, Calvin
                  Annapolis Brass Quintet
                  CRYS S 202
                        1-CR 3-75 P. 36
                        1-NR 1-75 P. 6
      Ballet # 4 (Petite Suite)
                  Nimbus 45006 (45 rpm)
                        1-FF 7/8-81 P. 222
                        1-GR 1-81 P. 959
Debussy, Claude (1862-1918)
      Berceuse heroique
                  Nimbus 45006 (45 rpm)
                        1-FF 7/8-81 P. 222
                        1-GR 1-81 P. 959
      Girl With the Flaxen Hair
                  Nimbus 45006 (45 rpm)
                        1-FF 7/8-81 P. 222
                        1-GR 1-81 P. 959
                  Philip Jones Brass Ensemble
                  London 410125-1LH
      Golliwog's Cakewalk
                  Nimbus 45006 (45 rpm)
                        1-FF 7/8-81 P. 222
                        1-GR 1-81 P. 959
                  Philip Jones Brass Ensemble
                  London 410125-1LH
            Page, Graeme
                  Canadian Brass Quintet
                  Boot BMC 3004
                  Canadian Brass Quintet
                  CBC:  RCI 403

Debussy, Claude (Cont'd)
      Golliwog's Cakewalk (Cont'd)
            van Aeken, Alex
                  Theo Mertens Chamber Brass Quintet
                  Eufoda 1082
      Le Petite Negre
                  Nimbus 45006 (45 rpm)
                        1-FF 7/8-81 P. 222
                        1-GR 1-81 P. 959
                  Philip Jones Brass Ensemble
                  Argo ZRG 895
                        2-FF 5/6-80
                        1-GR 1-79 P. 1334
      Minstrels
                  Philip Jones Brass Ensemble
                  London 410125-1LH
De Jong
      Humoristische Suite voor Koperensemble
            van Driessche, Andre
                  Theo Mertens Brass Ensemble
                  Eufoda 1051
Dering, Richard (1580-1630)
      Pavane
                  Philip Jones Brass Ensemble
                  Argo ZRG 717
                        1-GR 11-74 P. 910
                        2-ML 11-74 P. 5
Des Prez, Josquin (1440-1521)
      Heth Sold Ein Meisken Om Win
            Ohanian, David
                  Empire Brass Quintet
                  Sine Qua Non SA 2014
      Motet & Royal Fanfare
                  Baldwin-Wallace College Brass Choir
                  Mark Ed. Records MES 32565
      Royal Fanfare
                  Canadian Brass Quintet
                  Vanguard VSD 71254
                        4-FF 7/8-80 P. 186
                        2-NR 7-80 P. 6
            Happe, Richard
                  American Brass Quintet
                  Folkways FM 3651
                        4-NR 12-65 P. 8
            Ingraham, Paul
                  New York Brass Quintet
                  RCA AGL 1 3968
                        1-HF 9-67 P. 98B
                        4-NR 7-67 P. 9
            Page, Graeme
                  Canadian Brass Quintet
                  Boot BMC 3001
Dlugoszewski, Lucia (1931-    )
      Angels of the Inmost Heaven
            Smith, Martin
                  Schwartz Ensemble
                  Folkways FTS 33902
                        4-NYT 4-11-76 P. D24

Dlugoszewski, Lucia (Cont'd)
      Tender Theatre Flight Nageire
      (3 Tpt/Hn/Trb/B. Trb/Perc)
            Routch, Robert
                  CRI SD 388
Dodgson, Stephen (1924-      )
      Fantasy for 6 Brass
                  Philip Jones Brass Ensemble
                  London LDR 71100
                        1-AR 2-83 P. 77
                        1-FF 1/2-83 P. 338
                        1-NR 3-83 P. 3
      Sonata for Brass (1963)
                  Philip Jones Brass Ensemble
                  Argo ZRG 813
                        1-GR 12-75 P. 1066
                        1-ML 12-75 P. 6
                        1-NR 8-76 P. 6
      Suite for Brass Septet
                  Philip Jones Brass Ensemble
                  Argo ZRG 655
                        4-HF 11-71 P. 812
                        1-ML 11-70 P. 9
                        1-NR 9-71 P. 6
Dowland, John (1562-1626)
      3 Dances from Lachrimae
            Happe, Richard
                  American Brass Quintet
                  Folkways FMS 33652
                        2-AU 7-68 P. 46
                        4-NR 9-67 P. 6
      4 Dances
            Birdwell, Edward
                  American Brass Quintet
                  4-Desto 6474/7
                        1-ST 3-70 P. 120
      Pavane
                  Paris Brass Quintet
                  PLE 084
                        2-FF 9/10-79 P. 181
      Volta
            Wakefield, David
                  American Brass Quintet
                  Delos DMS 3003
                        1-NR 3-80 P. 7
                        1-NYT 5-18-80 P. D32
                        1-ST 7-80 P. 84
Dubois
      3 Fanfare Preludes
                  Locke Brass Consort
                  Unicorn UN 1-72012
                        1-FF 7/8-79 P. 133
                        2-GR 5-78 P. 1889
Dukas, Paul (1865-1935)
      La Peri:  Fanfare
                  Philip Jones Brass Ensemble
                  Argo ZRG 731

Dukas, Paul (Cont'd)
    La Peri:  Fanfare (Cont'd)
                Philip Jones Brass Ensemble (Cont'd)
                    4-GR 6-73 P. 62
                    1-ML 6-73 P. 4
                    1-NR 10-73 P. 13
                    1-ST 1-74 P. 118
          Osborne, Larry
             Vintage Brass Ensemble
             Ohlone Band Album CR 8242

Dupre
    Poeme heroique
             Atlanta Brass Ensemble
             Crystal Clear CCS 7011
                2-AR 11-79 P. 31
                1-NR 6-80 P. 14

Dvorak, Antonin (1841-1904)
    Humoresque
             Philip Jones Brass Ensemble
             Argo ZRG 928
    2 Waltzes from Op. 54
             Empire Brass Quintet
             Digitech DIGI 105
                2-FF 11/12-81 P. 295
    Slavonic Dance in g, Op. 46 # 8
          Leroy, C.
             Ades 14 032

East, Michael (1580-1648)
    Desperavi
          Happe, Richard
             American Brass Quintet
             Folkways FM 3651
                4-NR 12-65 P. 8
    Desperavi; Triumphavi
          Birdwell, Edward
             American Brass Quintet
             4-Desto 6474/7
                1-ST 3-70 P. 120
          Smith, Calvin
             Annapolis Brass Quintet
             2 CRYS S 202
                1-CR 3-75 P. 36
                1-NR 1-75 P. 6
    Peccavi
          Smith, Calvin
             Annapolis Brass Quintet
             CRYS S 206
                2-NR 11-76 P. 7

End, Jack (1918-   )
    3 Salutations (1965)
             Tidewater Brass Quintet
             Golden Crest CRS 4205
                1-NR 10-81 P. 5
          Strieby, Lawrence
             St. Louis Brass Quintet
             CRYS S 212
                2-FF 7/8-83 P. 283

Erb, Donald (1927-    )
    3 Pieces for Brass Quintet & Piano
            Ingraham, Paul
                New York Brass Quintet
                    CRI SD 323
                        1-NR 1-76 P. 7
    Sonneries (4 Tpt/4 Hn/3 Trb/Tba)
                Cleveland Orchestra Brass Section
                    CRYS S 531
                        2-NR 4-77 P. 5
    Spatial Fanfare for Brass & Percussion
                Louisville LOU 772
Etler, Alvin (1913-1973)
    Quintet for Brass Instruments (1964)
            Benjamin, Barry
                New York Brass Quintet
                    CRI SD 205
                        1-HSR 11-66 P. 100
                        4-NR 9-66 P. 7
                        1-NYT 5-8-66 P. X24
                        4-PP 3-67 P. 18
    Sonic Sequence for Brass Quintet (1967)
            Birdwell, Edward
                American Brass Quintet
                    CRI 229
                        1-HF 9-68 P. 84
                        1-HSR 9-68 P. 104
                        1-NR 8-68 P. 14
Ewald, Victor (1860-1935)
    Quintet # 3
                Philip Jones Brass Ensemble
                    ARGO ZRG 928
                Swedish Brass Quintet
                    BIS 248
    Quintet in Bb minor, Op. 5 (1912)
            Birdwell, Edward
                American Brass Quintet
                    4-Desto 6474/7
                        1-ST 3-70 P. 120
    Quintet in Bb, Op. 5
            Hackleman, Martin
                Tidewater Brass Quintet
                    Golden Crest CRSQ 4174
            James, Ifor
                Philip Jones Brass Ensemble
                    Argo ZRG 655
                        1-GR 11-70 P. 812
                        4-HF 11-71 P. 118
                        1-NR 9-71  P. 6
                        1-ML 11-70 P. 9
            Ohanian, David
                Empire Brass Quintet
                    Sine Qua Non SA 2012
                        1-FF 5/6-78 P. 106
                        1-HF 4-78 P. 94

Ewald, Victor (Cont'd)
    Quintet in Bb, Op. 5 (Cont'd)
            Talamantes, Nona
                    Mount Royal Brass Quintet
                    McGill University 77004
                            1-FF 5/6-82 P. 292
            Hackleman, Martin
                    Tidewater Brass Quintet
                    Golden Crest GC 4174
    Quintet in Eb, Op. 6
            Ohanian, David
                    Empire Brass Quintet
                    Sine Qua Non SA 2012
                            1-FF 5/6-78 P. 106
                            1-HF 4-78 P. 94
    Quintet in Db, Op. 7
            Ohanian, David
                    Empire Brass Quintet
                    Sine Qua Non SA 2012
                            1-FF 5/6-78 P. 106
                            1-HF 4-78 P. 94
            Wakefield, David
                    American Brass Quintet
                    CRYS S 214
    Symphony for 5 part Brass Choir
            Chambers, James
                    New York Philharmonic Brass Quintet
                    Golden Crest GC 4003
                            2-HF 12-57 P. 94
                            4-LJ 1-1-58 P. 70
                            4-SR 11-9-57 P. 38
de Falla/Mattern (1876-1946)
    Miller's Dance from Three Cornered Hat
            Boen, Jonathan
                    Chicago Brass Quintet
                    CRYS S 211
                            1-FF 11/12-82 P. 305
                            1-NR 11-82 P. 6
de Falla, Manuel
    Suite from El Amor Brujo
            Boen, Jonathan
                    Chicago Brass Quintet
                    CRYS S 211
                            1-FF 11/12-82 P. 305
                            1-NR 11-82 P. 6
Farberman, Harold (1929-    )
    Five Images for Brass (1964)
            Benjamin, Barry
                    New York Brass Quintet
                    Serenus SRE 12011
                            1-AR 11-65 P. 239
                            4-HF 9-65 P. 84
                            4-HSR 10-65 P. 84
                            4-NYT 11-28-65 P. HF 3

Farnaby, Giles (1565-1640)
        Giles Farnaby Suite
                        Philip Jones Brass Ensemble
                        Argo ZRG 823
                                1-GR 6-76 P. 61
                                2-ML 5-76 P. 7
                                1-NR 10-77 P. 7
Faure, Gabriel (1845-1924)
        Mi-a-ou from Dolly, Op. 56 # 2
                Neilson, Diana
                        Chicago Chamber Brass
                        Pro Arte Sinfonia S 616
Feld, Jindrich (1925-    )
        Quintette (1972)
                Smith, Calvin
                        Annapolis Brass Quintet
                        CRYS S 206
                                2-NR 11-76 P. 7
Fennelly, Brian (1932-    )
        Prelude & Elegy for Brass Quintet
                        Empire Brass Quintet
                        Advent ADV 19
Ferrabosco, Alfonso (1575-1628)
        Almayne & Dovehouse Pavanne
                Wakefield, David
                        American Brass Quintet
                        Delos DMS 3003
                                1-NR 3-80 P. 7
                                1-NYT 5-18-80 P. D32
                                1-ST 7-80 P. 84
Ferrabosco II
        4 Note Pavan
                Reynolds, Verne
                        Eastman Brass Quintet
                        Candide CE 31004
                                1-HF 11-68 P. 120
                                1-NR 5-69 P. 6
                                4-SR 8-31-68 P. 45
Ferrante, Joe (1929-1980)
        Three Scenes for Brass Quintet (1978)
                        Tidewater Brass Quintet
                        Golden Crest CRS 4205
                                1-NR 10-81 P. 5
Fillmore, Henry (1881-1956)
        'Lasses Trombone
                Page, Graeme
                        Canadian Brass Quintet
                        Boot BMC 3004
                        Canadian Brass Quintet
                        CBC: RCI 403
        Slim Trombone
                Page, Graeme
                        Canadian Brass Quintet
                        Boot BMC 3004
                        Canadian Brass Quintet
                        CBC: RCI 403

117

Finck, Heinrich (1445-1527)
        Greiner Zanner
                Happe, Richard
                        American Brass Quintet
                        Folkways FMS 33652
                                2-AU 7-68 P. 46
                                4-NR 9-67 P. 6
Flagello, Nicolas (1928-    )
        Lyra for Brass Sextet (3 Tpt/Hn/2 Trb)
                        Orchestra Sinfonica di Roma
                        Serenus SRS 12008
                                2-HSR 10-65 P. 96

        Philos
                        American Brass Quintet
                        Serenus SRS 12041
                                1-NR 9-72 P. 6
Ford, Thomas (1580-1648)
        Fantasy
                        Paris Brass Quintet
                        PLE 084
                                2-FF 9/10-79 P. 181
Forsyth, Malcolm (1936-    )
        Golyardes' Grounde (1972)
                        Canadian Brass Quintet
                        Vanguard VSD 71253
                                2-CR 5-79 P. 43
                                1-FF 7/8-79 P. 132
                                1-NR 3-79 P. 9
                Page, Graeme
                        Canadian Brass Quintet
                        Boot BMC 3003
Frackenpohl, Arthur (1924-    )
        Brass Quintet (1966)
                Covert, John
                        Mark Ed. Records MEC 32558
Franchois
        Trumpetta Introitus
                        Philip Jones Brass Ensemble
                        Argo ZRG 823
                                1-GR 6-76 P. 61
                                2-ML 5-76 P. 7
                                1-NR 10-77 P. 7
Franck, Melchoir (1579-1639)
        Intrada
                        Philip Jones Brass Ensemble
                        Argo ZRG 898
                                1-FF 1/2-80 P. 173
                                1-FU 5-80 P. 46
                                1-GR 8-79 P. 348
                                1-ML 5-79 P. 9
        (2) Pavannes
                        Ars Nova Brass Quintet
                        MHS 1446 Z
                                1-GR 1-72 P. 1233
Frescobaldi, Girolami (1583-1643)
        Toccata
                Page, Graeme
                        Canadian Brass Quintet

Frescobaldi, Girolami (Cont'd)
    Toccata (Cont'd)
        Page, Graeme (Cont'd)
                    2-AR 11-80 P. 39
                    1-CR 8-80 P. 43
                    1-FF 7/8-80 P. 186
                    1-NR 7-80 P. 6
                    2-NYT 5-18-80 P. D32
Friedman
    Parodie I (1974)
        Guy, Marc
            Annapolis Brass Quintet
            CRYS S 213
                    1-FF 9/10-83 P. 327
                    4-NR 8-83 P. 3
Friend
    American Folksong Medley
        Berger/Watson
            Kansas University Brass Choir
            Audio House AH 21473
Fux, Johann Joseph (1660-1741)
    Aria; Gigue
        Page, Graeme
            Canadian Brass Quintet
            Boot BMC 3003
    2 Serenades
            Vienna State Opera Brass Ensemble
            Westminister XWN 18931
                    4-AU 12-60 P. 67
Fux & Weelkes
    Renaissance Suite
            Canadian Brass Quintet
            Vanguard VSD 71253
                    2-CR 5-79 P. 43
                    1-FF 7/8-79 P. 132
                    1-NR 3-79 P. 9
Gabaye, Pierre (1930-     )
    Boutade (Original for Tpt & Pf)
        van Aeken, Alex
            Theo Mertens Chamber Brass Ensemble
            Eufoda 1082
Gabrieli, Andrea (1510-1586)
    Aria della Battaglia
            Philip Jones Brass Ensemble
            Odyssey 34605
            Vienna State Opera Brass Ensemble
            Westminister 8212
    Ricercar
            Paris Instrumental Ensemble
            Turnabout TVS 34540
            Weber Instrumental Ensemble
            Candide CE 31062
    Ricercar del Duodecimo Tono
            Chicago Chamber Brass
            Pro Arte Sinfonia SDS 632
            Philip Jones Brass Ensemble
            Argo ZRG 717
                    1-GR 11-74 P. 910

Gabrieli, Andrea (Cont'd)
    Ricercar del Duodecimo Tono (Cont'd)
        Katzen
            Empire Brass Quintet
            Digitech DIGI 102
                1-ST 7-80 P. 86
    Ricercar del Sesti Tono
        Wakefield, David
            American Brass Quintet
            Delos DMS 3003
                1-NR 3-80 P. 7
                1-NYT 5-18-80 P. D32
                1-ST 7-80 P. 84
abrieli, Giovanni (1557-1612)
    (4) Canzone
            American Brass Quintet
            BASF KMB 20812
                1-NR 2-74 P. 6
                4-NR 9-67 P. 6
    Canzon a 12
        Clevenger/Bloom/Jones
            Chicago/Cleveland/
            Philadelphia Brass Ensembles
            Columbia MS 7209
                1-GR 7-69 P. 151
                1-HF 7-69 P. 82
                2-ML 8-69 P. 2
                1-NR 4-69 P. 14
                1-ST 4-69 P. 94
    Canzon a 12 in echo
        Clevenger/Bloom/Jones
            Chicago/Cleveland/Philadelphia
            Brass Ensembles
            Columbia MS 7209
                1-GR 7-69 P. 151
                1-HF 7-69 P. 82
                2-ML 8-69 P. 2
                1-NR 4-69 P. 14
                1-ST 4-69 P. 94
    Canzon a 12 in double echo
            Chicago Chamber Brass
            Pro Arte Sinfonia SDS 632
    Canzon duodecimi toni
            Baldwin-Wallace College Brass Choir
            Mark Ed. Records MES 32565
            Vienna State Opera Brass Ensemble
            Westminister 8212
        Clevenger/Bloom/Jones
            Chicago/Cleveland/Philadelphia
            Brass Ensembles
            Columbia MS 7209
                1-GR 7-69 P. 151
                1-HF 7-69 P. 82
                2-ML 8-69 P. 2
                1-NR 4-69 P. 14
                1-ST 4-69 P. 94

Gabrieli, Giovanni (Cont'd)
    Canzon duodecimi toni a 10
                Chicago Chamber Brass
                  Pro Arte Sinfonia SDS 632
    Canzon per Sonare Prime a 4, # 4
        Wakefield, David
                American Brass Quintet
                Delos DMS 3003
                      1-NR 3-80 P. 7
                      1-NYT 5-18-80 P. D32
                      1-ST 7-80 P. 84
    Canzon per Sonare Prime a 4, "La Spiritata"
                London Gabrieli Brass Ensemble
                MHS 4635K
                      2-GR 2-79 P. 1440
                      2-GR 7-82 P. 142
                      2-MG 4-82 P. 17
        Happe, Richard
                American Brass Quintet
                Folkways FM 3651
                      4-NR 12-65 P. 8
        Tillotson, Brooks
                Chamber Brass Players
                Classic Editions CE 1039
        Wakefield, David
                American Brass Quintet
                Delos DMS 3003
                      1-NR 3-80 P. 7
                      1-NYT 5-18-80 P. D32
                      1-ST 7-80 P. 84
    Canzon per Sonare Prime a 5
                Canadian Brass Quintet
                Vanguard VSD 71254
                      4-FF 7/8-80 P. 186
                      2-NR 7-80 P. 6
                Chicago Chamber Brass
                Pro Arte Sinfonia SDS 632
        Happe, Richard
                American Brass Quintet
                Folkways FMS 33652
                      2-AU 7-68 P. 46
                      4-NR 9-67 P. 6
        Page, Graeme
                Canadian Brass Quintet
                Boot BMC 3001
                Canadian Brass Quintet
                CBC:  SM 239
        Wakefield, David
                American Brass Quintet
                Delos DMS 3003
                      1-NR 3-80 P. 7
                      1-NYT 5-18-80 P. D32
                      1-ST 7-80 P. 84
    Canzon per Sonare # 1
        Ward, Charles
                Metropolitan Brass Quintet
                CRYS S 208
                      2-NR 5-78 P. 5

Gabrieli, Giovanni (Cont'd)
    Canzon per Sonare # 1 (Cont'd)
             Metropolitan Brass Quintet
             CRYS S 208
                2-NR 5-78 P. 5
             Chicago Chamber Brass
             Pro Arte Sinfonia SDS 632
    Canzon per Sonare # 1, "La Spiritata"
        Schmitt, Frederick
             New York Brass Quintet
             Golden Crest GC S 4023
                1-AU 5-60 P. 53
                4-NR 4-60 P. 7
                4-NYT 4-3-60 P. X10
    Canzon per Sonare # 2
             Chicago Chamber Brass
             Pro Arte Sinfonia SDS 632
             Eastern Brass Quintet
             Klavier KS 536
                1-AU 12-75 P. 106
                1-NR 5-75 P. 8
        Clevenger/Bloom/Jones
             Chicago/Cleveland/Phila. Brass Ens.
             Columbia MS 7209
                1-GR 7-69 P. 151
                1-HF 7-69 P. 82
                2-ML 8-69 P. 2
                1-NR 4-69 P. 14
                1-ST 4-69 P. 94
        Cowden, Hugh
             Chicago Symphony Brass Ensemble
              Audiophile AP 21
        Ingraham, Paul
             New York Brass Quintet
              RCA AGL 1 3968
                1-HF 9-67 P. 98B
                4-NR 7-67 P. 9
        Ohanian, David
             Empire Brass Quintet
              Sine Qua Non SA 2014
        Tillotson, Brooks
             Chamber Brass Players
              Classic Editions CE 1039
        Ward, Charles
             Metropolitan Brass Quintet
             CRYS S 208
                2-NR 5-78 P. 5
    Canzon per Sonare # 3
             Chicago Chamber Brass
             Pro Arte Sinfonia SDS 632
    Canzon per Sonare # 4
             Chicago Chamber Brass
             Pro Arte Sinfonia SDS 632
    Canzon per Sonare # 27
        Clevenger/Bloom/Jones
             Chicago/Cleveland/Phila. Brass Ens.
             Columbia MS 7209

Gabrieli, Giovanni (Cont'd)
　Canzon per Sonare # 27 (Cont'd)
　　　Clevenger/Bloom/Jones (Cont'd)
　　　　　　　　1-GR 7-69 P. 151
　　　　　　　　1-HF 7-69 P. 82
　　　　　　　　2-ML 8-69 P. 2
　　　　　　　　1-NR 4-69 P. 14
　　　　　　　　1-ST 4-69 P. 94
　Canzon per Sonare # 28
　　　Clevenger/Bloom/Jones
　　　　　Chicago/Cleveland/Philadelphia
　　　　　Brass Ensembles
　　　　　　Columbia MS 7209
　　　　　　　　1-GR 7-69 P. 151
　　　　　　　　1-HF 7-69 P. 82
　　　　　　　　2-ML 8-69 P. 2
　　　　　　　　1-NR 4-69 P. 14
　　　　　　　　1-ST 4-69 P. 94
　Canzon primi toni
　　　Clevenger/Bloom/Jones
　　　　　Chicago/Cleveland/Philadelphia
　　　　　Brass Ensembles
　　　　　　Columbia MS 7209
　　　　　　　　1-GR 7-69 P. 151
　　　　　　　　1-HF 7-69 P. 82
　　　　　　　　2-ML 8-69 P. 2
　　　　　　　　1-NR 4-69 P. 14
　　　　　　　　1-ST 4-69 P. 94
　Canzon primi toni a 8
　　　Chicago Chamber Brass
　　　　Pro Arte Sinfonia SDS 632
　Canzon quarti toni
　　　Clevenger/Bloom/Jones
　　　　　Chicago/Cleveland/Philadelphia
　　　　　Brass Ensembles
　　　　　　Columbia MS 7209
　　　　　　　　1-GR 7-69 P. 151
　　　　　　　　1-HF 7-69 P. 82
　　　　　　　　2-ML 8-69 P. 2
　　　　　　　　1-NR 4-69 P. 14
　　　　　　　　1-ST 4-69 P. 94
　Canzon septimi toni
　　　Kjellden, Thomas
　　　　　Malmo Brass Ensemble
　　　　　BIS LP 59
　　　　　　1-FF 9-77 P. 61
　Canzon septimi toni # 1
　　　Clevenger/Jones
　　　　　Chicago/Philadelphia Brass Ensembles
　　　　　Columbia MS 7209
　　　　　　　　1-GR 7-69 P. 151
　　　　　　　　1-HF 7-69 P. 82
　　　　　　　　2-ML 8-69 P. 2
　　　　　　　　1-NR 4-69 P. 14
　　　　　　　　1-ST 4-69 P. 94

Gabrieli, Giovanni (Cont'd)
     Canzon septimi toni # 1 (Cont'd)
          Meek/Keaney
                    Voisin Brass Ensemble
                    Unicorn 1003
                         1-AR 2-55 P. 202
                         1-ET 3-55 P. 18
                         2-HF 3-55 P. 64-VII
                         1-LJ 5-15-55 P. 1205
                         11-MA 3-55 P. 22
                         2-NR 4-55 P. 6
     Canzon septimi toni # 2
          Bloom/Jones
                    Cleveland/Philadelphia Brass Ensembles
                    Columbia MS 7209
                         1-GR 7-69 P. 151
                         1-HF 7-69 P. 82
                         2-ML 8-69 P. 2
                         1-NR 4-69 P. 14
                         1-ST 4-69 P. 94
     Canzon septimi toni a 8
                    Chicago Chamber Brass
                    Pro Arte Sinfonia SDS 632
     Canzon octavi toni
          Clevenger/Jones
                    Chicago/Philadelphia Brass Ensembles
                    Columbia MS 7209
                         1-GR 7-69 P. 151
                         1-HF 7-69 P. 82
                         2-ML 8-69 P. 2
                         1-NR 4-69 P. 14
                         1-ST 4-69 P. 94
     Canzon noni toni
          Bloom/Jones
                    Cleveland/Philadelphia Brass Ensembles
                    Columbia MS 7209
                         1-GR 7-69 P. 151
                         1-HF 7-69 P. 82
                         2-ML 8-69 P. 2
                         1-NR 4-69 P. 14
                         1-ST 4-69 P. 94
     Canzon III
                    Canadian Brass Quintet
                    Moss Music Group MMG 1123
                         3-NR 3-81 P. 7
          Katzen
                    Empire Brass Quintet
                    Digitech DIGI 102
                         1-ST 7-80 P. 86
          Page, Graeme
                    Canadian Brass Quintet
                    Moss Music Group MMG 1139
     Canzon XIII
                    Berlin Philharmonic Brass Ensemble
                    DG 2532 066
                         1-FF 7/8-82 P. 268
                         1-FF 1/2-83 P. 336
                         1-NR 2-83 P. 4

Gabrieli, Giovanni (Cont'd)
    Canzon XIII (Cont'd)
                    Philip Jones Brass Ensemble
                    Argo ZRG 717
                        1-GR 11-74 P. 910
                        2-ML 11-74 P. 5
    Canzon XV
            Hagen/Hatfield/Thelander/Gullickson
            University of Minnesota Brass Choir
            UMBC:  001
    Canzon XVIII
            Hagen/Hatfield/Thelander/Gullickson
            University of Minnesota Brass Choir
            UMBC: 001
    Canzoni for Brass Choirs
                    Berlin Brass Quintet
                    CRYS S 201
                        1-CR 3-75 P. 36
                        1-NR 1-75 P. 6
                    Metropolitan Brass Quintet
                    CRYS S 208
                    New York Brass Quintet
                    Golden Crest GC S 4023
                        1-AU 5-60 P. 53
                        4-NR 4-60 P. 7
                        4-NYT 4-3-60 P. X10
                    Philip Jones Brass Ensemble
                    Argo ZRG 644
                        1-GR 3-70 P. 1444
                        2-ML 3-70 P. 5
                        3-NR 11-70 P. 9
                    Philip Jones Brass Ensemble
                    Odyssey Y 34605
                    Vienna State Opera Brass Ensemble
                        Westminister 8212
                    Chicago/Cleveland/Philadelphia
                    Brass Ensembles
                    CBS MP 38759
                    Weber Instrumental Ensemble
                        Candide CE 31062
                        Seraphim S 60324
    Canzonas for Single & Double Brass Choir
                    New York Brass Ensemble
                    Esoteric 503
                        1-AR 12-50 P. 124
                        2-GS 12-50 P. 3
                        1-LJ 8-51 P. 1245
                        4-NR 6-51 P. 16
                        1-SR 5-26-51 P. 52
    In Eccleiis
                    Canadian Brass Quintet
                    CBS 1M 39035
    Jubilate Deo
                    Canadian Brass Quintet
                    CBS 1M 39035

Gabrieli, Giovanni (Cont'd)
    Sinfonia Sacrae
                    Gabrieli Brass Ensemble
                        Nonesuch 71118
                            1-GR 2-66 P. 397
                            2-HF 11-66 P. 169
                            1-HSR 11-66 P. 72
                            1-NR 9-66 P. 5
        Sonata XIII
                    Berlin Philharmonic Brass Ensemble
                        DG 2741 011
                            1-FF 1/2-83 P. 336
                            1-GR 11-82 P. 591
                            3-HF 1-83 P. 76
                    Canadian Brass Quintet
                        CBS 1M 39035
        Sonata Pian e Forte
                    Berlin Philharmonic Brass Ensemble
                        DG 2532 066
                            1-FF 7/8-82 P. 268
                            1-FF 1/2-83 P. 336
                            1-NR 2-83 P. 4
                    Berlin Philharmonic Brass Ensemble
                        DG 2741 011
                            1-FF 1/2-83 P. 336
                            1-GR 11-82 P. 591
                            3-HF 11-83 P. 76
                            1-MG 7-82 P. 10
                    Canadian Brass Quintet
                        CBS 1M 39035
                    Philip Jones Brass Ensemble
                        Nonesuch 71118
                            1-GR 2-66 P. 397
                            2-HF 11-66 P. 169
                            1-HSR 11-66 P. 72
                            1-NR 9-66 P. 5
                    Vienna State Opera Brass Ensemble
                        Westminister 8212
                Clevenger/Jones
                    Chicago/Philadelphia Brass Ensembles
                        Columbia MS 7209
                            1-GR 7-69 P. 151
                            1-HF 7-69 P. 82
                            2-ML 8-69 P. 2
                            1-NR 4-69 P. 14
                            1-ST 4-69 P. 94
                Mayer/Lannutti/Pierson
                    Virtuosi Di Philharmonica
                        Columbia ML 5129
Gade, Jacob
    Jealousy
                    Philip Jones Brass Ensemble
                        London LDR 71100
                            1-AR 2-83 P. 77
                            1-FF 1/2-83 P. 338
                            1-NR 3-83 P. 3

Gardner, John (1917-    )
     Theme & Variations for Brass, Op. 7 (1951)
                    Philip Jones Brass Ensemble
                    Argo ZRG 813
                         1-GR 12-75 P. 1066
                         1-ML 12-75 P. 6
                         1-NR 8-76 P. 6
George, Thom Ritter (1942-    )
     Quintet # 1
               Strieby, Lawrence
                    St. Louis Brass Quintet
                    CRYS S 215
                    St. Louis Brass Quintet
                    CRYS S 212
                         2-FF 7/8-83 P. 283
Gershwin, George (1898-1937)
     Bess, You Is My Woman Now
               Halloin, Beth
                    Chicago Chamber Brass
                    Pro Arte Sinfonia S05616
                         1-AR 3-84 P. 62
                         1-FF 3/4-84 P. 324
               Neilson, Diana
                    Chicago Chamber Brass
                    Pro Arte Sinfonia S 616
     I Got Rhythm
                    Eastern Brass Quintet
                    Klavier KS 539
                         2-AU 2-76 P. 96
                         1-HF 11-75 P. 129
     Mine
                    Eastern Brass Quintet
                    Klavier KS 539
                         2-AU 2-76 P. 96
                         1-HF 11-75 P. 129
     Porgy & Bess Suite
                    Empire Brass Quintet
                    Digitech DIGI 104
     Summertime
               Barnett, George
                    Chestnut Brass Company
                    Chestnut Brass Company 3 0001 9
     The Man I Love
                    Eastern Brass Quintet
                    Klavier KS 539
                         2-AU 2-76 P. 96
                         1-HF 11-75 P. 129
     Variations On I Got Rhythm
               Barnett, George
                    Chestnut Brass Company
                    Chestnut Brass Company 3 0001 9
Gervaise, Claude
     (8) Bransles de Bourgobue
                    Ensemble de Cuivres
                    Societe Francaise du Son SXL 20093
                         2-AU 4-66 P. 59
                         1-NR 2-66 P. 6

Gervaise, Claude (Cont'd)
    (8) Bransles de Poictou
               Ensemble de Cuivres
                   Societe Francaise du Son SXL 20093
                       2-AU 4-66 P. 59
                       1-NR 2-66 P. 6
    (12) Bransles de Champagne
               Ensemble de Cuivres
                   Societe Francaise du Son SXL 20093
                       2-AU 4-66 P. 59
                       1-NR 2-66 P. 6
    Danceries
               Paris Brass Quintet
               PLE 084
                   2-FF 9/10-79 P. 181
Gesualdo, Don Carlo (1560-1613)
    4 Madrigals
        Page, Graeme
               Canadian Brass Quintet
                   CBC: SM 216
Ghiselin
    La Alfonsina
        Katzen
              Empire Brass Quintet
               Digitech DIGI
                   1-ST 7-80 P. 86
Gibbons, Orlando (1583-1625)
    Fantasia
        Reynolds, Verne
               Eastman Brass Quintet
               Candide CE 31004
                   1-HF 11-68 P. 120
                   1-NR 5-69 P. 6
                   4-SR 8-31-68 P. 45
    In Nomine
               Canadian Brass Quintet
               CBS 1M 39035
               Philip Jones Brass Ensemble
               Argo ZRG 823
                   1-GR 6-76 P. 61
                   2-ML 5-76 P. 7
                   1-NR 10-77 P. 7
        Reynolds, Verne
               Eastman Brass Quintet
               Candide CE 31004
                   1-HF 11-68 P. 120
                   1-NR 5-69 P. 6
                   4-SR 8-31-68 P. 45
    Royal Pavane
               Philip Jones Brass Ensemble
               Argo ZRG 823
                   1-GR 6-76 P. 61
                   2-ML 5-76 P. 7
                   1-NR 10-77 P. 7
Giovannelli, Ruggiero
    "You Defy Me, Beloved Foe"
               Chicago Chamber Brass
               Pro Arte Sinfonia SDS 632

Giuffre
     Pharoh (6 Tpt/4 Hn/3 Trb/2 Bar/Ta)
                         Brass Ensemble of Jazz &
                         Classical Music Society
                         Columbia CL 941
                              1-AR 5-57 P. 129
                              4-AU 7-57 P. 45
                              4-HF 6-57 P. 77
                              4-NYT 9-29-57 P. X15
                         Kansas University Brass Choir
                         Audio House AH 21473
Glasel, John (ed.)
     16th c. Carmina
                Ingraham, Paul
                     New York Brass Quintet
                     RCA AGL 1 3968
                          1-HF 9-67 P. 98B
                          4-NR 7-67 P. 9
                Schmitt, Frederick
                     New York Brass Quintet
                     Golden Crest GC S 4023
                          1-AU 5-60 P. 53
                          4-NR 4-60 P. 7
                          4-NYT 4-3-60 P. X10
Glazunov, Alexander (1865-1936)
     In Modo Religioso, Op. 38 (1892)
     (Tpt/Hn/Trb/Tba)
                Birdwell, Edward
                     American Brass Quintet
                     4-Desto 6474/7
                          1-ST 3-70 P. 120
Gould, Morton (1913-     )
     Suite for Tuba & 3 Horns
                     New York Horn Trio
                     Golden Crest GC 4122
                          4-ST 5-74 P. 111
Gounod, Charles (1818-1893)
     Petite Sinfonie
                     Nimbus 45006 (45 rpm)
                          1-FF 7/8-81 P. 222
                          1-GR 1-81 P. 959
Grant, Parks (1910-     )
     Brevities for Brass Suite # 3, Op. 44
     (2 Tpts/Hn/Trb)
                Wagnitz, Ralph
                     Coronet S 2738
                          4-NR 4-73 P. 8
     Excursions for 2 Trumpets, Horn & Trombone (1951)
                Birdwell, Edward
                     CRI S 222
                          2-NR 7-68 P. 7
     Laconic Suite # 1, Op. 31
     (2 Tpts/Hn/Trb)
                Wagnitz, Ralph
                     Coronet S 2738
                          4-NR 4-73 P. 8

Gregson, Edward (1945-      )
      Quintet For Brass
            Baker, Julian
                  Halle Brass Consort
                  PYE Golden Guinea GSGC 14114
Grieg, Edvard (1843-1907)
      Funeral March
                  Philip Jones Brass Ensemble
                  Argo ZRG 731
                        1-ML 6-73 P. 4
                        1-NR 10-73 P. 13
                        1-ST 1-74 P. 118
                  Locke Brass Consort
                  Unicorn RHS 339
                        1-GR 6-76 P. 58
            Leroy, C.
                  Ades 14 032
                        1-FF 5/6-83 P. 268
      Grieg for Brass
            Klinger/Worchester/Green/Bentley
                  University of Minnesota Brass Choir
                  UMBC:   002
      Homage for Brass
                  Locke Brass Consort
                  CRDD 1102
                        1-FF 5/6-83 P. 269
                        1-GR 3-83 P. 1059
                        1-MG 4-83 P. 6
                        2-NR 6-83 P. 6
      Suite
            Leroy, C.
                  Ades 14 032
                        1-FF 5/6-83 P. 268
Grillo
      Canzona I
                  Berlin Philharmonic Brass Ensemble
                  DG 2532 066
                        1-FF 7/8-82 P. 268
                        1-FF 1/2-83 P. 336
                        1-NR 2-83 P. 4
                  Berlin Philharmonic Brass Ensemble
                  DG 2741 011
                        1-FF 1/2-83 P. 336
                        1-GR 11-82 P. 591
                        3-HF 11-83 P. 76
                        1-MG 7-82 P. 10
      Canzona II
                  Berlin Philharmonic Brass Ensemble
                  DG 2532 066
                        1-FF 7/8-82 P. 268
                        1-FF 1/2-83 P. 336
                        1-NR 2-83 P. 4
                  Berlin Philharmonic Brass Ensemble
                  DG 2741 011
                        1-FF 1/2-83 P. 336
                        1-GR 11-82 P. 591
                        3-HF 11-83 P. 76
                        1-MG 7-82 P. 10

Guami
    Canzon # 19
        Katzen
                Empire Brass Quintet
                  Digitech DIGI 102
                      1-ST 7-80 P. 86
    Canzon # 25
                Ed Tarr Brass Ensemble
                  Nonesuch H 71385
                      1-CR 12-80 P. 43
Haines, Edmund (1914-    )
    Toccata
                Ars Nova Brass Quintet
                MHS 1446 Z
                      1-GR 1-72 P. 1233
        Battey, David
                Dallas Brass Quintet
                CRYS S 203
                      1-AR 6-79 P. 41
                      1-FF 7/8-79 P. 130
                      2-NR 5-79 P. 7
        Boen, Jonathan
                Chicago Brass Quintet
                CRYS S 211
                      1-FF 11/12-82 P. 305
                      1-NR 11-82 P. 6
        Cowden, Hugh
                Chicago Symphony Brass Ensemble
                Audiophile AP 21
        Schmitt, Frederick
                New York Brass Quintet
                Golden Crest GC S 4023
                      1-AU 5-60 P. 53
                      4-NR 4-60 P. 7
                      4-NYT 4-3-60 P. X10
Hammond, Don (1917-    )
    Quintet for Brass
        Schmitt, Frederick
                New York Brass Quintet
                Golden Crest CR 4017
                      1-AU 4-60 P. 48
                      1-NR 4-60 P. 7
                      4-NYT 4-3-60 P. X10
Handel, G. F. (1685-1759)
    Allegro Maestoso from Water Music
        Page, Graeme
                Canadian Brass Quintet
                RCA ARL 1 4733
    Aria
        van Aeken, Alex
                Theo Mertens Chamber Brass Quintet
                Eufoda 1082
    Arrival of Queen of Sheba
                Philip Jones Brass Ensemble
                London 411930-2LH
    Excerpts from Giulio Cesare
                Guy Touvron Brass Quintet
                MHS 4168

Handel, G. F. (Cont'd)
      Harmonious Blacksmith
            Halloin, Beth
                  Chicago Chamber Brass
                        Pro Arte Sinfonia S05616
                              1-AR 3-84 P. 62
                              1-FF 3/4-84 P. 324
      La Rejouissance
                  Philip Jones Brass Ensemble
                  London 411930-2LH
                  Philip Jones Brass Ensemble
                  London CS 7221
                        2-FF 11/12-81 P. 296
                        2-NR 1-82 P. 7
                        4-ST 5-82 P. 81
      Largo for Xerses
                  Philip Jones Brass Ensemble
                  London 411930-2LH
      Messiah:  Hallelujah Chorus
                  Canadian Brass Quintet
                  Vanguard VSD 71253
                        2-CR 5-79 P. 43
                        1-FF 7/8-79 P. 132
                        1-NR 3-79 P. 9
            Page, Graeme
                  Canadian Brass Quintet
                  Boot BMC 3003
                  Canadian Brass Quintet
                  RCA ARL 1 4733
      March
                  Philip Jones Brass Ensemble
                  London 411930-2LH
      Minuet
                  Philip Jones Brass Ensemble
                  London 411930-2LH
      Overture to Music for Royal Fireworks
            Halloin, Beth
                  Chicago Chamber Brass
                        Pro Arte Sinfonia S05616
                              1-AR 3-84 P. 62
                              1-FF 3/4-84 P. 324
      Royal Fireworks Music
                  Guy Touvron Brass Quintet
                  MHS 4168
                  Philip Jones Brass Ensemble
                  London 411930-2LH
      Water Music Suite
                  Philip Jones Brass Ensemble
                  London 411930-2LH
            Page, Graeme
                  Canadian Brass Quintet
                  ARL 1 3554
                        2-AR 11-80 P. 39
                        1-CR 8-80 P. 43
                        1-FF 7/8-80 P. 186
                        1-NR 7-80 P. 36
                        2-NYT 5-18-80 P. D32

Hansen/Andresen
    Quintet
        Hansen, Henning
            Royal Danish Brass
            Rondo Grammofon RLP 8304
Harris, Arthur (1927-    )
    4 Moods for Brass Quintet (1957)
            Schmitt, Frederick
                New York Brass Quintet
                Golden Crest GC S 4023
                    1-AU 5-60 P. 53
                    4-NR 4-60 P. 7
                    4-NYT 4-3-60 P. X10
        Ward, Charles
                Metropolitan Brass Quintet
                CRYS S 208
                    2-NR 5-78 P. 5
Harris, Roy (1898-1979)
    Chorale for Organ & Brass (1943)
    (3 Tpt/Hn/3 Trb/Org)
                UCLA Brass Ensemble
                VAR/SARA 81085
    Toccata for Organ & Brass (1943)
    (3 Tpt/Hn/3 Trb/Org)
                UCLA Brass Ensemble
                VAR/SARA 81085
Hartley, Walter (1927-    )
    Divertissement
        Covert, John
                 Ithaca Brass Quintet
                Mark Ed. Records MEC 32558
    Orpheus (1960)
            Smith, Calvin
                Annapolis Brass Quintet
                CRYS S 206
                    2-NR 11-76 P. 7
Hassler, Hans Leo (1564-1612)
    O Haupt Voll Blut Und Wundn
            Tillotson, Brooks
                 Chamber Brass Players
                Golden Crest CR 4008
                    4-HF 12-57 P. 94
                    2-LJ 1-1-58 P. 70
    Intrada 5
                Philip Jones Brass Ensemble
                Argo ZRG 898
                    1-FF 1/2-80 P. 173
                    1-FU 5-80 P. 46
                    1-GR 8-79 P. 348
                    1-ML 5-79 P. 9
Haufrecht, Herbert (1909-    )
    Symphony for Brass & Timpani (1956)
            Snyder, Vince
                New York Brass Ensemble Society
                CRI SD 192
                    2-HSR 10-65 P. 88

Haydn, F. J. (1732-1809)
      March for Prince of Wales
                        Locke Brass Consort
                        Unicorn RHS 339
                              1-GR 6-76 P. 58
Hazell
      Black Sam
                        Philip Jones Brass Ensemble
                        Argo ZRG 895
                              2-FF 5/6-80
                              1-GR 1-79 P. 1334
      Borage
                        Philip Jones Brass Ensemble
                        Argo ZRG 895
                              2-FF 5/6-80
                              1-GR 1-79 P. 1334
      Kraken
                        Philip Jones Brass Ensemble
                        Argo ZRG 895
                              2-FF 5/6-80
                              1-GR 1-79 P. 1334
      Mr. Jums
                        Philip Jones Brass Ensemble
                        Argo ZRG 895
                              2-FF 5/6-80
                              1-GR 1-79 P. 1334
Helmore/Schlabach
      O Come Emanuel
            La Bar, Arthur
                        Annapolis Brass Quintet
                        Richardson Records RRS-5
Henderson, Robert (1948-      )
      Fanfare 1964
      (3 Tpt/4 Hn/3 Trb/Ta/Ti/Perc)
                        Los Angeles Philharmonic Brass Ensemble
                        Avant AV 1005
                              1-NR 7-73 P. 12
Henderson, William
      Quintet for Brass Quintet
                        Modern Brass Quintet
                        Orion ORS 80399
Henze, Hans Werner (1926-      )
      Der langwierige Weg in die Wohnung
      der Natascha Ungeheuer
                        Philip Jones Brass Quintet
                        DG 2530 212
                              4-HF 1-73 P. 90
                              1-NR 12-72 P. 15
                              1-NYT 11-5-72 P. D30
                              4-ON 1-27-73 P. 28
                              4-SR 3-3-73 P. 48
                              1-ST 12-72 P. 126
Hermann
      Brass Quintet # 1
            Goldstein, Arthur
                        Grenadilla GS 1040
                              2-FF 7/8-80 P. 187
                              2-NR 7-78 P. 7

Hermansson
    Shadow Play
        Kjellden, Thomas
            Malmo Brass Ensemble
            BIS LP 59
                1-FF 9-77 P. 61
Hoffman/Andresen
    Valdemar's Castle Dances
        Hansen, Henning
            Royal Danish Brass
            Rondo Grammofon RLP 8304
Holborne, Anthony (    -1602)
    Allemande (Sonata # 59)
            Guy Touvron Brass Quintet
            MHS 4168
    Coranto
            Philip Jones Brass Ensemble
            Argo ZRG 717
                1-GR 11-74 P. 910
                2-ML 11-74 P. 5
    Galliard (Sonata # 34)
            Guy Touvron Brass Quintet
            MHS 4168
    Galliard
        Reynolds, Verne
            Eastman Brass Quintet
            Candide CE 31004
                1-HF 11-68 P. 120
                1-NR 5-69 P. 6
                4-SR 8-31-68 P. 45
            Eastman Brass Quintet
            Moss Music Group MMG 1139
    Muy Linda; Galliard
            Canadian Brass Quintet
            Vanguard VSD 71254
                4-FF 7/8-80 P. 186
                2-NR 7-80 P. 6
        Page, Graeme
            Canadian Brass Quintet
            Boot BMC 3001
    Night Watch
            Music Hall Brass Ensemble
            Monogram 817
                1-AR 7-54 P. 348
                1-HF 12-54 P. 77
                1-MA 12-15-54 P. 24
                2-NYT 7-25-54 P. X6
                2-SR 6-26-54 P. 52
    Pavens, Galliards, Almains & other short Aeirs
            Philadelphia Brass Ensemble
            Columbia MS 6941
    2 Pieces
        Tillotson, Brooks
            Chamber Brass Players
            Classic Editions CE 1039

135

Holborne, Anthony (Cont'd)
     3 Pieces
                         Eastern Classical Brass Quintet
                           Klavier KS 561
                               2-FF 7/8-79 P. 131
                         Pacific Brass Quintet
                           Avant AV 1004
                               2-NR 6-72 P. 8
                 Page, Graeme
                         Canadian Brass Quintet
                           CBC:  SM 239
                 Smith, Calvin
                         Annapolis Brass Quintet
                           2 CRYS S 202
                               1-CR 3-75 P. 36
                               1-NR 1-75 P. 6
                 Schmitt, Frederick
                         New York Brass Quintet
                           Golden Crest GC S 4023
                               1-AU 5-60 P. 53
                               4-NR 4-60 P. 7
                               4-NYT 4-3-60 P. X10
     5 Pieces
                 Ohanian, David
                         Empire Brass Quintet
                           Sine Qua Non SA 2014
     Suite
                         Gabrieli Brass Ensemble
                           Nonesuch 71118
                               1-GR 2-66 P. 397
                               2-HF 11-66 P. 169
                               1-HSR 11-66 P. 72
                               1-NR 9-66 P. 5
                 Ingraham, Paul
                         New York Brass Quintet
                           RCA AGL 1 3968
                               1-HF 9-67 P. 98B
                               4-NR 7-67 P. 9
     Suite of Dances
                         Paris Brass Quintet
                           PLE 084
                               2-FF 9/10-79 P. 181
     Suite of Elizabethan Dances
                 Happe, Richard
                         American Brass Quintet
                           Folkways FM 3651
                               4-NR 12-65 P. 8
     The Fairie Round
                 Katzen
                         Empire Brass Quintet
                           Digitech DIGI 102
                               1-ST 7-80 P. 86

Holborne, Anthony (Cont'd)
      The Honie Suckle
                        Music Hall Brass Ensemble
                        Monogram 817
                            1-AR 7-54 P. 348
                            1-HF 12-54 P. 77
                            1-MA 12-15-54 P. 24
                            2-NYT 7-25-54 P. X6
                            2-SR 6-26-54 P. 52
            Katzen
                        Empire Brass Quintet
                        Digitech DIGI 102
                            1-ST 7-80 P. 86
      The Image of Melancholy
            Katzen
                        Empire Brass Quintet
                        Digitech DIGI 102
                            1-ST 7-80 P. 86
      Wanton
                        Music Hall Brass Ensemble
                        Monogram 817
                            1-AR 7-54 P. 348
                            1-HF 12-54 P. 77
                            1-MA 12-15-54 P. 24
                            2-NYT 7-25-54 P. X6
                            2-SR 6-26-54 P. 52
            Katzen
                        Empire Brass Quintet
                        Digitech DIGI 102
                            1-ST 7-80 P. 86
      Widow's Myte
            Katzen
                        Empire Brass Quintet
                        Digitech DIGI 102
                            1-ST 7-80 P. 86
            Wakefield, David
                        American Brass Quintet
                        Delos DMS 3003
                            1-NR 3-80 P. 7
                            1-NYT 5-18-80 P. D32
                            1-ST 7-80 P. 84
Holmboe, Vagn (1909-    )
      Quintet for Brass, Op. 79 (1961)
                        Swedish Brass Quintet
                        BIS 248
            Hansen, Henning
                        Royal Danish Brass
                        Rondo Grammofon RLP 8303
Hopkins, James (1939-    )
      Brass Quintet # 1
            Boen, Jonathan
                        Chicago Brass Quintet
                        CRYS S 211
                            1-FF 11/12-82 P. 305
                            1-NR 11-82 P. 6

Hopkinson
    The Toast
            Smith, Calvin
                    Annapolis Brass Quintet
                    Richardson Records RRS-3
Horovitz, Joseph (1926-      )
        "Music Hall" Suite for Brass Quintet (1964)
                    Budapest Brass Quintet
                    Hungaroton SLPX 12486
                            1-FF 3/4-84 P. 322
                            2-NR 3-84 P. 6
                    Philip Jones Brass Ensemble
                    HNH 4037
                            1-HF 2-78 P. 100
                            2-ST 5-78 P. 110
            Baker, Julian
                    Halle Brass Consort
                    PYE Golden Guinea GSGC 14114
            James, Ifor
                    Philip Jones Brass Ensemble
                    Claves DPF 600
            Strieby, Lawrence
                    St. Louis Brass Quintet
                    CRYS S 212
                            2-FF 7/8-83 P. 283
            Ward, Charles
                    Metropolitan Brass Quintet
                    CRYS S 208
                            2-NR 5-78 P. 5
Hoskins
    Sonata for Brass Quartet (1st Movement)
            Gelston/Terry
                    Georgia State College Brass Ensemble
                    Golden Crest GC S 4084
Hovhaness, Alan (1911-      )
        Sharagan & Fugue, Op. 58
                    American Brass Quintet
                    BASF KMB 20812
                            1-NR 2-74 P. 6
                    Empire Brass Quintet
                    Digitech DIGI 105
                            2-FF 11/12-81 P. 295
                    MGM Brass Ensemble
                    MGM E 3517
                            2-AR 12-57 P. 150
                            1-AU 1-58 P. 50
                            1-HF 2-58 P. 66
                            4-SR 2-22-58 P. 43
            Goldstein, Arthur
                    Grenadilla GS 1040
                            2-FF 7/8-80 P. 187
                            2-NR 7-78 P. 7
            Ingraham, Paul
                    New York Brass Quintet
                    Desto 6401

Hovhaness, Alan (Cont'd)
    6 Dances for Brass Quintet
        Battey, David
            Dallas Brass Quintet
                CRYS S 203
                    1-AR 6-79 P. 41
                    1-FF 7/8-79 P. 130
Howarth, Elgar
    Pasce Tuos
        James, Ifor
            Philip Jones Brass Ensemble
                Argo ZRG 851
                    1-GR 7-77 P. 201
                    1-HF 5-78 P. 116
    Variations on Carnival of Venice
        Philip Jones Brass Ensemble
            HNH 4037
                1-HF 2-78 P. 100
                2-ST 5-78 P. 110
        James, Ifor
            Philip Jones Brass Ensemble
                Claves DPF 600
Huggler, John (1928-    )
    Op. 58 (3 Movements)
        Iowa Brass Quintet
            Trilogy/Composers Theatre
            Series CTS 1001
                1-NR 8-73 P. 6
    Quintet # 1 (1955)
        Johns, Michael
            Cambridge Brass Quintet
                CRYS S 204
                    2-HF 7-77 P. 118
                    1-NR 11-76 P. 7
Hummel, Johann Nepomuk (1778-1857)
    Andante & Rondo from Trumpet Concerto in Eb
        Neilson, Diana
            Chicago Chamber Brass
                Pro Arte Sinfonia S 616
Humphreys
    Showcase Five
        Pacific Brass Quintet
            Avant AVV 1004
                2-NR 6-72 P. 8
Husa, Karel (1921-    )
    Divertimento for Brass Quintet (1968)
        Anderson, Paul
            Iowa Brass Quintet
                University of Iowa Press 29001
                    2-HF 7-77 P. 118
        Covert, John
            Ithaca Brass Quintet
                Golden Crest GC 4114
    Landscapes for Brass Quintet (1977)
        Western Brass Quintet
            CRI S 192 (78)

Huston, Scott (1916-    )
     Sounds at Night for 13 Brass Instruments
                         Indianapolis Brass Ensemble
                         Serenus SRS 12066
                              1-NR 4-76 P. 7
     Suite for Our Times
                         Indianapolis Brass Ensemble
                         Serenus SRS 12066
                              1-NR 4-76 P. 7
Isaac, Heinrich (1450-1517)
     La Martinella
                         American Brass Quintet
                         BASF KMB 20812
                              1-NR 2-74 P. 6
     Der Hund
              Happe, Richard
                         American Brass Quintet
                         Folkways FMS 33652
                              2-AU 7-68 P. 46
                              4-NR 9-67 P. 6
     Der Welte Fundt
              Katzen
                         Empire Brass Quintet
                         Digitech DIGI 102
                              1-ST 7-80 P. 86
     Instrumental Piece Without Title
              Katzen
                         Empire Brass Quintet
                         Digitech DIGI 102
                              1-ST 7-80 P. 86
     La Mi La Sol
              Happe, Richard
                         American Brass Quintet
                         Folkways FMS 33652
                              2-AU 7-68 P. 46
                              4-NR 9-67 P. 6
     La Martinella
                         American Brass Quintet
                         BASF KMB 20812
                              1-NR 2-74 P. 6
     Maudit Soyt
              Katzen
                         Empire Brass Quintet
                         Digitech DIGI 102
                              1-ST 7-80 P. 86
Ives, Charles (1874-1954)
     On the Counter
                         Eastern Brass Quintet
                         Klavier KS 539
                              2-AU 2-76 P. 96
                              1-HF 11-75 P. 129
     Sideshow
                         Eastern Brass Quintet
                         Klavier KS 539
                              2-AU 2-76 P. 96
                              1-HF 11-75 P. 129

Ives, Charles (Cont'd)
    Slow March
                  Eastern Brass Quintet
                  Klavier KS 539
                      2-AU 2-76 P. 96
                      1-HF 11-75 P. 129
    Tarrant Mass
                  Eastern Brass Quintet
                  Klavier KS 539
                      2-AU 2-76 P. 96
                      1-HF 11-75 P. 129

Jacob, Gordon (1895-1984)
    Salute to USA
                  Locke Brass Consort
                  Unicorn UN 1-72012
                      1-FF 7/8-79 P. 133
                      2-GR 5-78 P. 1889

Jarrett, Keith (1945-    )
    Brass Quintet
                  American Brass Quintet
                  ECM/Polydor 1033-34

Jenkins
    Newark Siege
                  Philip Jones Brass Ensemble
                  London CS 7242
                      2-FF 7/8-82 P. 268
                  Philip Jones Brass Ensemble
                  London CS 7221
                      2-FF 11/12-81 P. 296
                      2-NR 1-82 P. 7
                      4-ST 5-82 P. 81

Johnson, J. J.
    Poem for Brass
    (7 Tpt/4 Hn/4 Trb/2 Bar/Ta)
                  Brass Ensemble of Jazz
                  & Classical Music Society
                  Columbia CL 941
                      1-AR 5-57 P. 129
                      4-AU 7-57 P. 45
                      4-HF 6-57 P. 77
                      4-NYT 9-29-57 P. X15

Jolivet, Andre (1905-1974)
    Fanfare: Narcisse
                  Philip Jones Brass Ensemble
                  Argo ZRG 731
                      4-GR 6-73 P. 62
                      1-ML 6-73 P. 4
                      1-NR 10-73 P. 13
                      1-ST 1-74 P. 118

Jones, Collier
    4 Movements for 5 Brass
            Ingraham, Paul
                  New York Brass Quintet
                  Desto DS 6401
          Soper, Kenneth
                  New York Brass Choir
                  Golden Crest CRS 4148
                      1-AR 3-77 P. 40

Jones, Kelsey (1922-    )
    Passacaglia & Fugue (1975)
        Talamantes, Nona
            Mount Royal Brass Quintet
            McGill University 77004
                1-FF 5/6-82 P. 292
Joplin, Scott (1868-1917)
    Cascades
        Soper, Kenneth
            New York Brass Quintet
            Golden Crest CRS 4148
                1-AR 3-77 P. 40
    Easy Winners
            Philip Jones Brass Ensemble
            Argo ZRG 895
                2-FF 5/6-80
                1-GR 1-79 P. 1334
        Page, Graeme
            Canadian Brass Quintet
            Boot BMC 3004
            Canadian Brass Quintet
            CBC: RCI 403
    Entertainer
            Eastern Brass Quintet
            Klavier KS 539
                2-AU 2-76 P. 96
                1-HF 11-75 P. 129
        Page, Graeme
            Canadian Brass Quintet
            CBC: RCI 403
            Canadian Brass Quintet
            Boot BMC 3004
    Euphonic Rag
        Page, Graeme
            Canadian Brass Quintet
            CBC: RCI 403
    Euphonic Sounds
        Page, Graeme
            Canadian Brass Quintet
            Boot BMC 3004
    The Favorite
        Page, Graeme
            Canadian Brass Quintet
            Boot BMC 3001
            Canadian Brass Quintet
            Boot BMC 3004
            Canadian Brass Quintet
            CBC: SM 239
            Canadian Brass Quintet
            CBC: RCI 403
    Figleaf Rag
        Page, Graeme
            Canadian Brass Quintet
            Boot BMC 3004
            Canadian Brass Quintet
            CBC: RCI 403

Joplin, Scott (Cont'd)
    Gladiolus Rag
                    Philip Jones Brass Ensemble
                    London LDR 71100
                        1-AR 2-83 P. 77
                        1-FF 1/2-83 P. 338
                        1-NR 3-83 P. 3
    Paragon Rag
                    Empire Brass Quintet
                    Digitech DIGI 104
    Pleasant Moments
            Page, Graeme
                    Canadian Brass Quintet
                    Boot BMC 3001
                    Canadian Brass Quintet
                    Boot BMC 3004
    Ragtime Dance
                    Philip Jones Brass Ensemble
                    Argo ZRG 895
                        2-FF 5/6-80
                        1-GR 1-79 P. 1334
    Ragtime Waltz
            Page, Graeme
                    Canadian Brass Quintet
                    CBC: RCI 403
    Rosebud March
            Page, Graeme
                    Canadian Brass Quintet
                    Boot BMC 3004
                    Canadian Brass Quintet
                    CBC:  RCI 403
    Sycamore Rag
            Page, Graeme
                    Canadian Brass Quintet
                    Boot BMC 3004
                    Canadian Brass Quintet
                    CBC:  RCI 403
Jorgensen/Andresen
    Quintet
            Hansen, Henning
                    Royal Danish Brass
                    Rondo Grammofon RLP 8304
Kauffmann, Leo Justinus (1901-1944)
    Music for Brass (1941)
    (3 Tpt/4 Hn/3 Trb/Ta)
                    Locke Brass Consort
                    Unicorn RHS 339
                        1-GR 6-76 P. 58
Kersters, Willem (1929-    )
    Drie Rondos voor Koperkwintet, Op. 48 (1969)
            van Driessche, Andre
                    Theo Mertens Brass Ensemble
                    Eufoda 1051

Kessel
      Sonata II (1672)
            Guy, Marc
                  Annapolis Brass Quintet
                  CRYS S 213
                        1-FF 9/10-83 P. 327
                        4-NR 8-83 P. 3
Knight, Morris (1933-    )
      Brass Quintet # 1
            Ingraham, Paul
                  New York Brass Quintet
                  Now Records RN 9
      Brass Quintet # 2
            Ingraham, Paul
                  New York Brass Quintet
                  Now Records RN 9
      Brass Quintet # 3
            Ingraham, Paul
                  New York Brass Quintet
                  Now Records RN 9
      Toccata for Brass Quintet & Tape
            Ingraham, Paul
                  New York Brass Quintet
                  Now Records RN 9
Knox, Charles (1929-    )
      Solo for Trumpet With Brass Trio (1964)
      (2 Tpt/ Hn/Trb)
                  Georgia State College Brass Ensemble
                  Golden Crest S 4084
      Symphony for Brass & Percussion (1965)
                  Georgia State College Brass Ensemble
                  Golden Crest S 4085
                  Baldwin-Wallace College Brass Choir
                  Mark Edition Records MES 32565
Kocsar, Miklos (1933-    )
      Brass Sextet (1972)
                  Hungarian Brass Ensemble
                  Hungaroton SLPX 11811
                        2-AR 8-77 P. 39
                        3-FF 9-77 P. 63
                        2-NR 9-77 P. 6
Koetsier, Jan (1911-    )
      Brass Symphony # 80
                  Philip Jones Brass Ensemble
                  London LDR 71100
                        1-AR 2-83 P. 77
                        1-FF 1/2-83 P. 338
                        1-NR 3-83 P. 3
      Petite Suite
                  Philip Jones Brass Ensemble
                  HNH 4037
                        1-HF 2-78 P. 100
                        2-ST 5-78 P. 110

Kraft, William (1923-    )
     Games, Collage # 1
                    Horn Club of Los Angeles
                    Angel S 36036
                         1-HF 8-70 P. 98
                         1-NR 7-70 P. 7
                         1-ST 9-70 P. 122
     Nonet for Brass & Percussion
             Pyle, Ralph
                    Los Angeles Brass Quintet
                    CRYS S 821
                         1-NR 7-71 P. 12
     Suite for Brass
             Goldstein, Arthur
                    Grenadilla GS 1040
                         2-FF 7/8-80 P. 187
                         2-NR 7-78 P. 7
Krush, Jay
     Puddle Jumper
             Barnett, George
                    Chestnut Brass Company
                    Chestnut Brass Company 3 0001 9
     Schuylkill Punch
             Barnett, George
                    Chestnut Brass Company
                    Chestnut Brass Company 3 0001 9
Kucera, Vaclav (1929-    )
     Argot drei Satze fur Blechblaserquintette (1970)
                    Supraphon 19 1054-56
Kuhnau, Johann (1660-1722)
     Biblical Sonata # 1
                    Philip Jones Brass Ensemble
                    London CS 7221
                         2-FF 11/12-81 P. 296
                         2-NR 1-82 P. 7
                         4-ST 5-82 P. 81
Kupferman, Meyer (1926-    )
     Madrigal for Brass Quintet
                    American Brass Quintet
                    Serenus SRS 12066
     Quintet
                    American Brass Quintet
                    Serenus SRS 12041
                         1-NR 9-72 P. 6
Lachner, Franz (1803-1890)
     Nonett (2 Tpt/4 Hn/3 Trb)
                    Locke Brass Consort
                    Unicorn UN 1-72012
                         1-FF 7/8-79 P. 133
                         2-GR 5-78 P. 1889
Lang, Istvan (1933-    )
     Canzon (La Seraphina)
                    Philip Jones Brass Ensemble
                    Argo ZRG 717
                         1-GR 11-74 P. 910
                         2-ML 11-74 P. 5

145

Lang, Istvan (Cont'd)
    Canzon # 26 a 8 (La Negrona)
    (3 Tpt/2 Hn/3 Trb)
                    Ed Tarr Brass Ensemble
                    Nonesuch H 71385
                        1-CR 12-80 P. 43
        Cassazione for Brass Sextet (1971)
                    Hungarian Brass Ensemble
                    Hungaroton SLPX 11811
Lassus, Orlando di (1532-1594)
    Adoramus Te
                    Gabrieli Brass Ensemble
                    Nonesuch 71118
                        1-GR 2-66 P. 397
                        2-HF 11-66 P. 169
                        1-HSR 11-66 P. 72
                        1-NR 9-66 P. 5
        De L'eterna
                    Philip Jones Brass Ensemble
                    Argo ZRG 823
                        1-GR 6-76 P. 61
                        2-ML 5-76 P. 7
                        1-NR 10-77 P. 7
        Echo Song
                    Canadian Brass Quintet
                    CBS 1M 39035
        Providebam Dominum (4 Tpt/Hn/Trb/Bar)
                Jones/Miller
                    Philadelphia Brass Ensemble
                    Columbia MS 6941
                        4-GR 5-67 P. 584
                        1-HF 5-67 P. 92
                        1-ML 4-67 P. 4
Lavalee
    Le rose nuptiale
                Leroy, C.
                    Ades 14 032
                        1-FF 5/6-83 P. 268
Lazarof, Henri (1932-     )
    Partita for Brass Quintet & Tape (1971)
                    Los Angeles Brass Quintet
                    Candide CE 31072
                        1-AU 10-73 P. 81
                        1-HF 11-73 P. 109
                        4-NR 9-73 P. 9
Lebow, Leonard
    Suite for Brass
                Farkas or Fitzpatrick
                    Chicago Brass Ensemble
                    Audiophile AP 32
                    Pacific Brass Quintet
                    Avant AV 1004
                        2-NR 6-72 P. 8
                Cowden, Hugh
                    Chicago Symphony Brass Ensemble
                    Audiophile Ap 21

LeClerc, Michel (1914-     )
      Par Monts et Par Vaux
            Anderson, Paul
                  Iowa Brass Quintet
                        University of Iowa Press 29001
                              2-HF 7-77 P. 118
                              1-NR 2-77 P. 7
                  Ingraham, Paul
                        New York Brass Quintet
                        CRYS S 210
                              1-AR 9-80 P. 50
                              1-FF 5/6-80 P. 129
                              1-NR 5-80 P. 8
Lee, W. F.
      Fanfare for Ralph
                  Tankersley, James
                        Houston Symphony Brass Quintet
                        Austin Custom Records SFM 33-6488
      Piece for Brass
                  Tankersley, James
                        Houston Symphony Brass Quintet
                        Austin Custom Records SFM 33-6488
      Regimentation
                  Tankersley, James
                        Houston Symphony Brass Quintet
                        Austin Custom Records SFM 33-6488
      Three Mosaics
                  Tankersley, James
                        Houston Symphony Brass Quintet
                        Austin Custom Records SFM 33-6488
Leisring
      Let All Nations Praise the Lord
                        Baldwin-Wallace College Brass Choir
                        Mark Ed. Records MES 32565
Le Jeune, Claude (1528-1600)
      Piece from Le Printemps
                  Soper, Kenneth
                        New York Brass Choir
                        Golden Crest CRS 4148
                              1-AR 3-77 P. 40
      Revecy Venir du Printemps
                        Canadian Brass Quintet
                        Vanguard VSD 71254
                              4-FF 7/8-80 P. 186
                              2-NR 7-80 P. 6
                        New York Brass Society
                        WIM 3
                              1-NR 5-72 P. 5
                  Page, Graeme
                        Canadian Brass Quintet
                        Boot BMC 3001
Lennon & McCartney
      Eleanor Rigby & Penny Lane
                  Soper, Kenneth
                        New York Brass Choir
                        Golden Crest CRS 4148
                              1-AR 3-77 P. 40

Lessard, John (1920-    )
     Quintet
                    American Brass Quintet
                       Serenus SRS 12041
                          1-NR 9-72 P. 6
Levy, Frank (1930-    )
     Brass Quintet (1965)
               Schneider, Vincent
                    Brass Arts Quintet
                       Grenadilla GS 1027
                          2-FF 7/8-79 P. 131
                          2-NR 10-79 P. 4
Lewis, John
     3 Little Feelings
                    Brass Ensemble of Jazz & Classical
                    Music
                       Columbia CL 941
                          1-AR 5-57 P. 129
                          4-AU 7-57 P. 45
                          4-HF 6-57 P. 77
                          1-NYT 6-2-57 P. X15
Lewis
     Movement for Brass Quintet & Piano
                    Ithaca Brass Quintet
                       Mark Edition Records MEC 32558
Liadov & Glazunov
     Fanfares for Jubilee of Rimsky-Korsakov
     (3 Tpt)4 Hn/3 Trb/Ta/Tp)
               Ward, Charles
                    Metropolitan Brass Quintet
                       CRYS S 208
                          2-NR 5-78 P. 5
Lieb
     Feature Suite
               Goldstein, Arthur
                    Brass Guild
                       Golden Crest GC 1040
                          2-FF 7/8-80 P. 187
                          2-NR 7-78 P. 7
Lindberg/Andresen
     Chalet Psalm
               Hansen, Henning
                    Royal Danish Brass
                       Rondo Grammofon RLP 8304
Linn, Robert (1925-    )
     Quintet For Brass Instruments (1963)
               Henderson, Robert
                    Fine Arts Brass Quintet
                       CRYS S 205
                          2-CR 3-81 P. 43
                          2-NR 3-81 P. 7
Locke, Matthew (1630-1677)
     Music For His Majesty's Cornetts & Sackbuts
                    Ars Nova Brass Quintet
                       MHS 3635
                    Ed Tarr Brass Ensemble
                       Nonesuch H 71385
                          1-CR 12-80 P. 43

Locke, Matthew (Cont'd)
    Music For His Majesty's Cornetts & Sackbuts (Cont'd)
                Gabrieli Brass Ensemble
                    Nonesuch 71118
                          1-GR 2-66 P. 397
                          2-HF 11-66 P. 169
                          1-HSR 11-66 P. 72
                          1-NR 9-66 P. 5
                Guy Touvron Brass Quintet
                    MHS 4168
                London Gabrieli Brass Ensemble
                    MHS 4635 K
                          2-GR 2-79 P. 1440
                          2-GR 7-82 P. 142
                          2-MG 4-82 P. 17
                Philip Jones Brass Ensemble
                    Argo ZRG 717
                          1-GR 11-74 P. 910
                          2-ML 11-74 P. 5
                Philip Jones Brass Ensemble
                    London CS 7242
                          2-FF 7/8-82 P. 268
           Katzen
                Empire Brass Quintet
                Digitech DIGI 102
                    1-ST 7-80 P. 86
           Kjellden, Thomas
                Malmo Brass Ensemble
                BIS LP 59
                    1-FF 9-77 P. 61
    Music for King Charles II
        Meek/Keaney
                Voisin Brass Ensemble
                Unicorn 1003
                  1-AR 2-55 P. 202
                  1-ET 3-55 P. 18
                  2-HF 3-55 P. 64-VII
                  1-LJ 5-15-55 P. 1205
                  11-MA 3-55 P. 22
                  2-NR 4-55 P. 6
Lockwood, Normand (1906-    )
    Concerto for Organ & Brass (1952)
                Members/New York Philharmonic
                Varese 81047
    Encore Piece # 4
        Barnett, George
             Chestnut Brass Company
             Chestnut Brass Company 3 0001 9
    St. Paul's Bicycle
        Barnett, George
             Chestnut Brass Company
             Chestnut Brass Company 3 0001 9
London, Edwin (1929-    )
    Brass Quintet (1965)
                CRI S 470

Lovelock, William (1899-    )
     Suite for Brass Instruments (1968)
               Wakefield, David
                    American Brass Quintet
                    CRYS S 214
Luckhardt
     Brass Quintet # 1
               Becknell, Nancy
                    Wisconsin Brass Quintet
                    University of Wisconsin UW 103
Lully, Jean Baptiste (1632-1687)
     March from Thesee
                    Ars Nova Brass Quintet
                    MHS 1446 Z
                         1-GR 1-72 P. 1233
     Prelude
                    American Brass Quintet
                    BASF KMB 20812
                         1-NR 2-74 P. 6
     Prelude, Menuet & Gigue
               Barboteu, Georges
                    Brass Ensemble of Paris
                    Music Guild 120
                         4-HF 8-65 P. 82
                         1-HSR 9-65 P. 102
Luther/J. S. Bach/Schlabach
     Von Himmel Hoch, Da Komm' Ich Her
               La Bar, Arthur
                    Annapolis Brass Quintet
                    Richardson Records RRS-5
Luzzachi
     Dolorosi Martin
                    New York Brass Society
                    WIM 3
                         1-NR 5-72 P. 5
     Fieri Tormenti
                    New York Brass Society
                    WIM 3
                         1-NR 5-72 P. 5
MacEnulty, John (1940-    )
     3 Poems
               Strieby, Lawrence
                    St. Louis Brass Quintet
                    CRYS S 215
MacInnis, Donald (1923-    )
     Collide-A-Scope for 12 Brass Instruments & Tape(1968)
                    Georgia State College Brass Ensemble
                    Golden Crest GC 4085
     Variations for Brass & Percussion
                    Georgia State College Brass Ensemble
                    Golden Crest GC 4084
Maes, Jef (1905-    )
     Prelude en Allegro (1959)
               van Driessche, Andre
                    Theo Mertens Brass Ensemble
                    Eufoda 1051

Malipiero, Riccardo
    Musica da Camera
               Philips 6500 261
Manzoni, Giacomo
    Quadruplum
        Birdwell, Edward
                American Brass Quintet
                4-Desto 6474/7
                      1-ST 3-70 P. 120
Marenzio
    Spring Returns
                Chicago Chamber Brass
                Pro Arte Sinfonia SDS 632
Massaino
    Canzon XXXV
        Hagen/Hatfield/Thelander/Gullickson
                University of Minnesota Brass Choir
                UMBC:  001
Mattern, James
    Sonata Breve
        Boen, Jonathan
                Chicago Brass Quintet
                CRYS S 211
                      1-FF 11/12-82 P. 305
                      1-NR 11-82 P. 6
Maurer, Ludwig W.
    Fanfares
        Soper, Kenneth
                New York Brass Quintet
                Golden Crest CRS 4148
                      1-AR 3-77 P. 40
    (3)   Pieces
        Ward, Charles
                Metropolitan Brass Quintet
                CRYS S 208
                      2-NR 5-78 P. 5
    (3)   Pieces for Brass Quintet
        Leroy, C.
                Ades 14 032
                      1-FF 5/6-83 P. 268
    4 Pieces for Brass Quintet
        James, Ifor
                Philip Jones Brass Ensemble
                Argo ZRG 851
                      1-GR 7-77 P. 201
                      1-HF 5-78 P. 116
                      1-ML 8-77 P. 6
                      1-NR 7-78 P. 7
    4 Songs
        Strieby, Lawrence
                St. Louis Brass Quintet
                CRYS S 212
                      2-FF 7/8-83 P. 283
Mayer, William (1925-    )
    Brass Quintet
        Anderson, Paul

Mayer, William (Cont'd)
    Brass Quintet (Continued)
        Anderson, Paul
           Iowa Brass Quintet
           CRI SD 291
               2-ON 4-14-73 P. 32
               1-NR 11-72 P. 8
               2-SR 11-4-72 P. 67
McBeth, Francis
    Four Frescoes for 5 Brass (1969)
        Smith, Calvin
           Annapolis Brass Quintet
           CRYS S 206
               2-NR 11-76 P. 7
McCabe, John (1939-    )
    Rounds for Brass Quintet (1967)
        Baker, Julian
           Halle Brass Consort
           PYE Golden Guinea GSGC 14114
McCauley, William A. (1917-    )
    Miniature Overture for Brass Quintet
           Canadian Brass Quintet
           Vanguard VSD 71254
               4-FF 7/8-80 P. 186
               2-NR 7-80 P. 6
        Page, Graeme
           Canadian Brass Quintet
           Boot BMC 3001
    Staggering
           Canadian Brass Quintet
           Vanguard VSD 71253
               2-CR 5-79 P. 43
               1-FF 7/8-79 P. 132
               1-NR 3-79 P. 9
        Page, Graeme
           Canadian Brass Quintet
           Boot BMC 3003
McGarth, Joseph (1889-1968)
    Six Brevities for Brass Quintet, Op. 81
        Ingraham, Paul
           New York Brass Quintet
           Desto 6401
McPeek, Benjamin D. (1934-    )
    Paul Bunyan Suite
        Page, Graeme
           Canadian Brass Quintet
           Boot BMC 3004
           Canadian Brass Quintet
           CBC: RCI 403
    Ragtime for Brass
        Page, Graeme
           Canadian Brass Quintet
           Boot BMC 3004
           Canadian Brass Quintet
           CBC: RCI 403

Melby, John (1941-    )
    91 Plus 5 for Brass Quintet & Tape
            Curenton, Edward
                    Contemporary Brass Quintet
                    CRI SD 310
                            1-NR 10-73 P. 7
                            2-ST 1-74 P. 116
Mendelssohn, Felix (1809-1847)
    Funeral March (3 Tpt/4 Hn/3 Trb/Bar/Ta)
                    Locke Brass Consort
                    Unicorn UN 1-72012
                            1-FF 7/8-79 P. 133
                            2-GR 5-78 P. 1889
    Tarantella
                    Philip Jones Brass Ensemble
                    ARGO ZRG 928
            Leroy, C.
                    Ades 14 032
                            1-FF 5/6-83 P. 268
Mendez, Raphael (1906-    )
    La Virgen de La Macarena
                    Canadian Brass Quintet
                    Vanguard VSD 71254
                            4-FF 7/8-80 P. 186
                            2-NR 7-80 P. 6
            Page, Graeme
                    Canadian Brass Quintet
                    Boot BMC 3001
Michalsky, Donal (1928-1975)
    Fantasia alla Marcia
            Henderson, Robert
                    Fine Arts Brass Quintet
                    CRYS S 205
                            2-CR 3-81 P. 43
                            2-NR 3-81 P. 7
    Fantasia sopra M.F.V.
            Henderson, Robert
                    Fine Arts Brass Quintet
                    CRYS S 205
                            2-CR 3-81 P. 43
                            2-NR 3-81 P. 7
Miller, Edward (1930-    )
    The Folly Stone (1966)
            Ingraham, Paul
                    New York Brass Quintet
                    CRI SD 302
                            4-NR 6-73 P. 6
Molineaux, Allen (1950-    )
    Encounter (1972)
            La Bar, Arthur
                    Annapolis Brass Quintet
                    CRYS S 207
                            2-AR 6-79 P. 41
                            2-CR 9-79 P. 43
                            1-NR 5-79 P. 7

Monteverdi, Claudio (1567-1643)
    Concertato, Qui Rise Tirsi
                Eastern Brass Quintet
                Klavier KS 536
                    1-AU 12-75 P. 106
                    1-NR 5-75 P. 8
    2 Madrigals
                Eastern Classical Brass Quintet
                Klavier KS 561
                    2-FF 7/8-79 P. 131
    Suite for Brass Instruments
        Ingraham, Paul
                New York Brass Quintet
                RCA AGL 1 3968
                    1-HF 9-67 P. 98B
                    4-NR 7-67 P. 9
    Suite of 5 Sinfonias
                Music Hall Brass Ensemble
                Monogram 817
                    1-AR 7-54 P. 348
                    1-HF 12-54 P. 77
                    1-MA 12-15-54 P. 24
                    2-NYT 7-25-54 P. X6
                    2-SR 6-26-54 P. 52
Monti
    Czardas
                Philip Jones Brass Ensemble
                Argo ZRG 895
                    2-FF 5/6-80
                    1-GR 1-79 P. 1334
Morel, Francois (1926-   )
    Quintet for Brass
        Page, Graeme
                Canadian Brass Quintet
                CBC: SM 216
Moritz, Edvard (1891-   )
    Suite of Dances
                Ars Nova Brass Quintet
                MHS 3635
Morley, Thomas (1557-1602)
    Joyne Hands
        Wakefield, David
                American Brass Quintet
                Delos DMS 3003
                    1-NR 3-80 P. 7
                    1-NYT 5-18-80 P. D32
                    1-ST 7-80 P. 84
Moross, Jerome (1913-   )
    Brass Quintet
                London Pro Musica
                Desto 6469
Morton, Ferdinand (Jelly Roll)
    Grandpa's Spells
        Page, Graeme
                Canadian Brass Quintet
                    Brassworks Music Umbrella 05862
                Canadian Brass Quintet
                RCA ARL 1 4733

Mouret, Jean Joseph (1682-1738)
      Rondeau
                        Eastern Brass Quintet
                           Klavier KS 536
                               1-AU 12-75 P. 106
                               1-NR 5-75 P. 8
                  Anderson, Paul
                        Iowa Brass Quintet
                           University of Iowa Press 29001
                               2-HF 7-77 P. 118
                               1-NR 2-77 P. 7
                  Page, Graeme
                        Canadian Brass Quintet
                           RCA ARC 1 4574
                               2-FF 7/8-83 P. 284
                               4-NR 6-83 P. 6
                        Canadian Brass Quintet
                           RCA ARL 1 4733
                  Soper, Kenneth
                        New York Brass Choir
                           Golden Crest CR S 4148
                  Strieby, Lawrence
                        St. Louis Brass Quintet
                           CRYS S 212
                               2-FF 7/8-83 P. 283
                  Klinger/Worchester/Green/Bentley
                        University of Minnesota Brass Choir
                           UMBC: 002
                  Osborne, Larry
                        Vintage Brass Ensemble
                           Ohlone Band Album CR 8242
      Rondelay
                        Atlanta Brass Ensemble
                           Crystal Clear CCS 7011
                               2-AR 11-79 P. 31
                               1-NR 6-80 P. 14
Mozart, W. A. (1756-1791)
      Divertimento, K. 252
                  Halloin, Beth
                        Chicago Chamber Brass
                           Pro Arte Sinfonia S05616
                               1-AR 3-84 P. 62
                               1-FF 3/4-84 P. 324
      March of the Priests
                        Locke Brass Consort
                           CRDD 1102
                               1-FF 5/6-83 P. 269
                               1-GR 3-83 P. 1059
                               1-MG 4-83 P. 6
                               2-NR 6-83 P. 6
      Tuba Serenade
                        Philip Jones Brass Ensemble
                           Argo ZRG 895
                               2-FF 5/6-80 P. 197
                               1-GR 1-79 P. 1334

Muffat, Georg (1653-1704)
    Suite
                        Berlin Philharmonic Brass Ensemble
                        DG 2532 066
                            1-FF 7/8-82 P. 268
                            1-FF 1/2-83 P. 336
                            1-NR 2-83 P. 4
                        Berlin Philharmonic Brass Ensemble
                        DG 2741 011
                            1-FF 1/2-83 P. 336
                            1-GR 11-82 P. 591
                            3-HF 11-83 P. 76
                            1-MG 7-82 P. 10
Mussorgsky, Modeste (1839-1881)
    Hopak from the Fair at Sorochintzy
            Boen, Jonathan
                        Chicago Brass Quintet
                        CRYS S 211
                            1-FF 11/12-82 P. 305
                            1-NR 11-82 P. 6
    March
                        Locke Brass Consort
                        CRDD 1102
                            1-FF 5/6-83 P. 269
                            1-GR 3-83 P. 1059
                            1-MG 4-83 P. 6
                            2-NR 6-83 P. 6
Nelhybel, Vaclav (1919-    )
    Chorale for Brass & Percussion
                        Orchestra Sinfonica di Roma
                        Serenus SRS 12008
                            2-HSR 10-65 P. 96
    Brass Quartet (Tpt/Hn/Trb/Pf)
                        Orchestra Sinfonica di Roma
                        Serenus SRS 12006
                            2-HF 9-65 P. 94
                            1-NR 8-65 P. 15
    3 Intradas for Brass (3 Tpt/3 Hn/3 Trb)
                        Orchestra Sinfonica di Roma
                        Serenus SRS 12006
                            2-HF 9-65 P. 94
                            1-NR 8-65 P. 15
    Numismata for 7 Brass
    (2 Tpt/2 Hn/2 Trb/Ta)
                        Orchestra Sinfonica di Roma
                        Serenus SRS 12008
                            2-HSR 10-65 P. 96
Nielsen/Andresen
    Lur Signals
            Hansen, Henning
                        Royal Danish Brass
                        Rondo Grammofon RLP 8304
    5 Preludes
            Hansen, Henning
                        Royal Danish Brass
                        Rondo Grammofon RLP 8303

O'Koever
      Fantasie
            Reynolds, Verne
                  Eastman Brass Quintet
                  Candide CE 31004
                        1-HF 11-68 P. 120
                        1-NR 5-69 P. 6
                        4-SR 8-31-68 P. 45
Pachelbel, Johann (1653-1706)
      Canon in D
                  Ars Nova Brass Quintet
                  MHS 4244
                        1-GR 5-80 P. 1689
                  Canadian Brass Quintet
                  CBS 1M 39035
                  Canadian Brass Quintet
                  Chandos 1069
            Page, Graeme
                  Canadian Brass Quintet
                  RCA ARL 1 3554
                        2-AR 11-80 P. 39
                        1-CR 8-80 P. 43
                        1-FF 7/8-80 P. 186
                        1-NR 7-80 P. 6
                        2-NYT 5-18-80 P. D32
                  Canadian Brass Quintet
                  RCA ARL 1 4733
                  Canadian Brass Quintet
                  Boot BMC 3003
      Madrigal
                  Canadian Brass Quintet
                  Vanguard VSD 71253
                        2-CR 5-79 P. 43
                        1-FF 7/8-79 P. 132
                        1-NR 3-79 P. 9
      Magnificat
                  Canadian Brass Quintet
                  CBS 1M 39035
      2 Magnificat Fugues (7 Tpt/2 Hn/4 Trb/Bar/Ta)
            Andrus/Haines
                  Georgia State College Brass Ensemble
                  Golden Crest GC S 4083
      Suite in Bb
                  Ars Nova Brass Quintet
                  MHS 4244
                        1-GR 5-80 P. 1689
      Suite in G
                  Ars Nova Brass Quintet
                  MHS 4244
                        1-GR 5-80 P. 1689
Paganini, Niccolo (1782-1840)
      Caprices
            Pyle, Ralph
                  Los Angeles Brass Quintet
                  CRYS S 102

Palestrina, Giovanni (1525-1594)
    Jubilate Deo
            Canadian Brass Quintet
            CBS 1M 39035
    Ricercar del Primo Tuono
            Chicago Chamber Brass
                Pro Arte Sinfonia SDS 632
        Ohanian, David
            Empire Brass Quintet
            Sine Qua Non SA 2014
    Ricercar Sopra il Primo Tuono
        Birdwell, Edward
            American Brass Quintet
            4-Desto 6474/7
                1-ST 3-70 P. 120
Passereau, Pierre
    Il est Bel et Bon
            Philip Jones Brass Ensemble
            Argo ZRG 823
                1-GR 6-76 P. 61
                2-ML 5-76 P. 7
                1-NR 10-77 P. 7
        van Aeken, Alex
            Theo Mertens Chamber Brass Quintet
            Eufoda 1082
Pauer, Jiri (1919-    )
    Charaktery (1978)
        La Bar, Arthur
            Annapolis Brass Quintet
            CRYS S 207
                2-AR 6-79 P. 41
                2-CR 9-79 P. 43
                1-NR 5-79 P. 7
        Suchanek, Stanislav
            Panton 8111 0045
Penn, William (1943-    )
    Ultra Mensuram for 3 Brass Quintets
        Felt/Grahm/Mosier
            Western Michigan U. Brass Ensemble
            CRI SD 340
Persichetti, Vincent (1915-    )
    Parable for Brass Quintet (1968)
        Battey, David
            Dallas Brass Quintet
            CRYS S 203
                1-AR 6-79 P. 41
                1-FF 7/8-79 P. 130
                2-NR 5-79 P. 7
        Ingraham, Paul
            New York Brass Quintet
            CRYS S 210
                1-AR 9-80 P. 50
                1-FF 5/6-80 P. 129
                1-NR 5-80 P. 8

Petrovics, Emil (1930-    )
     Cassazione (1953)
                         Hungarian Brass Ensemble
                           Hungaroton SLPX 11811
                                2-AR 8-77 P. 39
                                3-FF 9-77 P. 63
                                2-NR 9-77 P. 6
Peuerl, Paul (1570-1625)
     Canzon # 1
                         Canadian Brass
                           Moss Music Group MMG 1123
                                3-NR 3-81 P. 7
                     Page, Graeme
                         Canadian Brass
                           Moss Music Group MMG 1139
                   Ohanian, David
                         Empire Brass Quintet
                           Sine Qua Non SA 2014
     Canzon # 2
                         Chicago Chamber Brass
                           Pro Arte Sinfonia SDS 632
Pezel, Johann (1639-1694)
     Bal
                 Barboteu, Georges
                         Brass Ensemble of Paris
                           Music Guild 120
                                4-HF 8-65 P. 82
                                1-HSR 9-65 P. 102
     Ceremonial Brass Music
                         London Gabrieli Brass Ensemble
                           MHS 4635K
                                2-GR 2-79 P. 1440
                                2-GR 7-82 P. 142
                                2-MG 4-82 P. 17
     3 Dances
                         Eastern Classical Brass Quintet
                           Klavier KS 561
                                2-FF 7/8-79 P. 131
                 Andrus/Haines
                         Georgia State College Brass Ensemble
                           Golden Crest GC S 4083
     6 17th Century Dances
                 Birdwell, Edward
                         American Brass Quintet
                           4-Desto 6474/7
                                1-ST 3-70 P. 120
                 Happe, Richard
                         American Brass Quintet
                           Folkways FMS 33652
                                2-AU 7-68 P. 46
                                4-NR 9-67 P. 6
     German Dance Suite
                 Page, Graeme
                         Canadian Brass Quintet
                           CBC: SM 239

Pezel, Johann (Cont'd)
    Gigue, Intrada, & Sarabande
                    Music Hall Brass Ensemble
                    Monogram 817
                            1-AR 7-54 P. 348
                            1-HF 12-54 P. 77
                            1-MA 12-15-54 P. 24
                            2-NYT 7-25-54 P. X6
                            2-SR 6-26-54 P. 52
    Hora Decima
        Katzen
                    Empire Brass Quintet
                    Digitech DIGI 102
                            1-ST 7-80 P. 86
    Intradas 1, 3, 10 & 11
        Page, Graeme
                    Canadian Brass Quintet
                    Boot BMC 3001
    Intradas 1, 3, 10 & 13
                    Canadian Brass Quintet
                    Vanguard VSD 71254
                            4-FF 7/8-80 P. 186
                            2-NR 7-80 P. 6
    Intrade, Sarabande, Bal
        Meek/Keaney
                    Voisin Brass Ensemble
                    Unicorn 1003
                            1-AR 2-55 P. 202
                            1-ET 3-55 P. 18
                            2-HF 3-55 P. 64-VII
                            1-LJ 5-15-55 P. 1205
                            11-MA 3-55 P. 22
                            2-NR 4-55 P. 6
    3 Pieces
                    Kansas University Brass Choir
                    Audio House AH 21473
                    Pacific Brass Quintet
                    Avant AV 1004
                            2-NR 6-72 P. 8
        Ohanian, David
                    Empire Brass Quintet
                    Sine Qua Non SA 2014
        Soper, Kenneth
                    New York Brass Choir
                    Golden Crest CRS 4148
                            1-AR 3-77 P. 40
    4 Pieces
        Tillotson, Brooks
                    Chamber Brass Players
                    Classic Editions CE 1039
    Ceremonial Brass Music
                    London Gabrieli Brass Ensemble
                    MHS 4635K
                            2-GR 2-79 P. 1440
                            2-GR 7-82 P. 142
                            2-MG 4-82 P. 17

Pezel, Johann (Cont'd)
    Sarabande
                Canadian Brass Quintet
                Vanquard VSD 71254
                        4-FF 7/8-80 P. 186
                        2-NR 7-80 P. 6
        Barboteu, Georges
                Brass Ensemble of Paris
                Music Guild 120
                        4-HF 8-65 P. 82
                        1-HSR 9-65  P. 102
        Page, Graeme
                Canadian Brass Quintet
                Boot BMC 3001
    Sonata # 2
        Meek/Keaney
                Voisin Brass Ensemble
                Unicorn 1003
                        1-AR 2-55 P. 202
                        1-ET 3-55 P. 18
                        2-HF 3-55 P. 64-VII
                        1-LJ 5-15-55 P. 1205
                        11-MA 3-55 P. 22
                        2-NR 4-55 P. 6
        Tillotson, Brooks
                Chamber Brass Players
                Classic Editions CE 1039
    Sonata # 3
                 Music Hall Brass Ensemble
                Monogram 817
                        1-AR 7-54 P. 348
                        1-HF 12-54 P. 77
                        1-MA 12-15-54 P. 24
                        2-NYT 7-25-54 P. X6
                        2-SR 6-26-54 P. 52
    Sonata # 14
        Barboteu, Georges
                Brass Ensemble of Paris
                Music Guild 120
                        4-HF 8-65 P. 82
                        1-HSR 9-65 P. 102
    Sonata # 22
        Ingraham, Paul
                New York Brass Quintet
                RCA AGL 1 3968
                        1-HF 9-67 P. 98B
                        4-NR 7-67 P. 9
        Katzen
                Empire Brass Quintet
                Digitech DIGI 102
                        1-ST 7-80 P. 86
        Tillotson, Brooks
                Chamber Brass Players
                Classic Editions CE 1039
    Sonatas (# 12, # 13, # 42)
                Budapest Brass Quintet
                Hungaroton 12486

Pezel, Johann (Cont'd)
    Suite for Brass
                Ars Nova Brass Quintet
                    MHS 1446 Z
                            1-GR1-72 P. 1233
                Ars Nova Brass Quintet
                    MHS 3635
        Suite
                Berlin Philharmonic Brass Ensemble
                    DG 2532 066
                            1-FF 7/8-82 P. 268
                            1-FF 1/2-83 P. 336
                            1-NR 2-83 P. 4
                Berlin Philharmonic Brass Ensemble
                    DG 2741 011
                            1-FF 1/2-83 P. 336
                            1-GR 11-82 P. 591
                            3-HF 11-83 P. 76
                New York Brass Society
                    WIMR 3
                            1-NR 5-72 P. 5
                Philadelphia Brass Ensemble
                    Columbia MS 6941
                            4-GR 5-67 P. 584
                            1-HF 5-67 P. 92
            Schmitt, Frederick
                New York Brass Quintet
                    Golden Crest GC S 4023
                            1-AU 5-60 P. 53
                            4-NR 4-60 P. 7
    Suite I
        Tillotson, Brooks
                Chamber Brass Players
                    Golden Crest CR 4008
                            4-HF 12-57 P. 94
                            2-LJ 1-1-58 P. 70
    Suite II
        Tillotson, Brooks
                Chamber Brass Players
                    Golden Crest CR 4008
                            4-HF 12-57 P. 94
                            2-LJ 1-1-58 P. 70
    Tower Music
                Los Angeles Brass Quintet
                    CRYS S 102
            Happe, Richard
                American Brass Quintet
                    Folkways FMS 33652
                            2-AU 7-68 P. 46
                            4-NR 9-67 P. 6
    Tower Sonata # 14 & # 30
            Tillotson, Brooks
                Chamber Brass Players
                    Golden Crest CR 4008
                            4-HF 12-57 P. 94
                            2-LJ 1-1-58 P. 70

Phillips, Peter (1930-    )
     Music for Brass Quintet
                         American Brass Quintet
                         Nonesuch H 71222
                              4-AR 6-69 P. 941
                              1-HF 7-69 P. 98
                              4-NR 7-69 P. 7
                              1-ST 9-69 P. 120
Phyle
     The President's March
                  Smith, Calvin
                         Annapolis Brass Quintet
                         Richardson Records RRS-3
Pilss, Karl (1902-    )
     Capriccio  (1976)
                  La Bar, Arthur
                         Annapolis Brass Quintet
                         CRYS S 207
                              2-AR 6-79 P. 41
                              2-CR 9-79 P. 43
                              1-NR 5-79 P. 7

     Scherzo
                  Soper, Kenneth
                         New York Brass Quintet
                         Golden Crest CRS 4148
                              1-AR 3-77 P. 40
Plog, Anthony (1947-    )
     Mini-Suite
                         Fine Arts Brass Quintet
                         WIM 4
                              1-NR 11-74 P. 7
Polin, Claire (1926-    )
     Cader Idris for Brass Quintet
                         Apple Brass Quintet
                         Opus One 61
                              2-FF 9/19-82 P. 459
Pollack
     That's A-Plenty
                  Halloin, Beth
                         Chicago Chamber Brass
                           Pro Arte Sinfonia S05616
                              1-AR 3-84 P. 62
                              1-FF 3/4-84 P. 324
Powell, Morgan (1938-    )
     Darkness II
                         University of Illinois
                         Faculty Brass Quintet
                         UBRE S 203

     Music for Brass
                         University of Illinois Brass Ensemble
                         UBRE S 203
     Windows for Brass Quintet (1977)
                  Strieby, Lawrence
                         St. Louis Brass Quintet
                         CRYS S 215

Praetorius, Michael (1571-1621)
      Danses from Terpsichore
            Snyder, Kurt
                  Las Vegas Brass Quintet
                  Ashland Records AR 7118
      Es ist ein Ros' entsprungen
                  Baldwin-Wallace College Brass Choir
                  Mark Ed. Records MES 32565
      Terpsichorean Suite
                  Philip Jones Brass Ensemble
                  London LDR 71100
                        1-AR 2-83 P. 77
                        1-FF 1/2-83 P. 338
                        1-NR 3-83 P. 3
Premru, Raymond (1934-    )
      Blues March
                  Philip Jones Brass Ensemble
                  Argo ZRG 895
                        2-FF 5/6-80
                        1-GR 1-79 P. 1334
      Le Bateau sur Leman
                  Philip Jones Brass Ensemble
                  Argo ZRG 895
                        2-FF 5/6-80
                        1-GR 1-79 P. 1334
      Music from Harter Fell
                  Philip Jones Brass Ensemble
                  Argo ZRG 906
                        4-FF 1/2-81 P. 801
                        1-GR 11-79 P. 801
                        1-ML 12-79 P. 7
      Of Nights & Castle
                  Philip Jones Brass Ensemble
                  Argo ZRG 895
                        2-FF 5/6-80
                        1-GR 1-79 P. 1334
      Tissington Variations
            Kjellden, Thomas
                  Malmo Brass Ensemble
                  BIS LP 59
                        1-FF 9-77 P. 61
Presser, William (1916-    )
      Suite for Brass Quartet (1964)
                  Golden Crest GC 4084
Previn
      4 Outings for Brass
            James, Ifor
                  Philip Jones Brass Ensemble
                  Argo ZRG 851
                        1-GR 7-77 P. 201
                        1-HF 5-78 P. 116
                        1-ML 8-77 P. 6
                        1-NR 7-78 P. 7
Puccini, Giacomo (1858-1924)
      March Sequence

Puccini, Giacomo (Cont'd)
    March Sequence (Cont'd)
                Locke Brass Consort
                CRDD 1102
                    1-FF 5/6-83 P. 269
                    1-GR 3-83 P. 1059
                    1-MG 4-83 P. 6
                    2-NR 6-83 P. 6
Purcell, Henry (1659-1695)
    Allegro & Air for King Arthur
                Kansas University Brass Choir
                Audio House AH 21473
            Ingraham, Paul
                New York Brass Quintet
                RCA AGL 1 3968
                    1-HF 9-67 P. 98B
                    4-NR 7-67 P. 9
            Ohanian, David
                Empire Brass Quintet
                Sine Qua Non SA 2014
    Anthem (Man That Is Born of a Woman)
                London Gabrieli Brass Ensemble
                MHS 4635K
                    2-GR 2-79 P. 1440
                    2-GR 7-82 P. 142
                    2-MG 4-82 P. 17
    Anthem (Thou Knowest, Lord, The Secrets of Our Hearts)
                London Gabrieli Brass Ensemble
                MHS 4635K
                    2-GR 2-79 P. 1440
                    2-GR 7-82 P. 142
                    2-MG 4-82 P. 17
    2 Anthems
                Philip Jones Brass Ensemble
                Angel S 37282
    Canzona
                London Gabrieli Brass Ensemble
                MHS 4635K
                    2-GR 2-79 P. 1440
                    2-GR 7-82 P. 142
                    2-MG 4-82 P. 17
    Funeral Music for Queen Mary
                Philip Jones Brass Ensemble
                Angel S 37282
    March
                London Gabrieli Brass Ensemble
                MHS 4635K
                    2-GR 2-79 P. 1440
                    2-GR 7-82 P. 142
                    2-MG 4-82 P. 17
    March for the Funeral of Queen Mary
                London Gabrieli Brass Ensemble
                MHS 4635K
                    2-GR 2-79 P. 1440
                    2-GR 7-82 P. 142
                    2-MG 4-82 P. 17

Purcell, Henry (Cont'd)
         March & Canzona for the Funeral of Queen Mary
                        Paris Brass Quintet
                        PLE 084
                            2-FF 9/10-79 P. 181
         Music for Queen Mary II
                 Meek/Keaney
                        Voisin Brass Ensemble
                        Unicorn 1003
                            1-AR 2-55 P. 202
                            1-ET 3-55 P. 18
                            2-HF 3-55 P. 64-VII
                            1-LJ 5-15-55 P. 1205
                            11-MA 3-55 P. 22
                            2-NR 4-55 P. 6
         The Queen's Funeral March
                 Barboteu, Georges
                        Brass Ensemble of Paris
                        Music Guild 120
                            4-HF 8-65 P. 82
                            1-HSR 9-65 P. 102
         Sonata
                 Page, Graeme
                        Canadian Brass Quintet
                        Boot BMC 3003
         Sonata in D for Trumpet
                 Page, Graeme
                        Canadian Brass Quintet
                        Umbrella 05862
         Suite
                 Page, Graeme
                        Canadian Brass Quintet
                        RCA ARC 14574
                            2-FF 7/8-83 P. 284
                            4-NR 6-83 P. 6
         Suite from Bonduca
                        Ars Nova Brass Quintet
                        MHS 3635
         Symphony from "Fairy Queen,"Act IV(6Tpt/2Hn/3Trb/Bar)
                 Berger/Watson
                        Kansas University Brass Choir
                        Audio House AH 21473
         Trumpet Tunes
                 Tillotson, Brooks
                        Chamber Brass Players
                        Classic Editions CE 1039
         Trumpet Tune & Air (2Tpt/Hn/Trb/Bar/Ta)
                        London Gabrieli Brass Ensemble
                        MHS 4635K
                            2-GR 2-79 P. 1440
                            2-GR 7-82 P. 142
                            2-MG 4-82 P. 17
         2 Trumpet Tunes & Air
                 Ingraham, Paul
                        New York Brass Quintet
                        RCA AGL 1 3968
                            1-HF 9-67 P. 98B
                            4-NR 7-67 P. 9

Purcell, Henry (Cont'd)
      Voluntary on Old 100th
      (2 Tpt/Hn/Trb/Bar)
                        Eastern Brass Quintet
                          Klavier KS 536
                                1-AU 12-75 P. 106
                                1-NR 5-75 P. 8
Ramsoe, Wilhelm (1837-1897)
      Quintet # 3
                        Philip Jones Brass Ensemble
                          ARGO ZRG 928
      Quintet # 5
                        Philip Jones Brass Ensemble
                          ARGO ZRG 928
Ramsoe/Andresen
      Valve Fanfares
              Hansen, Henning
                        Royal Danish Brass
                          Rondo Grammofon RLP 8304
Raphling, Sam (1910-      )
      Movement for Piano & Brass Quintet
                        American Brass Quintet
                          Serenus SRS 12061
                                4-NR 4-76 P. 6
Rathburn, Eldon (1916-      )
      Canadian Brass Rag
              Page, Graeme
                        Canadian Brass Quintet
                          Boot BMC 3004
                        Canadian Brass Quintet
                          CBC: RCI 403
Raymond
      Short Suite (2 Tpt/Hn/Trb)
                        Fine Arts Brass Quintet
                          WIM 4
                                1-NR 11-74 P. 7
Reicha, Gottfried (1667-1734)
      Baroque Suite (2 Tpt/Hn/Trb/Ta)
              Birdwell, Edward
                        American Brass Quintet
                          4-Desto 6474/7
                                1-ST 3-70 P. 120
      Fanfare "Abblasen"
              Page, Graeme
                        Canadian Brass Quintet
                          RCA ARC 1 4574
                                4-FF 7/8-83 P. 284
                                4-NR 6-83 P. 6
                        Canadian Brass Quintet
                          RCA ARL 1 4733
      Sonata # 15 (Tpt/Hn/Trb/Bar)
              Cowden, Hugh
                        Chicago Symphony Brass Ensemble
                          Audiophile AP 21

Reicha, Gottfried (Cont'd)
    Sonata # 18 (Tpt/Hn/Trb/Bar)
        Meek/Keaney
            Voisin Brass Ensemble
            Unicorn 1003
                1-AR 2-55 P. 202
                1-ET 3-55 P. 18
                2-HF 3-55 P. 64-VII
                1-LJ 5-15-55 P. 1205
                11-MA 3-55 P. 22
                2-NR 4-55 P. 6
    Sonata # 19 (Tpt/Hn/Trb/Bar)
        Ingraham, Paul
            New York Brass Quintet
            RCA AGL 1 3968
                1-HF 9-67 P. 98B
                4-NR 7-67 P. 9
        Meek/Keaney
            Voisin Brass Ensemble
            Unicorn 1003
                1-AR 2-55 P. 202
                1-ET 3-55 P. 18
                2-HF 3-55 P. 64-VII
                1-LJ 5-15-55 P. 1205
                11-MA 3-55 P. 22
                2-NR 4-55 P. 6
        Tillotson, Brooks
            Chamber Brass Players
            Classic Editions CE 1039
    3 Sonatas (21, 22, 24) (Tpt/Hn/Trb/Bar)
        Jones/Miller
            Philadelphia Brass Ensemble
            Columbia MS 6941
                4-GR 5-67 P. 584
                1-HF 5-67 P. 92
                1-ML 4-67 P. 4
    Sonatina # 18
        Page, Graeme
            Canadian Brass Quintet
            CBC: SM 216
    Tower Sonata # 15 & # 19
        Tillotson, Brooks
            Chamber Brass Players
            Golden Crest CR 4008
                4-HF 12-57 P. 94
                2-LJ 1-1-58 P. 70
Reinagle, Alexander (1756-1809)
    Gavotte
        Smith, Calvin
            Annapolis Brass Quintet
              Richardson Records RRS-3
Renwick, Wilke
    Dance
        Osborne, Larry
            Vintage Brass Ensemble
            Ohlone Band Album CR 8242

Renwicke, Wilke (Cont'd)
    Dance (Cont'd)
            van Aeken, Alex
                    Theo Mertens Chamber Brass Quintet
                    Eufoda 1082
    Dance (1973)
            Smith, Calvin
                    Annapolis Brass Quintet
                    CRYS S 206
                        2-NR 11-76 P. 7
Reynolds, Verne (1926-    )
    Centone I
            Battey, David
                    Dallas Brass Quintet
                    CRYS S 203
                        1-AR 6-79 P. 41
                        1-FF 7/8-79 P. 130
            Reynolds, Verne
                    Eastman Brass Quintet
                    Mark Records MES 57577
    Centone II
            Reynolds, Verne
                    Eastman Brass Quintet
                    Mark Records MES 57577
    Centone III
            Reynolds, Verne
                    Eastman Brass Quintet
                    Mark Records MES 57577
    Concertare I (Brass Quintet & Organ)
            Reynolds, Verne
                    Eastman Brass Quintet
                    Mark Records MES 57577
    Signals for Trumpet,Tuba & Brass Choir(5Tpt/5Hn)
            Duke/Lane/Miller/Hyde/Brieglab
                    CRYS S 392
    Suite for Brass Quintet (1963) (2Tpt/Hn/Trb/Ta)
                    Iowa Brass Quintet
                        Trilogy/Composers Theatre
                        Service CTS 1001
                            1-NR 8-73 P. 6
            Covert, John
                    Ithaca Brass Quintet
                    Golden Crest GC 4114
Reigger, Wallingford (1885-1961)
    Music for Brass Choir Op. 45
    (10 Tpt/8 Hn/10 Trb/2 Ta/Perc)
                    Lehigh Ensemble
                        Lehigh University 1103
            Birdwell/Carabella/Happe/Ingraham/
            Johnson/Salomon/Secon/Sussman
                    National Orchestra Association
                    Alumni Brass Ensemble
                    CRI 229 USD
                        1-HF 9-68 P. 84
                        1-HSR 9-68 P. 104
                        1-NR 8-68 P. 14

Riegger, Wallingford (Cont'd)
        Nonet for Brass, Op. 49
        (3 Tpt/2 Hn/3 Trb/Ta)
                Birdwell/Ingraham
                        National Orchestra Association
                        Alumni Brass Ensemble
                        CRI 229 USD
                                1-HF 9-68 P. 84
                                1-HSR 9-68 P. 104
                                1-NR 8-68 P. 14
Rieti, Vittorio (1898-    )
        Incisioni for Brass Quintet (1967)
                        American Brass Quintet
                        Serenus SRS 12023
                Johns, Michael
                        Cambridge Brass Quintet
                        CRYS S 204
                                2-HF 7-77 P. 118
                                1-NR 11-76 P. 7
Rimsky-Korsakov, Nicolai (1844-1908)
        Flight of the Bumblebee
                Page, Graeme
                        Canadian Brass Quintet
                        RCA ARL 1 4733
                van Driessche, Andre
                        Theo Mertens Brass Ensemble
                        Eufoda 1029
        Procession of Nobles
        (Picc Tpt/4 Tpt/2 Hn/3 Trb/Ta/Perc)
                        Philip Jones Brass Ensemble
                        London LDR 71100
                                1-AR 2-83 P. 77
                                1-FF 1/2-83 P. 338
                                1-NR 3-83 P. 3
Rodrigo, Joaquin (1902-    )
        Adagio
                van Driessche, Andre
                        Theo Mertens Chamber Brass Quintet
                        Eufoda 1082
Rose, Gustav (1854-    )
        Holiday for Brass
                van Driessche, Andre
                        Theo Mertens Chamber Brass Quintet
                        Eufoda 1082
Rossi, Salamon (1570-1630)
        Psalm 92
                        Locke Brass Consort
                        Unicorn UN 1-72012
                                1-FF 7/8-70 P. 133
                                2-GR 5-78 P. 1889
Roussel, Albert (1869-1937)
        Fanfare pour une Sacre paien(4 Tpt/4 Hn/3 Trb/Ti)
                Barboteu, Georges
                        Brass Ensemble of Paris
                        Music Guild 120
                                4-HF 8-65 P. 82
                                1-Hsr 9-65 P. 102

Ruggles, Carl (1876-1971)
      Angels
                        Lehigh Ensemble
                        Lehigh University 1103
Saint-Saens, Camille (1835-1921)
      Carnival of the Animals
                        Philip Jones Brass Ensemble
                        London 410125-1LH
                        Philip Jones Brass Ensemble
                        London LDR 71094-1
Salzedo, Leonard (1921-    )
      Cappriccio, Op. 90
                        Philip Jones Brass Ensemble
                        Argo ZRG 906
                              4-FF 1/2-81 P. 801
                              1-GR 11-79 P. 801
                              1-ML 12-79 P. 7
Sanders, Robert (1906-    )
      Quintet in Bb for Brass Instruments
      (2 Tpt/Hn/2 Trb)
                  Keaney/McConathy
                        Voisin Brass Ensemble
                        Unicorn 1031
                              1-AR 11-56 P. 40
                              4-HA 1-57 P. 96
                              1-HF 12-56 P. 104
                              1-MH 11/12-56 P. 49
      Quintet in Bb for Brass Instruments
      (3rd Movement)
                  Chambers, James
                        New York Philharmonic Brass Quintet
                        Golden Crest GC 4003
                              2-HF 12-57 P. 94
                              4-LJ 1-1-58 P. 70
                              4-SR 11-9-57 P. 38
Satie, Erik (1866-1925)
      Gymnopedie # 1
                        Philip Jones Brass Ensemble
                        London 410125-1LH
      Trois Gymnopedies
                        Philip Jones Brass Ensemble
                        London LDR 71094-1
                        Nimbus 45006 (45 rpm)
                              1-FF 7/8-81 P. 222
                              1-GR 1-81 P. 949
Scarlatti, Domenico (1685-1757)
      Sonata in D, K.430
                        Philip Jones Brass Ensemble
                        Argo ZRG 898
                              1-FF 1/2-80 P. 173
                              1-FU 5-80 P. 46
                              1-GR 8-79 P. 348
                              1-ML 5-79 P. 9
      Sonata in D, K.443
                        Philip Jones Brass Ensemble
                        Argo ZRG 898

Scarlatti, Domenico (Cont'd)
        Sonata in D, K.443 (Cont'd)
                        1-FF 1/2-80 P. 173
                        1-FU 5-80 P. 46
                        1-GR 8-79 P. 348
                        1-ML 5-79 P. 9
        Sonata in E, K.380
                        Philip Jones Brass Ensemble
                        Argo ZRG 898
                        1-FF 1/2-80 P. 173
                        1-FU 5-80 P. 46
                        1-GR 8-79 P. 348
                        1-ML 5-79 P. 9
                        Philip Jones Brass Ensemble
                        London CS 7242
                        2-FF 7/8-82 P. 268
Scheidt, Samuel (1587-1654)
        Battle Suite
                        Guy Touvron Brass Quintet
                        MHS 4168
                        Philip Jones Brass Ensemble
                        Argo ZRG 717
                        1-GR 11-74 P. 910
                        2-ML 11-74 P. 5
                Happe, Richard
                        American Brass Quintet
                        Folkways FMS 33652
                        2-AU 7-68 P. 46
                        4-NR 9-67 P. 6
                Wakefield, David
                        American Brass Quintet
                        Delos DMS 3003
                        1-NR 3-80 P. 7
                        1-NYT 5-18-80 P. D32
                        1-ST 7-80 P. 84
        Benedicamus Domino
                Page, Graeme
                        Canadian Brass Quintet
                        CBC: SM 239
                        Canadian Brass Quintet
                        Moss Music Group MMG 1139
        Canzona a 10
                        Philip Jones Brass Ensemble
                        ARGO ZRG 898
                        1-FF 1/2-80 P. 173
                        1-FU 5-80 P. 46
                        1-GR 8-79 P. 348
                        1-ML 5-79 P. 9
        Canzon Aechiopican
                        Canadian Brass Quintet
                        Vanguard VSD 71254
                        4-FF 7/8-80 P. 186
                        2-NR 7-80 P. 6
                Page, Graeme
                        Canadian Brass Quintet
                        Boot BMC 3001
                        Canadian Brass Quintet
                        CBC: SM 239

Scheidt, Samuel (Cont'd)
  Canzon Bergamasca
      Philip Jones Brass Ensemble
      London CS 7242
        2-FF 7/8-82 P. 268
     Kjellden, Thomas
      Malmo Brass Ensemble
      BIS LP 59
        1-FF 9-77 P. 61
     Happe, Richard
      American Brass Quintet
      Folkways FMS 33652
        2-AU 7-68 P. 46
        4-NR 9-67 P. 6
     Ohanian, David
      Empire Brass Quintet
      Sine Qua Non SA 2014
     Osborne, Larry
      Vintage Brass Ensemble
      Ohlone Band Album CR 8242
     Page, Graeme
      Canadian Brass Quintet
      CBC: SM 216
     Talamantes, Nona
      Mount Royal Brass Quintet
      McGill University 77004
        1-FF 5/6-82 P. 292
  Canzon Cornetto
      Philip Jones Brass Ensemble
      London CS 7242
        2-FF 7/8-82 P. 268
  Canzon Gallican
    Page, Graeme
      Canadian Brass Quintet
      CBC: SM 239
    Page, Graeme
      Canadian Brass Quintet
      Moss Music Group MMG 1139
      Canadian Brass Quintet
      Moss Music Group MMG 1123
        3-NR 3-81 P. 7
  Canzona on a French Theme
    Katzen
      Empire Brass Quintet
      Digitech DIGI 102
        1-ST 7-80 P. 86
  Centone # 5
    Page, Graeme
      Canadian Brass Quintet
      CBC: SM 216
  Christus ist erstanden
    Tillotson, Brooks
      Chamber Brass Players
      Golden Crest CR 4008
        4-HF 12-57 P. 94
        2-LJ 1-1-58 P. 70

Scheidt, Samuel (Cont'd)
    Courant Dolorosa
                  Philip Jones Brass Ensemble
                  London CS 7242
                      2-FF 7/8-82 P. 268
    Galliard Battaglia
                  Canadian Brass Quintet
                  Vanguard VSD 71254
                      4-FF 7/8-80 P. 186
                      2-NR 7-80 P. 6
        Page, Graeme
                  Canadian Brass Quintet
                  Boot BMC 3001
                  Canadian Brass Quintet
                  CBC: SM 203
                  Canadian Brass Quintet
                  RCA ARC 1 4574
                      2-FF 7/8-83 P. 284
                      4-NR 6-83 P. 6
   6 Works
        Reynolds, Verne
                  Eastman Brass Quintet
                  Candide CE 31004
                      1-HF 11-68 P. 120
                      1-NR 5-69 P. 6
                      4-SR 8-31-68 P. 45
    Suite (2 Tpt/Hn/Trb/Bar or Ta)
                  Berlin Philharmonic Brass Ensemble
                  DG 2532 066
                      1-FF 7/8-82 P. 268
                      1-FF 1/2-83 P. 336
                      1-NR 2-83 P. 4
                  Berlin Philharmonic Brass Ensemble
                  DG 2741 011
                      1-FF 1/2-83 P. 336
                      1-GR 11-82 P. 591
                      3-HF 11-83 P. 76
                      1-MG 7-82 P. 10
                  London Gabrieli Brass Ensemble
                  MHS 4635K
                      2-GR 2-79 P. 1440
                      2-GR 7-82 P. 142
                      2-MG 4-82 P. 17
Schein, Johann Hermann (1586-1630)
    Die Mit Tranen Saen
                  Eastern Brass Quintet
                  Klavier KS 536
                      1-AU 12-75 P. 106
                      1-NR 5-75 P. 8
                  Eastern Classical Brass Quintet
                  Klavier KS 561
                      2-FF 7/8-79 P. 131
    Intrada & Paduana
                  Music Hall Brass Ensemble
                  Monogram 817
                      1-AR 7-54 P. 348
                      1-HF 12-54 P. 77

Schein, Johann Hermann (Cont'd)
    Intrada & Paduana (Cont'd)
                    1-MA 12-15-54 P. 24
                    2-NYT 7-25-54 P. X6
                    2-SR 6-26-54 P. 52
        Madrigal
            Page, Graeme
                    Canadian Brass Quintet
                    Boot BMC 3003
        Paduanna
                    Gabrieli Brass Ensemble
                    Nonesuch 71118
                        1-GR 2-66 P. 397
                        2-HF 11-66 P. 169
                        1-HSR 11-66 P. 72
                        1-NR 9-66 P. 5
        Paduanna & Galliard
                    Vienna State Opera Brass Ensemble
                    Westminister XWN 18931
                        4-AU 12-60 P. 67
        2 Pieces
            Ohanian, David
                    Empire Brass Quintet
                    Sine Qua Non SA 2014
            Tillotson, Brooks
                    Chamber Brass Players
                    Classic Editions CE 1039
        Suite # 3
            Smith, Calvin
                    Annapolis Brass Quintet
                    2 CRYS S 202
                        1-CR 3-75 P. 36
                        1-NR 1-75 P. 6
Scheurer, Rolf (1929-    )
    Scherzo (2 Tpt/2 Hn/2 Trb/Ta/Ti)
                    Locke Brass Consort
                    Unicorn UN 1-72012
                        1-FF 7/8-79 P. 133
                        2-GR 5-78 P. 1889
Schlabach/arr.
    Crisp English Carol Medley
            La Bar, Arthur
                    Annapolis Brass Quintet
                    Richardson Records RRS-5
Schmidt, William (1926-    )
    7 Variations on a Hexachord
                    Fine Arts Brass Quintet
                    WIM 4
                        1-NR 11-74 P. 7
    Concertino for Piano & Brass Quintet
            Pyle, Ralph
                    Los Angeles Brass Quintet
                    CRYS S 821
                        1-NR 7-71 P. 12

Schmidt, William (Cont'd)
    Sequential Fanfares for Brass
                Los Angeles Philharmonic Brass Ensemble
                Avant 1005
                    1-NR 7-73 P. 12
    Suite # 1
                New York Brass Society
                WIM 3
                    1-NR 5-72 P. 5
    Suite # 2
                Los Angeles Brass Society
                WIM 6
                    4-NR 6-72 P. 8
    Spiritual Phantasy for Organ & Brass
                Los Angeles Brass Society
                WIM 6
                    4-NR 6-72 P. 8
    Variations on a Negro Folk Song
    (2 Tpt/Hn/Trb/Ta)
                Los Angeles Brass Quintet
                CRYS S 602
                    2-NR 10-68 P. 5
Schmitt, Florent (1870-1958)
    Fanfare for Anthony & Cleopatra
    (3 Tpt/4 Hn/3 Trb/Ta/Perc)
            Barboteu, Georges
                Brass Ensemble of Paris
                Music Guild 120
                    4-HF 8-65 P. 82
                    1-HSR 9-65 P. 102
Schuller, Gunther (1925-    )
    Music for Brass Quintet (1961)
            Alonge, Ray
                New York Brass Quintet
                CRI 144
                    4-HF 2-62 P. 92
                    2-HSR 3-62 P. 80
                    1-NYT 1-21-62 P. X14
                    4-MQ 4-62 P. 271
                    4-NR 2-62 P. 6
            Gainsforth, Nona
                Mount Royal Brass Quintet
                McGill University 80012
    Symphony for Brass & Percussion
                Jones Brass Ensemble
                Argo ZRG 731
                    4-GR 6-73 P. 62
                    1-ML 6-73 P. 4
                    1-NR 10-73 P. 13
                    1-ST 1-74 P. 118
            Schuller/Singer/Alonge/Sussman
                Columbia CL 941
                    1-AR 5-57 P. 129
                    4-AU 7-57 P. 45
                    4-HF 6-57 P. 77
                    4-NYT 9-29-57 P. X15

Shahan, Paul (1923-     )
    Leipzig Towers
    (4 Tpt/4 Hn/4 Trb/Ta/Bar/Ti/Perc)
                    Vienna State Opera Brass Ensemble
                    Westminister XWN 18931
                    4-AU 12-60 P. 67
Shostakovich, Dimitri (1906-1975)
    Satirical Dance
            van Driessche, Andre
                    Theo Mertens Brass Ensemble
                    Eufoda 1029
Siegmeister, Elie
    Brass Sextet (2 Tpt/Hn/Trb/Ta/Perc)
            Birdwell, Edward
                    American Brass Quintet
                    Desto DC 6467
                    1-AR 3-70 P. 520
Simmes, G.
    Fantasia (2 Tpt/Hn/Trb/Tba)
            Reynolds, Verne
                    Eastman Brass Quintet
                    Candide CE 31004
                    1-HF 11-68 P. 120
                    1-NR 5-69 P. 6
                    4-SR 8-31-68 P. 45
Simon, Anton (1858-1916)
    Quatuor en forme de Sonatine, Op. 23 # 1
                    Philip Jones Brass Ensemble
                    Argo ZRG 851
                    1-GR 7-77 P. 201
                    1-HF 5-78 P. 116
                    1-ML 8-77 P. 66
                    1-NR 7-78 P. 7
            Birdwell, Edward
                    American Brass Quintet
                    4-Desto 6474/7
                    1-ST 3-70 P. 120
Simpson, Thomas (1582-1630)
    Allemande
            Wakefield, David
                    American Brass Quintet
                    Delos DMS 3003
                    1-NR 3-80 P. 7
                    1-NYT 5-18-80 P. D32
                    1-ST 7-80 P. 84
Smoker
    Brass in Spirit
            Anderson, Paul
                    Iowa Brass Quintet
                    University of Iowa Press 29001
                    2-HF 7-77 P. 118
                    1-NR 2-77 P. 7

Sousa, John Philip (1854-1932)
        Stars & Stripes Forever
                Halloin, Beth
                        Chicago Chamber Brass
                                Pro Arte Sinfonia S05616
                                        1-AR 3-84 P. 62
                                        1-FF 3/4-84 P. 324
                        Neilson, Diana
                                Chicago Chamber Brass
                                Pro Arte Sinfonia S 616
        Washington Post March
                                Empire Brass Quintet
                                Digitech DIGI 104
Sousa/Cable
        A Sousa Collection
                Page, Graeme
                        Canadian Brass Quintet
                                RCA ARL 1 4733
Speer, Daniel (1636-1707)
        Musickalisch Turckischer
        Eulen-Spiegel (1688)
                                Budapest Brass Quintet
                                Hungaroton SLPX 12486
                                        1-FF 3/4-84 P. 322
                                        2-NR 3-84 P. 6
        Sonata 1
                                MHS 1804
        Sonata a 4
                Wakefield, David
                        American Brass Quintet
                                Delos DMS 3003
                                        1-NR 3-80 P. 7
                                        1-NYT 5-18-80 P. D32
                                        1-ST 7-80 P. 84
        Sonata In C
                Johns,Michael
                        Cambridge Brass Quintet
                                CRYS S 204
                                        2-HF 7-77 P. 118
                                        1-NR 11-76 P. 7
        Sonata In G
                Johns,Michael
                        Cambridge Brass Quintet
                                CRYS S 204
                                        2-HF 7-77 P. 118
                                        1-NR 11-76 P. 7
        Three Sonatas (1688)
                Smith, Calvin
                        Annapolis Brass Quintet
                                CRYS S 206
                                        2-NR 11-76 P. 7
        Three Sonatas (# 4, 5, 6)
                Guy, Marc
                        Annapolis Brass Quintet
                                CRYS S 213
                                        1-FF 9/10-83 P. 327
                                        4-NR 8-83 P. 3

Speer, Daniel (Cont'd)
      Three Sonatas (# 4, 5, 6)
            Strieby, Lawrence
                  St. Louis Brass Quintet
                  CRYS S 212
                        2-FF 7/8-83 P. 283
      Sonatas 1-4
                  Philip Jones Brass Ensemble
                  Argo ZRG 898
                        1-FF 1/2-80 P. 173
                        1-FU 5-80 P. 46
                        1-GR 8-79 P. 348
                        1-ML 5-79 P. 9
Staigers, D.
      Carnival of Venice
            Page, Graeme
                  Canadian Brass Quintet
                  RCA ARL 1 4733
Stanley, John (1713-1786)
      Trumpet Tune
                  London Gabrieli Brass Ensemble
                  MHS 4635K
                        2-GR 2-79 P. 1440
                        2-GR 7-82 P. 142
                        2-MG 4-82 P. 17
      Trumpet Tune & Airs
                  Atlanta Brass Ensemble
                  Crystal Clear CCS 7011
                        2-AR 11-79 P. 31
                        1-NR 6-80 P. 14
Starer, Robert (1924-    )
      5 Miniatures for Brass (1952)
      (2 Tpt/2 Hn/Trb)
                  Schumann Brass Choir
                  Circle L-51-102
            Birdwell, Edward
                  American Brass Quintet
                  4-Desto 6474/7
                        1-ST 3-70 P. 120
            Chambers, James
                  New York Philharmonic Brass Quintet
                  Golden Crest GC 4003
                        2-HF 12-57 P. 94
                        4-LJ 1-1-58 P. 70
                        4-SR 11-9-57 P. 38
Stein
      Mock March (1960)
            La Bar, Arthur
                  Annapolis Brass Quintet
                  CRYS S 207
                        2-AR 6-79 P. 41
                        2-CR 9-79 P. 43
                        1-NR 5-79 P. 7
Steven
      Rainy Day Afternoon
            Gainsforth, Nona
                  Mount Royal Brass Quintet
                  McGill University 80012
                        179

Stewart, Robert
    Music for Brass, No. 4
                  Georgia State College Brass Ensemble
                  Golden Crest CR 4085
    Three Pieces for Brass Quintet
                  Georgia State College Brass Ensemble
                  Golden Crest CR 4084
Stoerl, Johann Georg Christian (1675-1719)
    Sonata
          Wakefield, David
                American Brass Quintet
                Delos DMS 3003
                      1-NR 3-80 P. 7
                      1-NYT 5-18-80 P. D32
                      1-ST 7-80 P. 84
    Sonata # 1 (Tpt/Hn/Trb/Bar)
          Tillotson, Brooks
                Chamber Brass Players
                Classic Editions CE 1039
    (3) Sonatas #1, 3, & 4
                  Berlin Philharmonic Brass Ensemble
                      1-FF 7/8-82 P. 268
                      1-FF 1/2-83 P. 336
                      1-NR 2-83 P. 4
                  Berlin Philharmonic Brass Ensemble
                  DG 2741 011
                      1-FF 1/2-83 P. 336
                      1-GR 11-82 P. 591
                      3-HF 11-83 P. 76
                      1-MG 7-82 P. 10
Strauss, Johann, Sr. (1804-1849)
    Radetzky March, Op. 228
                  Locke Brass Consort
                  CRDD 1102
                      1-FF 5/6-83 P. 269
                      1-GR 3-83 P. 1059
                      1-MG 4-83 P. 6
                      2-NR 6-83 P. 6
Strauss, Richard (1864-1949)
    Allerseelen Op. 10 # 8
          Leroy, C.
                Ades 14 032
                      1-FF 5/6-83 P. 268
    Feierlicher Einzug
    (5 Tpt/4 Hn/4 Trb/2 Ta/Ti)
          Hagen/Hatfield/Thelander/Gullickson
                University of Minnesota Brass Choir
                UMBC: 001
    Festmusic Der Stadt Wien for Brass & Timpani (1943)
                  Locke Brass Consort
                  Chandos ABR 1002
    Festmusic Der Stadt Wien:  Short Fanfare
                  Philip Jones Brass Ensemble
                  Argo ZRG 731
                      4-GR 6-73 P. 62
                      1-ML 6-73 P. 4
                      1-ST 1-74 P. 118

Susato, Tilman (1500-1561)
   3 Dances (Tpt/Hn/Trb/Bar)
               Georgia State College Brass Ensemble
               Golden Crest GC S 4083
   3 Dances
       Ingraham, Paul
           New York Brass Quintet
           RCA AGL 1 3968
               1-HF 9-67 P. 98B
               4-NR 7-67 P. 9
       Tillotson, Brooks
           Chamber Brass Players
           Classic Editions CE 1039
   4 Flemish Dances
       Happe, Richard
           American Brass Quintet
           Folkways FMS 33652
               2-AU 7-68 P. 46
               4-NR 9-67 P. 6
   5 Flemish Dances
       Birdwell, Edward
           American Brass Quintet
           4-Desto 6474/7
               1-ST 3-70 P. 120
   Susato Suite
       Philip Jones Brass Ensemble
        Argo ZRG 823
               1-GR 6-76 P. 61
               2-ML 5-76 P. 7
               1-NR 10-77 P. 7
Sydeman, William (1928-    )
   Brass Quintet
       Schneider, Vincent
           Brass Arts Quintet
           Grenadilla GS 1027
               2-FF 7/8-79 P. 131
               2-NR 10-79 P. 4
Symonds, Norman (1920-    )
   A Diversion
           Canadian Brass Quintet
           Moss Music Group MMG 1123
               3-NR 3-81 P. 7
       Page, Graeme
           Canadian Brass Quintet
           Umbrella 05862
Tanenbaum, Elias (1924-    )
   Improvisations and Patterns for Brass Quintet & Tape
       Birdwell, Edward
           American Brass Quintet
           4-Desto 6474/7
               1-ST 3-70 P. 120
Tchaikowsky, P. I. (1840-1893)
   Coronation March
       Halloin, Beth
           Chicago Chamber Brass
           Pro Arte Sinfonia S05616
               1-AR 3-84 P. 62
               1-FF 3/4-84 P. 324

Tchaikowsky, P. I.   (Cont'd)
     Symphony # 6 (3rd Movement)
                    Locke Brass Consort
                         CRDD 1102
                              1-FF 5/6-83 P. 269
                              1-GR 3-83 P. 1059
                              1-MG 4-83 P. 6
                              2-NR 6-83 P. 6
     Waltz from Sleeping Beauty
               James, Ifor
                    Philip Jones Brass Ensemble
                         ARGO ZRG 851
                              1-GR 7-77 P. 201
                              1-HF 5-78 P. 116
                              1-ML 8-77 P. 6
                              1-NR 7-78 P. 7
Tcherepnin, Nicholas (1899-1977)
     Brass Quintet, Op. 105 (1972)
               La Bar, Arthur
                    Annapolis Brass Quintet
                         CRYS S 207
                              2-AR 6-79 P. 41
                              2-CR 9-79 P. 43
                              1-NR 5-79 P. 7
     Fanfare (3 Tpt/4 Hn/3 Trb/Ta/Perc)
                    Locke Brass Consort
                         Unicorn RHS 339
                              1-GR 6-76 P. 58
Thomson, Virgil (1896-    )
     Family Portrait for Brass Quintet
                    American Brass Quintet
                         Nonesuch 79024
Tillis, Frederick (1930-     )
     Quintet for Brass
                    New York Brass Quintet
                         Serenus SRS 12066
                              1-NR 4-76 P. 7
Tomasi, Henri (1901-1971)
     Procession du Vendredi-Saint
                    Baldwin-Wallace College Brass Choir
                    Mark Ed. Records MES 32565
Tomkins, Thomas
     Pavan
                    Philip Jones Brass Ensemble
                    Argo ZRG 717
                              1-GR 11-74 P. 910
                              2-ML 11-74 P. 5
Topff/Baldwin
     Danket dem Hernn; Lobet den Hernn
               Hagen/Hatfield/Thelander/Gullickson
                    University of Minnesota Brass Choir
                         UMBC: 001
Trabaci, Giovanni (1580-1647)
     (8) Galliards (2 Tpt/Hn/Trb)
                    Ensemble de Cuivres
                    Societe Francaise du Son SXL 20093
                              2-AU 4-66 P. 59
                              1-NR 2-66 P. 6

Traditional
    Amazing Grace
                    Eastern Brass Quintet
                    Klavier KS 539
                        2-AU 2-76 P. 96
                        1-HF 11-75 P. 129
    Frere Jacques
                    Philip Jones Brass Ensemble
                    Argo ZRG 895
                        2-FF 5/6-80
                        1-GR 1-79 P. 1334
    Londonderry Air
                    Philip Jones Brass Ensemble
                    London LDR 71100
                        1-AR 2-83 P. 77
                        1-FF 1/2-83 P. 338
                        1-NR 3-83 P. 3
    Scarborough Fair
            Soper, Kenneth
                    New York Brass Quintet
                    Golden Crest CRS 4148
                        1-AR 3-77 P. 40
    The Cuckoo
                    Philip Jones Brass Ensemble
                    London LDR 71100
                        1-AR 2-83 P. 77
                        1-FF 1/2-83 P. 338
                        1-NR 3-83 P. 3
Tromboncino, Bartolomeo (1470-1535)
    Frottola
                    Gabrieli Brass Ensemble
                    Nonesuch 71118
                        1-GR 2-66 P. 397
                        2-HF 11-66 P. 169
                        1-HSR 11-66 P. 72
                        1-NR 9-66 P. 5
Tull, Fischer (1934-    )
    Exhibition
                    Fine Arts Brass Quintet
                    WIM 4
                        1-NR 11-74 P. 7
    Liturgical Symphony
    (6 Tpt/4 Hn/4 Trb/2 Bar/2 Ta/Ti/Perc)
                    Los Angeles Brass Society
                    Avant AV 1001
                        2-HF 4-72 P. 104
                        1-NR 9-71 P. 14
    Variations on an Advent Hymn
    (6 Tpt/4 Hn/4 Trb/2 Bar/2 Ta/Ti)
                    Los Angeles Philharmonic Brass Ensemble
                    Avant 1005
                        1-NR 7-73 P. 12
Van Vactor, David (1909-    )
    Octet (2 Tpt/2 Hn/2 Trb/2 Ta)
                    Soloists/Hessian Symphony Orchestra
                    Everest 3236
                        3-NR 3-69 P. 4

Vecchi, Orazio (1550-1605)
     Salterello
                    Philip Jones Brass Ensemble
                    Argo ZRG 823
                         1-GR 6-76 P. 61
                         2-ML 5-76 P. 7
                         1-NR 10-77 P. 7
Verdi, Giuseppe (1813-1908)
     Triumphal Scene (Aida)
                    Locke Brass Consort
                    CRDD 1102
                         1-FF 5/6-83 P. 269
                         1-GR 3-83 P. 1059
                         1-MG 4-83 P. 6
                         2-NR 6-83 P. 6
Viadana, Lodovico (1560-1620)
     La Padovana
                    Berlin Philharmonic Brass Ensemble
                    DG 2532 066
                         1-FF 7/8-82 P. 268
                         1-FF 1/2-83 P. 336
                         1-NR 2-83 P. 4
                    Berlin Philharmonic Brass Ensemble
                    DG 2741 011
                         1-FF 1/2-83 P. 336
                         1-GR 11-82 P. 591
                         3-HF 11-83 P. 76
                         1-MG 7-82 P. 10
     Sinfonia
                    Berlin Philharmonic Brass Ensemble
                    DG 2532 066
                         1-FF 7/8-82 P. 268
                         1-FF 1/2-83 P. 336
                         1-NR 2-83 P. 4
                    Berlin Philharmonic Brass Ensemble
                    DG 2741 011
                         1-FF 1/2-83 P. 336
                         1-GR 11-82 P. 591
                         3-HF 11-83 P. 76
                         1-MG 7-82 P. 10
Villa-Lobos, Heitor (1887-1959)
     Choros # 4 (3 Hns/Trb) (1926)
                    Leningrad State Philharmonic
                    Wind Quintet
                    Westminister WGS 8322
                         1-NR 10-76 P. 7
          Brain, A./Lott/Perissi
                    Capitol CTL 7014
          Bujanovski/ ? / ?
                    Melodiya CM 01953-4
          Bujanovski/Yevstignejev/Sukhorukov
                    Melodiya CM 04399-400
          Da Silva/De Mello/Svab
                    (Brazilian) Caravelle 004
          Hustis/Larson/Scharnberg
                    CRYS S 378

184

Vitali, G. B. (1644-1692)
        Capriccio (2 Tpt/Hn/Bar/2 Trb/Ta)
                        Baldwin-Wallace College Brass Choir
                        Mark Ed. Records MES 32565
Wade/Schlabach
        Adeste Fideles
                La Bar, Arthur
                        Annapolis Brass Quintet
                        Richardson Records RRS-5
Walker, George (1922-    )
        Music for Brass
                        American Brass Quintet
                        Serenus SRS 12077
                                2-NR 6-78 P. 15
Waller, "Fats" (1904-1943)
        Lounging at the Waldorf; Handful of Keys
                Page, Graeme
                        Canadian Brass Quintet
                        RCA ARL 1 4733
Washburn, Robert (1928-    )
        5 Miniatures for 5 Brasses
                Guy, Marc
                        Annapolis Brass Quintet
                        CRYS S 213
                                1-FF 9/10-83 P. 327
                                4-NR 8-83 P. 3
Watt/Schlabach
        Joy to the World
                La Bar, Arthur
                        Annapolis Brass Quintet
                        Richardson Records RRS-5
Weelkes, Thomas (1575-1623)
        A Gay Tune
                Cowden, Hugh
                        Chicago Symphony Brass Ensemble
                        Audiophile AP 21
        Hark I Hear Some Dancing
                Wakefield, David
                        American Brass Quintet
                        Delos DMS 3003
                                1-NR 3-80 P. 7
                                1-NYT 5-18-80 P. D32
                                1-ST 7-80 P. 84
        In Pride of May
                Page, Graeme
                        Canadian Brass Quintet
                        Boot BMC 3003
                        Canadian Brass Quintet
                        Moss Music Group MMG 1139
        5 Madrigals
                Reynolds, Verne
                        Eastman Brass Quintet
                        Candide CE 31004
                                1-HF 11-68 P. 120
                                1-NR 5-69 P. 6
                                4-SR 8-31-68 P. 45

Weelkes, Thomas (Cont'd)
    Why Are You Ladies Staying (Cont'd)
            Wakefield, David
                    American Brass Quintet
                    Delos DMS 3003
                            1-NR 3-80 P. 7
                            1-NYT 5-18-80 P. D32
                            1-ST 7-80 P. 84
Weiner, Stanley (1925-    )
    Suite for Brass Quintet, Op. 40
            van Driessche, Andre
                    Theo Mertens Brass Ensemble
                    Eufoda 1051
Welffens
    Vier Miniaturen
            van Driessche, Andre
                    Theo Mertens Brass Ensemble
                    Eufoda 1051
Whittenberg, Charles (1927-    )
    Triptych for Brass Quintet (1962)
            Birdwell, Edward
                    American Brass Quintet
                    4-Desto 6474/7
                            1-ST 3-70 P. 120
            Happe, Richard
                    American Brass Quintet
                    Folkways FM 3651
                            4-NR 12-65 P. 8
Widor, Charles-Marie (1844-1937)
    Toccata from Symphony # 5 in f, Op. 42 # 1
                    Atlanta Brass Ensemble
                    Crystal Clear CCS 7011
                            2-AR 11-79 P. 31
                            1-NR 6-80 P. 14
Wilby, John (1574-1638)
    Down In A Valley
                    Eastern Brass Quintet
                    Klavier KS 536
                            1-AU 12-75 P. 106
                            1-NR 5-75 P. 8
    (2) Madrigals
            Anderson, Paul
                    Iowa Brass Quintet
                    University of Iowa Press 29001
                            2-HF 7-77 P. 118
                            1-NR 2-77 P. 7
Wilder, Alec (1907-1980)
    Brassinity
            Hackleman, Martin
                    Tidewater Brass Quintet
                    Golden Crest CRS Q 4156
    Nonet for Brass (1969) (8 Hn/Tba)
                    Angel S 36036
                            1-HF 8-70 P. 98
                            1-NR 7-70 P. 7
                            1-ST 9-70 P. 122

Wilder, Alec (Cont'd)
    Quintet # 4 (1973)
        Hackleman, Martin
            Tidewater Brass Quintet
              Golden Crest CRS Q 4156
    Quintet # 5 (1975)
        Hackleman, Martin
            Tidewater Brass Quintet
              Golden Crest CRS Q 4156
    Quintet # 6 (1977)
        Hackleman, Martin
            Tidewater Brass Quintet
              Golden Crest GC 4174
    Quintet # 8 (1980)
            Tidewater Brass Quintet
              Golden Crest CRS 4205
                  1-NR 10-81 P. 5
    Suite for Brass Quintet (1959)
        Pyle, Ralph
            Los Angeles Brass Quintet
              CRYS S 102
        Schmitt, Frederick
            New York Brass Quintet
              Golden Crest CR 4017
                  1-AU 4-60 P. 48
                  1-NR 4-60 P. 7
                  4-NYT 4-3-60 P. X10
Witkin, Beatrice (1916-    )
    Triads & Things
            New York Brass Society
              Opus One 12
Zador, Eugene (1894-1977)
    Quintet for Brass (1973)
            Modern Brass Quintet
              Orion ORS 74140
                  1-NR 5-74 P. 6
    (9) Dances
            Ensemble de Cuivres
              Societe Francaise du Son SXL 20093
                  2-AU 4-66 P. 59
                  1-NR 2-66 P. 6
    (4) Parties
            Ensemble de Cuivres
              Societe Francaise du Son SXL 20093
                  2-AU 4-66 P. 59
                  1-NR 2-66 P. 6
Zelenka, Istran (1936-    )
    Calvary Fanfare
            Berlin Philharmonic Brass Ensemble
              DG 2532 066
                  1-FF 7/8-82 P. 268
                  1-FF 1/2-83 P. 336
                  1-NR 2-83 P. 4

Zelenka, Istran (Cont'd)
    Calvary Fanfare (Cont'd)
                    Berlin Philharmonic Brass Ensemble
                    DG 2741 011
                        1-FF 1/2-83 P. 336
                        1-GR 11-82 P. 591
                        3-HF 11-83 P. 76
                        1-MG 7-82 P. 10
Zielenski
    Laetentur Coeli
            Covert, John
                    Ithaca Brass Quintet
                    Golden Crest GC 4114
Zindars, Earl (1927-    )
    Suite for Brass
            Cowden, Hugh
                    Chicago Symphony Brass Ensemble
                    Audiophile AP 21
Zipoli, Domenico (1688-1762)
    Allegro Offertorio
            van Driessche, Andre
                    Theo Mertens Ensemble
                    Eufoda 1029
Zupko, Ramon (1932-    )
    Masques for Brass Quintet & Piano
                    Western Brass Quintet
                    CRI S 425

# Woodwind Ensemble

Addison, John
      Serenade for Woodwind Quintet & Harp
            Kittich, Eugene
                  CBC SM 186
Aitken
      Folia
                  Hennigar, Harcus
                        York Winds
                              Centrediscs CMC 0482
                                    1-HF 4-83 P. 61
                        York Winds
                              Centrediscs WRC 1-2304 (Canadian)
Allen, Judith Shatin
      Wind Songs for Wind Quintet (1980)
                        Clarion Wind Quintet
                              Opus One 87
Amram, David (1930-    )
      Quintet for Winds (1968)
                        Clarion Wind Quintet
                              Golden Crest GC 4125
                                    1-MJ 3-74 P. 10
Andersen, Karl
      Variations over Theme & Rhythm for Wind Quintet
                              Philips 6507 018
Andriessen, Jurriaan (1925-    )
      Sciarada Spagnuola
                        Wingra Quintet
                              Golden Crest GC 4150
Arnold, Malcolm (1921-    )
      3 Shanties for Wind Quintet, Op. 4 (1943)
                        Frosunda Quintet
                        BIS 136
                              2-ML 2-80 P. 9
                              1-NR 3-80 P. 8
                              1-ST 4-80 P. 136
                  Bujanovski, Vitali
                        Melodiya CM 02249-50

Arnold, Malcolm (Cont'd)
   3 Shanties for Wind Quintet, Op. 4 (1943) (Cont'd)
        Civil, Alan
             London Wind Quintet
             ARGO ZRG 5326
                  1-GR 2-63 P. 391
                  1-HF 8-64 P. 88
                  1-ML 1-63 P. 10
                  1-NR 8-64 P. 5
                  1-NYT 5-24-64 P. X18
        Tuckwell, Barry
             Tuckwell Wind Quintet
             Nonesuch 78022-1
                  1-AR 7-84 P. 53
                  1-FF 5/6-84 P. 351
                  1-HF 5-84 P. 72
                  1-NR 5-84 P. 7
                  3-OV 8-84 P. 59
Arrieu, Claude (1903-    )
    Quintet in C (1955)
             Cambini Wind Quintet
              Coronet 3060
             French Wind Quintet
             L'Oiseau Lyre 50122
                  4-AR 1/2-57 P. 77
                  1-GR 9-56 P. 128
                  1-ML 9-56 P. 8
                  1-SR 12-29-56 P. 42
            Soni Ventorum Wind Quintet
             CRYS S 253
                  1-CR 1-79 P. 43
                  1-FF 1/2-79 P. 109
                  1-NR 9-78 P. 7
Bach, C.P.E./Wilder
    Rondo Andantino
            New York Woodwind Quintet
             Golden Crest GC 3019
                  2-HF 11-57 P. 82
                  4-LJ 8-58 P. 2149
Bach, J. C. (1735-1782)
    4 Quintets for 2 Clarinets, 2 Horns & Bassoon
        Coursier/Fournier
             L'Oiseau Lyre OL 50135
    Symphony in Bb for 2 Clarinets, 2 Horns & Bassoon
        Freund/Sungler
             Eichendorff Wind Group
             MHS 0581Y
    The Six Symphonies for Winds (2 Cl/2 Hn/2 Bsn)
        Civil/Harper
             London Wind Soloists
               (Eng) Decca SXL 6337
Bach/Baron
    Art of the Fugue (Fugues 1-9)
        Froelich, Ralph
            New York Wind Quintet
            Concert Disc M 1230

Bach/Baron (Cont'd)
                        1-CR 1-63 P. 48
                        1-HF 3-63 P. 73
                        2-HSR 3-63 P. 63
                        1-NR 12-62 P. 4
    Art of the Fugue (Contrapuncti 12-19)
                New York Wind Quintet
                Concert Disc M 1250
                        4-AR 2-64 P. 533
                        2-CR 12-64 P. 10
                        1-HF 8-65 P. 67
                        1-NR 1-65 P. 7
    Art of the Fugue S 1080
                New York Wind Quintet
                2-Everest 3335
Bach, J. S. (1685-1750)
    Concerto # 2 BWV 593
                Israel Woodwind Quintet
                RCA (Israel) YJRL 1003
    Fughetta on "Dies sind die Heil 'gen zehn Gebot"
    BWV 679
                Israel Woodwind Quintet
                RCA (Israel) YJRL 1003
    Prelude # 22 in Bb from WTC
                Clarion Wind Quintet
                Golden Crest CRS 4146
    Prelude & Fugue in d BWV 539
                Israel Woodwind Quintet
                RCA (Israel) YJRL 1003
    Sarabande in d
                Oberlin Faculty Woodwind Quintet
                Coronet S 1408
                        1-HF 1-70 P. 126
                        1-NR 10-69 P. 7
Bach/Maros
    Quintet in Bb
                Hungarian Wind Quintet
                Qualiton SLPX 11379
                        1-GR 6-69 P. 51
                        1-ML 5-69 P. 8
                        1-NR 6-70 P. 6
Bach/Nakagawa
    Prelude & Fugue XXII
            Hennigar, Harcus
                York Winds
                Era 105
Bach/Stevens
    Fugue in g
            Watt, Robert
                Los Angeles Philharmonic Wind Quintet
                WIM 9
                        1-NR 6-73 P. 6
Balai, Leonid
    Divertissement, Op. 7 (Quintet with Harp)
                Leningrad State Philharmonic
                Wind Quintet
                Westminister WGS 8322
                        1-NR 10-76 P. 7
                    191

Balai, Leonid (Cont'd)
     Divertissement, Op. 7 (Quintet with Harp) (Cont'd)
          Bujanovski, Vitali
               Melodiya CM 01953-4
Barber, Samuel (1910-1981)
     Summer Music Op. 31 (1956)
                    Dorian Quintet
                    Vox SVBX 5307
                         1-AR 12-77 P. 51
                         1-FF 1-78 P. 73
                         1-HF 12-77 P. 110
                         1-NR 11-77 P. 8
                    Philadelphia Woodwind Quintet
                    Columbia ML 5441
                         1-AR 5-60 P. 714
                         1-HSR 5-60 P. 65
                         2-NR 4-60 P. 7
                         1-SR 3-26-60 P. 52
                    Soni Ventorum Wind Quintet
                    MHS 4782
                         2-FF 3/4-84 P. 323
               Barrows, John
                    New York Woodwind Quintet
                    Concert Disc CS 216
                         1-HF 1-60 P. 68
                         1-HSR 3-60 P. 99
                         4-NR 12-59 P. 7
                         1-NYT 12-13-59 P. X18
                         4-SR 12-12-59 P. 44
               Bujanovski, Vitali
                    Melodiya D 10533-41; C 357-8
               Tuckwell, Barry
                    Tuckwell Wind Quintet
                    Nonesuch 78 022 1
                         1-AR 7-84 P. 53
                         1-FF 5/6-84 P. 351
                         1-HF 5-84 P. 72
                         1-NR 5-84 P. 7
                         1-OV 8-84 P. 59
Barrows, John (1913-    )
     March
               Barrows, John
                    New York Woodwind Quintet
                    Everest EV 3092
Barta, Lubor (1928-    )
     Wind Quintet # 2 (1969)
                    Prague Wind Quintet
                    Supraphon 111 1426
                         2-NR 7-76 P. 5
Barthe, A.
     Passacaille
                    Wingra Quintet
                    Golden Crest GC 4150
                    Wisconsin Arts Quintet
                    Redwood ES 16

Bazelon, Irwin (1922-    )
    Woodwind Quintet (1975)
                    Boehm Quintet
                        Orion ORS 78291
                            2-NR 12-78 P. 8
Beach, H. H. A. (1867-1945)
    Pastorale from Woodwind Quintet
            Tillotson, Brooks
                MHS 3578
Bechler, Stanworth (1923-    )
    Little Suite, Op. 59 (1963)
                    Pacific Arts Woodwind Quintet
                        Orion 79345
                            2-FF 7/8-80 P. 182
                            2-NR 6-80 P. 8
Beethoven, L. Van (1770-1827)
    Five Pieces for Mechanical Organ
                    Soni Ventorum Wind Quintet
                        Lyrichord 7143
                            2-GR 5-67 P. 584
                            1-HF 11-65 P. 88
                            1-ML 4-67 P. 8
                            4-NR 7-65 P. 7
    March in Bb for 2 Clarinets, 2 Horns, & 2 Bassoons
                        London STS 15387
                            1-GR 4-74 P. 1901
                            1-ML 3-74 P. 12
                    London Wind Soloists
                        London CM 9442
                            1-GR 6-65 P. 17
                            1-HF 4-66 P. 92
                            1-LJ 3-1-67 P. 993
                            1-ML 6-65 P. 7
                            1-NR 9-66 P. 7
                    Netherlands Wind Ensemble
                        Philips 9500 87
            Sanders/   ?
                        HMV ASD 2671
    Octet in Eb, Op. 103 (2 Ob/2 Cl/2 Hn/2 Bsn)
                    Czech Philharmonic Chamber Ensemble
                        Supraphon 111 0703
                            3-GR 9-72 P. 485
                            3-HFN 8-72 P. 1456
                            3-R&R 8-72 P. 68
                            1-SFC 11-24-74 P. 32
                    Soloists/Leningrad Symphonic Orchestra
                        Westminister WGS 8220
                            2-NR 6-73 P. 8
                    Little Symphony Orchestra
                        Elaine Music Shop 1
                            2-AR 3-50 P. 226
                            2-GS 6-50 P. 3
                            1-JR 5/6-50 P. 12
                            1-LJ 5-15-50 P. 887
                            2-SR 5-13-50 P. 54
                            1-SR 3-25-50 P. 55

Beethoven, L. Van (Cont'd)
    Octet in Eb, Op. 103 (Cont'd)
        London Wind Soloists
          London CM 9442
              1-GR 6-65 P. 17
              1-HF 4-66 P. 92
              1-LJ 3-1-67 P. 993
              1-ML 6-65 P. 7
              1-NR 9-66 P. 7
        Netherlands Wind Ensemble
          Philips 9500 087
        Paris Wind Ensemble
          Nonesuch H 1054
              2-AR 8-65 P. 1148
              3-GR 9-65 P. 152
              2-HSR 9-65 P. 74
              2-ML 8-65 P. 6
              1-SR 9-25-65 P. 64
        Vienna Philharmonic Wind Group
          Westminister XWN 18189
              1-AU 10-56 P. 75
        Vienna Philharmonic Wind Group
          Westminister 50 03
              1-AR 6-50 P. 332
              2-GS 6-50 P. 3
              2-JR 5/6-50 P. 12
              2-LJ 10-1-50 P. 1680
              1-NR 10-50 P. 10
              2-SR 6-24-50 P. 63
      Barrows/Buffington
        New York Wind Ensemble
          Counterpoint 559
              1-AR 11-58 P. 176
              1-MH 9-58 P. 30
              1-NYT 8-31-58 P. X14
              2-SR 8-30-58 P. 42
      Bloom/Mackey
        Columbia MS 6116
              1-AR 6-60 P. 817
              1-AU 7-60 P. 42
              4-HF 6-60 P. 59
              1-HSR 10-60 P. 76
              2-LJ 2-15-61 P. 786
              1-NR 5-60 P. 6
        Columbia M 33527
              1-HF 2-76 P. 89
              1-NR 8-75 P. 7
      Bujanovski/  ?
        Melodiya CM 02529-30
      Sanders/  ?
        HMV ASD 2671
    Quintet in Eb, Op. 16 (Ob/Cl/Hn/Bsn/Pf)
        Decca SDD 256
        BIS 61
        Claves D 805
        CRD 1067
        Denon 7009
        MMO 105

Beethoven, L. Van (Cont'd)
    Quintet in Eb, Op. 16 (Cont'd)
                    4-NR 6-54 P. 1
            Paris Wind Ensemble
            Nonesuch H 1054
                2-AR 8-65 P. 1148
                3-GR 9-65 P. 152
                2-HSR 9-65 P. 74
                2-ML 8-65 P. 6
            Orion 76224
            Philips 6500 326
            Seraphim M 60368
                1-FF 7/8-82 P. 156
            Westminister WGS 8220
                2-NR 6-73 P. 8
            Vox SVBX 579
                2-LJ 4-1-70 P. 1348
        Brain, Dennis
            Angel 35303
                1-AR 4-56 P. 137
                1-GR 1-56 P. 316
                1-HF 3-56 P. 67
                1-MA 5-56 P. 34
                1-NR 3-56 P. 7
                1-SR 6-30-56 P. 46
            Arabesque 8071
                4-HF 5-81 P. 64
                1-NR 11-80 P. 8
            Bruno Walter Society I GI 370
                4-HF 5-81 P. 64
                1-NR 11-81 P. 7
        Bujanovski, Vitali
            Melodiya D 016087-8
        Coursier, Gilbert
            Vox PLP 6040
                1-AR 5-50 P. 304
                3-GS 3-50 P. 8
                2-JR 2-50 P. 10
                1-NR 2-50 P. 4
                2-SR 3-11-50 P. 39
        Jones, Mason
            Columbia ML 4834
                1-AR 4-54 P. 268
                1-HF 6-54 P. 47
                1-MA 4-54 P. 17
                3-NA 3-27-54 P. 267
                1-NYT 3-28-54 P. X8
                2-SR 3-27-54 P. 54
        Kappy, David
            MHS 4375 K
        Klein, Fred
            Stradivari 616
                1-AR 7-53 P. 355
                2-CR 8-53 P. 35
                2-GS 9-53 P. 2
                2-HF 11/12-53 P. 67
                4-NR 10-53 P. 8
                1-NYT 5-24-53 P. X9

Beethoven, L. Van (Cont'd)
    Quintet in Eb, Op. 16 (Cont'd)
        Pandolfi
                Phillips 9500 672
                        1-FF 9/10-80 P. 78
                        1-GR 11-80 P. 684
                        1-NR 7-80 P. 7
                        1-ST 10-80 P.109
                Turnabout 37004
        Routch, Robert
                Columbia M 33527
                        3-HF 2-76 P. 89
                        1-NR 8-75 P. 7
                RCA ARL 1-2217
                        1-NR 8-78 P. 9
                        1-ST 9-78 P. 104
        Sanders, Neill
                HMV ASD 2256
        Singer, Joseph
                AS 1004
                        2-AR 5-60 P. 700
                        2-HF 10-60 P. 72
                        2-HSR 5-60 P. 70
                        2-NYT 4-10-60 P. X19
                        3-SR 6-25-60 P. 54
        Tarjani, Ferenc
                Hungaroton SLPX 11637
                        1-ML 10-74 P. 8
                Fidelio 3347
    Quintet in Eb for Oboe, 3 Horns & Bassoon(Op.Posth.)
            London Wind Soloists
                London CM 9442
                        1-GR 6-65 P. 17
                        1-HF 4-66 P. 92
                        1-LJ 3-1-67 P. 993
                        1-ML 6-65 P. 7
                        1-NR 9-66 P. 7
            London Wind Soloists
                London STS 15387
                        1-GR 4-74 P. 1901
                        1-ML 3-74 P. 12
            Netherlands Wind Ensemble
                Philips 9500 087
                        1-GR 6-77 P. 68
                        1-HFN 6-77 P. 117
                        1-MJ 1-79 P. 46
                        2-MT 10-77 P. 825
                        1-NR 10-77 P. 7
        Baumann/Van Woudenberg/Meyendorf
                Telefunken SAWT 9547
                        1-AU 8-70 P. 54
                        1-GR 7-70 P. 179
                        2-HF 10-70 P. 94
                        1-NR 8-70 P. 6
                        2-SR 6-27-70 P. 52
                        1-ST 12-70 P. 86

Beethoven, L. Van (Cont'd)
    Quintet in Eb for Oboe (Cont'd)
        Baumann/ ?/ ?
            Telefunken 642321 AP
        Bujanovski/ ? / ?
            Melodiya CM 02529-30
        Civil/Bush/Beers
            Decca SXL 6170
        Meek/McConathy/Keaney
            Unicorn LP 1024
                1-AR 9-56 P. 10
                2-HF 12-56 P. 99
                2-MH 1/2-57 P. 41
    Rondino for Winds, Op. 146 (2 Ob/2 Cl/2 Hn/2 Bsn)
        London Wind Soloists
            London CM 9442
                1-GR 6-65 P. 17
                1-HF 4-66 P. 92
                1-LJ 3-1-67 P. 993
                1-ML 6-65 P. 7
                1-NR 9-66 P. 7
        Members/Little Symphony Orchestra
            Elaine Music Shop 1
                2-AR 3-50 P. 226
                2-GS 6-50 P. 3
                1-JR 5/6-50 P. 12
                1-LJ 5-15-50 P. 887
                2-SR 5-13-50 P. 54
                1-SR 3-25-50 P. 55
        Netherlands Wind Ensemble
            Philips 9500 087
        Vienna Philharmonic Wind Group
            Westminister XWN 18189
                1-AU 10-56 P. 75
        Barrows/Buffington
        New York Wind Ensemble
            Counterpoint CPST 559
                1-AR 11-58 P. 176
                1-MH 9-58 P. 30
                1-NYT 8-31-58 P. X14
                2-SR 8-30-58 P. 42
        Bujanovski/Shalyt
            Melodiya CM 02949-50
        Sanders/ ?
            HMV ASD 2671
    Sextet in Eb for 2 Clarinets, 2 Horns & 2 Bassoons,
    Op. 71
            London STS 15387
                1-GR 4-74 P. 1901
                1-ML 3-74 P. 12
            Philips 9500 087
        London Wind Soloists
            London CM 9442
                1-GR 6-65 P. 17
                1-HF 4-66 P. 92
                1-LJ 3-1-67 P. 993
                1-ML 6-65 P. 7
                1-NR 9-66 P. 7

Beethoven, L. Van (Cont'd)
    Sextet in Eb (Cont'd)
              Vienna Philharmonic Wind Group
              Westministter XWN 18189
                  1-AU 10-56 P. 75
              Vienna Philharmonic Wind Group
              Westministter 50-03
                  1-AR 6-50 P. 332
                  2-GS 6-50 P. 3
                  2-JR 5/6-50 P. 12
                  2-LJ 10-1-50 P. 1680
                  1-NR 10-50 P. 10
                  2-SR 6-24-50 P. 63
          Barrows/Buffington
           New York Wind Ensemble
              Counterpoint CPST 559
                  1-AR 11-58 P. 176
                  1-MH 9-58 P. 30
                  1-NYT 8-31-58 P. X14
                  2-SR 8-30-58 P. 41
          Bujanovski/ ?
              Melodiya CM 02949-50
          Berges/Barboteu
              Nonesuch 71025
                  1-HF 12-64 P. 80
                  1-ML 1-65 P. 4
                  1-NR 12-64 P. 9
          Jones/ ?
              Philadelphia Woodwind Quintet
              Columbia ML 5093
                  1-AR 7-56 P. 179
                  1-HA 11-56 P. 110
                  2-HF 12-56 P. 104
                  1-NR 10-56 P. 8
Benson, Warren (1924-    )
    Marche
          Farkas, Philip
              American Woodwind Quintet
              Golden Crest GC 4075
                  4-NR 8-66 P. 5
Berezowsky, N. (1900-1953)
    Suite for Wind Quintet, Op. 11
          New Art Wind Quintet
              Classic Edition 1003
                  2-NR 2-52 P. 7
                  4-SR 9-15-51 P. 30
                  4-SR 7-28-51 P. 40
Berge, Sigurd
    Yang Guan for Wind Quintet
              Philips 6507 018
Bergsma, William (1921-    )
    Concerto for Wind Quintet (1958)
          Clarion Quintet
              Golden Crest GC S 4076
                  1-NR 7-67 P. 7

Berio, Luciano (1925-    )
     Children's Play, Op. Z00
                    Dorian Quintet
                    Vox SVBX 5307
                              1-AR 12-77 P. 51
                              1-FF 1-78 P. 73
                              1-HF 12-77 P. 110
                              1-NR 11-77 P. 8
            Smith, Calvin
                    Westwood Wind Quintet
                    CRYS S 250
                              1-CR 3-82 P. 43
                              1-FF 1/2-82 P. 257
                              1-NR 12-81 P. 11
Berkeley, Lennox (1903-    )
     Quintet for Wind & Piano, Op. 90 (Ob/Cl/Hn/Bsn/Pf)
            Baker, Julian
                    Meridian E 77017
                              4-FF 9/10-82 P. 162
                              1-GR 2-79 P. 7
Besozzi, Carlo (1702-1775)
     Sonata XX for 2 Oboes, 2 Horns & Bassoon
            Freund/Sungler
                    Eichendorff Wind Group
                    MHS 0581Y
Bialosky
     Suite
            Watt, Robert
                    Los Angeles Philharmonic Wind Quintet
                    WIM 9
                              1-NR 6-73 P. 6
Bibalo, Antonio (1922-    )
     Sonantina 1 A "Semplice" for Wind Quintet (1971)
                    Norwegian Wind Quintet
                    Simax PS 1003
Blumenfeld, Harold (1923-    )
     Expansions for Woodwind Quintet (1964)
                    York Wind Quintet
                    Washington University T3-XM 708
                              3-NR 10-68 P. 5
Borowski, Felix (1872-1956)
     Madrigal to the Moon
                    Ohio State University
                    Faculty Woodwind Quintet
                    Coronet 543
Bozay, Attila (1939-    )
     Wind Quintet, Op. 6
            Tarjani, Ferenc
                    Hungarian Wind Quintet
                    Hungaroton SLPX 11 630
                              1-ML 3-75 P. 7
                              2-NR 5-75 P. 9
Bozza, Eugene (1905-    )
     Scherzo, Op. 48
                    Dorian Woodwind Quintet
                    Turnabout 34507
                              1-HF 9-73 P. 120
                              1-NR 9-73 P. 9

Bozza, Eugene (Cont'd)
    Scherzo, Op. 48 (Cont'd)
        Jones, Mason
            Philadelphia Woodwind Quintet
            Columbia ML 5093
                1-AR 7-56 P. 179
                1-HA 11-56 P. 110
                2-HF 12-56 P. 104
                1-NR 10-56 P. 8
    Variations sur un Theme libre, Op. 42
            Copenhagen Wind Quintet
            London LLP 734
                3-AR 9-53 P. 22
                1-CR 8-53 P. 20
                3-GR 10-53 P. 133
                1-GS 7-53 P. 8
                2-ML 8-53 P. 5
            New York Woodwind Quintet
            Esoteric 505
                1-AR 12-51 P. 118
                4-GS 10-51 P. 9
                1-SR 8-25-51 P. 50
            New York Woodwind Quintet
            Counterpoint 505
                1-HSR 10-65 P. 109
Brahms, Johannes (1833-1897)
    Variations & Fugue on a Theme by Handel
            Clarion Wind Quintet
            Golden Crest CRS 4146
Bright, Houston (1916-1970)
    3 Short Dances
        Farkas, Philip
            American Woodwind Quintet
            Golden Crest GC 4075
                4-NR 8-66 P. 5
Buxtehude, Dietrich/Wilder
    Jesu, Joy & Treasure
            New York Woodwind Quintet
            Golden Crest GC 3019
                2-HF 11-57 P. 82
                4-LJ 8-58 P. 2149
Cambini, Giovanni (1746-1825)
    Quintet # 1
            Cambini Wind Quintet
            Coronet 3060
    Quintet # 3 in F, Op. 4
            Oberlin Faculty Woodwind Quintet
            Coronet S 1408
                1-HF 1-70 P. 126
                1-NR 10-69 P. 7
            Philadelphia Woodwind Quintet
            Columbia MS 6799
                2-HF 4-66 P. 118
                1-HSR 6-66 P. 82
                1-NR 3-66 P. 6
                4-SR 2-26-66 P. 56

Cambini, Giovanni (Cont'd)
   3 Quintets for Winds
       Leuba, Christopher
           Soni Ventorum Wind Quintet
             University of Washington Press
             Rav. 701
                1-HF 8-72 P. 94
Campo, Frank (1922-   )
   5 Pieces for 5 Winds (1958)
       Watt, Robert
           Los Angeles Philharmonic Wind Quintet
             WIM 9
                1-NR 6-73 P. 6
Cantrell (Transcriber)
   4 Elizabethan Pieces
       Watt, Robert
           Los Angeles Philharmonic Wind Quintet
             WIM 9
                1-NR 6-73 P. 6
Carlstedt, Jan (1926-   )
   Sinfonietta for 5 Wind Instruments (1959)
       Linder, Albert
           Gothenburg Quintet
             BIS LP 24
                4-GR 3-77 P. 1457
Carter, Elliott (1908-   )
   Eight Etudes and a Fantasy for Woodwind Quartet (1950)
       Barrows, John
           New York Woodwind Quintet
             Concert Disc CS 229
                1-HF 11-63 P. 83
                1-HSR 12-63 P. 78
                2-NR 10-63 P. 7
                1-NYT 1-26-64 P. X18
   Woodwind Quintet (1948)
             Candide CE 31016
                1-NR 9-69 P. 7
             Boston Symphony Chamber Players
             Victor LM 6167
                4-GR 2-67 P. 431
                1-HF 12-66 P. 81
                2-ML 3-67 P. 9
                1-NR 10-66 P. 6
             Dorian Quintet
             Vox SVBX 5307
                1-AR 12-77 P. 51
                1-FF 1-78 P. 73
                1-HF 12-77 P. 110
                1-NR 11-77 P. 8
             New Art Wind Quintet
             Classic Edition 2003
                2-AR 5-54 P. 302
                1-HF 7-54 P. 57
                4-NYT 3-14-54 P. X8
                4-SR 2-27-54 P. 71
             Soni Ventorum Wind Quintet
             MHS 4782
                2-FF 3/4-84 P. 323

Carter, Elliott (Cont'd)
     Woodwind Quintet (1948) (Cont'd)
          Hennigar, Harcus
               York Winds
                    Melbourne SMLP 4040
Casadeus, Robert
     Sextuor in E, Op. 58 (1958)(Pf/Fl/Ob/Cl/Bsn/Hn)
          Guerin, Roger
               Columbia ML 5448
                    4-AR 6-60 P. 814
                    4-HF 4-60 P. 62
                    4-HSR 1-61 P. 62
                    1-NR 5-60 P. 6
                    2-NYT 6-5-60 P. X17
                    1-SR 5-28-60 P. 66
Chavez, Carlos (1899-1978)
     Soli II for Wind Quintet
          Henderson, Roger
               Westwood Wind Quintet
               CRYS S 812
                    1-HF 2-73 P. 102
                    2-NR 12-72 P. 8
          Zarzo, Vincente
               Odyssey Y 31534
                    2-HF 1-73 P. 82
Cherney, Brian (1942-    )
     Notturno for Wind Quintet & Piano (1974)
          Hennigar, Harcus
               York Winds
                    Melbourne SMLP 4040
     Woodwind Quintet
          Hennigar, Harcus
               York Winds
                    Centrediscs CMC 0482
                    1-HF 4-83 P. 61
               York Winds
                    Centrediscs WRC 1-2304 (Canadian)
Chou, Wen-Chung (1923-    )
     Suite for Harp & Wind Quintet
          Rose
               Otis Quintet
               New W 237
Coleman, Ornette (1930-    )
     Forms & Sounds for Wind Quintet (1965)
          Virtuoso Ensemble
          Victor LM 2982
                    1-AR 9-68 P. 24
                    4-AU 6-68 P. 44
                    2-HSR 6-68 P. 80
                    1-NR 5-68 P. 6
                    4-NYT 2-25-68 P. D30
Colomer, B. M.
     Menuet

               Wisconsin Arts Quintet
               Redwood ES 16

Cortes, Ramiro (1933-    )
    3 Movements for 5 Winds
           Henderson, Roger
                  Westwood Wind Quintet
                      CRYS S 812
                          1-HF 2-73 P. 102
                          2-NR 12-72 P. 8
Cowell, Henry (1897-1965)
    Suite for Wind Quintet (1933)
                  New Art Wind Quintet
                      Classic Edition 2003
                        2-AR 5-54 P. 302
                        1-HF 7-54 P. 57
                        4-NYT 3-14-54 P. X8
                        4-SR 2-27-54 P. 71
Custer, Arthur (1923-    )
    2 Movements for Woodwind Quintet
                  Interlochen Arts Quintet
                      CRI S 253
                        1-NR 5-70 P. 5
Dahl, Ingolf (1912-1970)
    Allegro & Arioso (1942)
                  New Art Wind Quintet
                      Classic Edition 2003
                        2-AR 5-54 P. 302
                        1-HF 7-54 P. 57
                        4-NYT 3-14-54 P. X8
                        4-SR 2-27-54 P. 71
                Hill, Douglas
                  Wingra Quintet
                      Golden Crest GC 4150
                Barrows, John
                  New York Woodwind Quintet
                      Concert Disc CS 216
                        1-HF 1-60 P. 68
                        1-HSR 3-60 P. 99
                        4-NR 12-59 P. 7
                        1-NYT 12-13-59 P. X18
                        4-SR 12-12-59 P. 44
Damase, J. M. (1928-    )
    (17) Variations, Op. 22 (1950)
                  Var/Sera 81002
                  French Wind Quintet
                  L'Oiseau Lyre 50122
                      4-AR 1/2-57 P. 77
                      1-GR 9-56 P. 128
                      1-ML 9-56 P. 8
                      1-SR 12-29-56 P. 42
                Buddle, Anthony
                  Sydney Wind Ensemble
                      Cherry Pie LA 07889
                Bujanovski, Vitali
                  Melodiya D 018529-30/ CM 02321-22

Danzi, Franz (1763-1826)
    Gypsy Dance
            Farkas, Philip
                    Chicago Symphony Woodwind Quintet
                    Audiophile Records AP 16
    Quintet in d for Oboe, Clarinet, Horn, Bassoon
    & Piano, Op. 41
                    Claves D 8101
                        1-GR 6-81 P. 48
    Quintet in Bb, Op. 56 # 1
                    DGG 2530 077
                        2-HF 4-71 P. 114
                        1-NR 3-71 P. 3
                    Eichendorff Wind Quintet
                    Baroque (Canada) 2869
                        2-NR 12-67 P. 10
                    Haifa Wind Quintet
                    Mace MCM 9053
                        1-GR 8-65 P. 112
                        3-ML 8-65 P. 7
                        2-NR 3-67 P. 8
                    Residenz Quintet
                    Claves D 611
            Coursier, Gilbert
                    French Wind Quintet
                    L'Oiseau Lyre-London 53005
                        1-CR 10-54  P. 58
                        2-GR 12-54  P. 306
                        2-HF 6-55 P. 55
                        4-MA 5-55 P. 16
                        2-ML 10-54 P. 10
                        2-NYT 4-24-55 P. X15
            Froelich, Ralph
                    New York Woodwind Quintet
                    Nonesuch 71108
                        2-AR 5-66 P. 843
                        1-CR 8-66 P. 25
                        1-HF 9-66 P. 94
                        1-HSR 9-66 P. 88
                        1-NR 6-66 P. 7
            Kappy, David
                    Soni Ventorum Wind Quintet
                    MHS 4621
                        2-FF 5/6-83 P. 129
            Raphaeli, Giora
                    Haifa Wind Quintet
                    PYE GSGC 14034
    Quintet in g, Op. 56 # 2
            Coursier, Gilbert
                    French Wind Quintet
                    L'Oiseau Lyre-London 53005
                        1-CR 10-54 P. 58
                        2-GR 12-54 P. 306
                        2-HF 6-55 P. 55
                        4-MA 5-55 P. 16
                        2-ML 10-54 P. 10
                        2-NYT 4-24-55 P. X15

Danzi, Franz (Cont'd)
    Quintet in g, Op. 56 # 2 (Cont'd)
        Froelich, Ralph
            New York Woodwind Quintet
            Nonesuch 71108
                2-AR 5-66 P. 843
                1-CR 8-66 P. 25
                1-HF 9-66 P. 94
                1-HSR 9-66 P. 88
                1-NR 6-66 P. 7
        Kappy, David
            Soni Ventorum Wind Quintet
            MHS 4621
                2-FF 5/6-83 P. 129
    Quintet in F, Op. 56 # 3
        Soni Ventorum Wind Quintet
        Lyrichord LLST 7216
            1-NR 5-70 P. 6
    Quintet in G, Op. 67 # 1
        Boehm Quintette
        Orion ORS 78291
            2-NR 12-78 P. 8
        New Art Wind Quintet
        Classic Edition 2010
            2-AR 3-53 P. 229
            1-GS 12-52 P. 5
            1-NR 7-53 P. 8
            1-NYT 1-18-53 P. X19
        Kappy, David
            Soni Ventorum Wind Quintet
            MHS 4621
                2-FF 5/6-83 P. 129
    Quintet in e, Op. 67 # 2 (1824)
        Barrows, John
            New York Woodwind Quintet
            Concert Disc CS 205
                1-HF 6-59 P. 64
                1-HMR 7-59 P. 45
                4-NR 7-59 P. 7
                1-NYT 4-19-59 P. X15
                1-SR 7-25-59 P. 43
        Froelich, Ralph
            New York Woodwind Quintet
            Nonesuch 71108
                2-AR 5-66 P. 843
                1-CR 8-66 P. 25
                1-HF 9-66 P. 94
                1-HSR 9-66 P. 88
                1-NR 6-66 P. 7
        Kappy, David
            Soni Ventorum Wind Quintet
            MHS 4621
                2-FF 5/6-83 P. 129
        Leuba, Christopher
            Soni Ventorum Wind Quintet
            CRYS S 251
                2-NR 6-76 P. 9

Danzi, Franz (Cont'd)
    Quintet in e, Op. 67 # 2 (1824) (Cont'd)
        Van Woudenberg, Adriaan
           Danzi Quintet
             Philips 839 703 LY
    Quintet in f, Op. 68 # 2
        Leuba, Christopher
           Soni Ventorum Wind Quintet
             CRYS S 251
                2-NR 6-76 P. 9
    Quintet in d, Op. 68 # 3
        Leuba, Christopher
           Soni Ventorum Wind Quintet
             CRYS S 251
                2-NR 6-76 P. 9
    Sinfonia Concertante in Eb (Fl/Ob/Hn/Bsn/Pf)
        Muhlbacher, Ernst
             Westminister XWN 19100
                2-HF 12-66 P. 91
                1-NR 11-66 P. 4
                1-SR 10-29-66 P. 58
Davidovsky, Mario (1934-    )
    Synchronisms # 8 (1975)
           Dorian Quintet
             Vox SVBX 5307
                1-AR 12-77 P. 51
                1-FF 1-78 P. 73
                1-HF 12-77 P. 110
                1-NR 11-77 P. 8
Debussy, Claude (1862-1918)
    Arabesque # 2
           Wisconsin Arts Quintet
           Redwood ES 16
D'Indy, Vincent (1857-1931)
    Chansons et Danses for 7 Winds, Op. 50
    (Fl/Ob/2 Cl/Hn/2 Bsn)
           Bourgue Wind Ensemble
           Nonesuch 71382
    Sarabande et Minuet, Op. 72 for Wind Quintet & Piano
           Paris Wind Quintet
           4 Ades 7084/7
Dittersdorf, Carl (1739-1799)
    Partita in D for 2 Oboes, 2 Horns & Bassoon
           Eichendorff Wind Group
           MHS 524
                1-AR 1-64 P. 419
                1-HF 5-64 P. 78
           Seraphim 60040
                1-GR 10-66 P. 225
                1-HSR 10-67 P. 159
                1-ML 11-66 P. 7
                1-NR 9-67 P. 13
                1-NYT 8-6-67 P. D17
    Partita in F
           Musica Rara Mus 16

Downey, John (1927-    )
    Agort (1972)
                Woodwind Arts Quintet
                    Orion 73123
                        1-NR 11-73 P. 6
Druckman, Jacob (1928-    )
    Delizie contente che L'alma beate
                Dorian Quintet
                    Vox SVBX 5307
                        1-AR 12-77 P. 51
                        1-FF 1-78 P. 73
                        1-HF 12-77 P. 110
                        1-NR 11-77 P. 8
Druschetzky, Georg (1745-1819)
    Partita in Dis
                Supraphon SUA 59764
Dubois, Pierre-Max (1930-    )
    Sinfonia da Camera (1965)
    (Saxophone & Wind Quintet)
            Pittle
                Westwood Wind Quintet
                CRYS S 353
Durey, Louis (1889-1979)
    Les Soirees de Valfere for Wind Quintet
                Paris Wind Quintet
                4 Ades 7084/7
Dussek, Franz (1731-1799)
    Partita in F for 2 Oboes, 2 Horns & Bassoon
                Freund/Sungler
                    MHS 0528H
                        1-AR 3-64 P. 627
                  Prague Collegium Ensemble
                    Supraphon 111 0614
                        1-GR 4-74 P. 1862
                        1-HFN 3-74 P. 119
                        1-NR 8-72 P. 115
                        1-R&R 2-74 P. 29
Egge, Klaus (1906-    )
    Wind Quintet Op. 13 (1939)
              Ullberg, Odd
                Norwegian Wind Quintet
                (Norwegian) Philips 839 249 AY
Etler, Alvin (1913-1973)
    Quintet # 1 (1955)
              Barrows, John
                New York Woodwind Quintet
                  Concert Disc CS 216
                      1-HF 1-60 P. 68
                      1-HSR 3-60 P. 99
                      4-NR 12-59 P. 7
                      1-NYT 12-13-59 P. X18
                      4-SR 12-12-59 P. 44
Farberman, Harold (1929-    )
    Quintessence (1963)
                Dorian Woodwind Quintet
                Serenus SRS 12011

Farberman, Harold (Cont'd)
    Quintessence (1963)(Cont'd)
                            1-AR 11-65 P. 239
                            4-HF 9-65 P. 84
                            4-HSR 10-65 P. 84
                            4-NYT 11-28-65 P. HF3
Farkas, Ferenc (1905-    )
    Ancient Hungarian Dances (1959)
                Pacific Arts Woodwind Quintet
                Orion 79345
                      2-FF 7/8-80 P. 182
                      2-NR 6-80 P. 8
                Frosunda Quintet
                BIS 136
                      2-ML 2-80 P. 9
                      1-NR 3-80 P. 8
                      1-ST 4-80 P. 136
            Hennigar, Harcus
                York Winds
                Era 105
Feld, Jindrich (1925-    )
    Wind Quintet #2 (1968)
                Prague Wind Quintet
                Serenus 12075
                Prague Wind Quintet
                Supraphon 111 1426
                      2-NR 7-76 P. 5
Fennelly, Brian (1937-    )
    Wind Quintet (1967)
                Dorian Woodwind Quintet
                CRI S 318
                      4-NR 8-74 P. 6
Fernstrom, John (1897-1961)
    Quintet for Winds, Op. 59 (1943)
                Norwegian Wind Quintet
                Simax PS 1003
Fiala, George
    Chamber Music for 5 Woodwind Instruments
                Rittich, Eugene
                CBC SM 186
Fine, Irving (1914-1962)
    Partita for Wind Quintet (1948)
                Dorian Woodwind Quintet
                3 Vox SVBX 5307
                      1-AR 12-77 P. 51
                      1-FF 1-78 P. 73
                      1-HF 12-77 P. 110
                      1-NR 11-77 P. 8
              New Art Wind Quintet
                Classic Edition 1003
                      2-NR 2-52 P. 7
                      4-SR 9-15-51 P. 30
                      4-SR 7-28-51 P. 40
                New York Woodwind Quintet
                Concert Disc CS 229
                      1-HF 11-63 P. 83
                      1-HSR 12-63 P. 78

Fine, Irving (Cont'd)
      Partita for Wind Quintet (1948) (Cont'd)
                        Soni Ventorum Wind Quintet
                        MHS 4782
                              2-FF 3/4-84 P. 323
Flosman, Oldrich (1925-    )
      Sonata for Winds & Piano
                        Prague Wind Quintet
                        Supraphon 111 1426
                              2-NR 7-76 P. 5
Foerster, Josef Bohuslav (1859-1951)
      Quintet, Op. 95 (1909)
                        Boehm Quintette
                        Orion ORS 76254
Fortner, Wolfgang
      Funf Bagateller
                        Philips 6500 261
Foss, Lukas (1922-    )
      "Cave of the Winds" for Wind Quintet (1972)
                        Dorian Woodwind Quintet
                        3 Vox SVBX 5307
                              1-AR 12-77 P. 51
                              1-FF 1-78 P. 73
                              1-HF 12-77 P. 110
                              1-NR 11-77 P. 8
Francaix, Jean (1912-    )
      Quintette a vent (1948)
                        Dorian Woodwind Quintet
                        Turnabout 34507
                              1-HF 9-73 P. 120
                              1-NR 9-73 P. 9
                        New Art Wind Quintet
                        Classic Edition 2001
                              4-GS 5-53 P. 1
                              4-HF 1/2-54 P. 58
                              1-LJ 8-54 P. 1392
                              1-MA 11-15-53 P. 18
                              1-NR 7-53 P. 8
                              1-NYT 4-19-53 P. X10
                        Southwest German Radio Wind Quintet
                        Mace M 9034
                              1-NR 3-67 P. 8
                        Taffanel Wind Quintet
                        Denon & Denon/PCM OX 7217-ND
                              2-FF 11/12-81 P. 295
                        Vienna Symphony Woodwinds
                        Westminister XWN 19097
                              2-HF 8-63 P. 83
                              1-HSR 10-65 P. 100
                              2-SR 5-29-65 P. 56
                        Wind Quintet of Orchestra National
                        de La Radio Francaise
                        Angel 35133
                              1-AR 1-55 P. 167
                              4-HF 1-55 P. 57
                              1-NR 3-55 P. 9
                              2-NYT 2-13-55 P. X10

Francaix, Jean (Cont'd)
    Quintette a vent (1948) (Cont'd)
                    Woodwind Arts Quintet
                        Orion 73123
                            1-NR 11-73 P. 6
                Jolley, David
                    MHS 3286
    Quintet (1949)
                    New York Woodwind Quintet
                        CRI CS 222
                            1-AR 10-61 P. 114
                            4-HF 10-61 P. 102
                            1-HSR 10-61 P. 82
                            1-NR 7-61 P. 9
                    New York Woodwind Quintet
                        Everest EV 3080; 6080
                            1-CR 11-63 P. 27
                            1-HF 2-64 P. 89
                            1-HSR 12-63 P. 82
                            2-NR 10-63 P. 7
                Bujanovski, Vitali
                    Melodiya CM 02249 50
Fricker, Peter (1920-    )
    Quintet, Op. 5 (1947)
                Civil, Alan
                    London Wind Quintet
                        ARGO ZRG 5326
                            1-GR 2-63 P. 391
                            1-HF 8-64 P. 88
                            1-ML 1-63 P. 10
                            1-NR 8-64 P. 5
                            1-NYT 5-24-64 P. X18
Gebauer, Francois (1773-1844)
    Quintet Concertante # 1 in Bb
                    Danzi Quintet
                        Philips World Series PHC 9136
                            1-NR 4-70 P. 8
Gerhard, Roberto (1896-1970)
    Quintet (1928)
                Civil, Alan
                    London Wind Quintet
                        ARGO ZRG 5326
                            1-GR 2-63 P. 391
                            1-HF 8-64 P. 88
                            1-ML 1-63 P. 10
                            1-NR 8-64 P. 5
                            1-NYT 5-24-64 P. X18
Gershwin/Wilder
    Dinah
                    New York Woodwind Quintet
                        Golden Crest GC 3019
                            2-HF 11-57 P. 82
                            4-LJ 8-58 P. 2149

Gibson
    Quintet for Winds (1974)
                        Clarion Woodwind Quintet
                        Golden Crest CRS 4191
                            1-AR 11-80 P. 49
                            2-FF 9/10-81 P. 278
                            1-NYT 4-27-80 P. D27
Goeb, Roger (1914-    )
    Prairie Songs for Woodwind Quintet (1947)
                        American Recording Society 10
                        Desto 6422 E
    Quintet for Woodwinds
                        New Art Wind Quintet
                        Classic Edition 2003
                            2-AR 5-54 P. 302
                            1-HF 7-54 P. 57
                            4-NYT 3-14-65 P. X8
                            4-SR 2-27-54 P. 71
    Quintet for Woodwinds # 2 (1956)
                        New Art Wind Quintet
                        CRI 158
                            1-HF 8-62 P. 86
                            1-HSR 8-62 P. 66
                            4-LJ 10-1-62 P. 3432
                            1-MA 10-62 P. 25
                            2-MQ 1-63 P. 121
                            4-NR 9-62 P. 9
Goodman, Joseph (1918-    )
    Scherzo for Wind Quintet
                        Soni Ventorum Wind Quintet
                        MHS 4782 F
                            2-FF 3/4-84 P. 323
    Quintet for Wind Instruments (1954)
            Bonnevie, Robert
                        Soni Ventorum Wind Quintet
                        Lyrichord LYR S 158
                            1-HF 10-66 P. 140
                            2-HSR 12-66 P. 88
                            2-NR 11-66 P. 9
                            1-SR 9-24-66 P. 76
Gounod, Charles
    Petit Sinfonie (Fl/2 Ob/2 Cl/2 Hn/2 Bsn)
                        Members/Halle Orchestra
                        PYE GSGC 4082
                        Netherlands Wind Ensemble
                        Philips 6500 163
Guentzel, Gus
    Scherzo
            Farkas, Philip
                        Chicago Symphony Woodwind Quintet
                        Audiophile Records AP 16
Haddad, Don
    Blues au vent
            Farkas, Philip
                        American Woodwind Quintet
                        Golden Crest GC 4075
                            4-NR 8-66 P. 5

211

Hall, Pauline
    Suite for 5 Winds
                Philips 839 256 AY
Hambraeus, Bengt (1928-    )
    Jeu de Cinq (1976)
            Hennigar, Harcus
                York Winds
                    Centrediscs CMC 0482
                York Winds
                    Centrediscs WRC 1-2304 (Canadian)
Hamerick, Ebbe (1898-1951)
    Quintet for Winds (1942)
                Soni Ventorum Wind Quintet
                Desto 6401
Handel, G. F.  (1685-1759)
    Two Arias for 2 Oboes, 2 Horns & Bassoon
            Freund/Sungler
                Eichendorff Wind Group
                MHS 0581Y
            Brain/  ?
                Decca DL 4070
                    2-CR 11-53 P. 35
                    1-GS 10-53 P. 9
                    1-HA 11-53 P. 112
                    2-HF 11/12-53 P. 74
                    1-NYT 9-27-53 P. X8
                    1-SR 12-26-53 P. 56
Harbison, John (1938-    )
    Quintet for Winds
                Aulos Wind Quintet
                CRI S 436
Hartley, Gerald (1921-    )
    Divertissement
                Ohio State University
                Faculty Woodwind Quintet
                Coronet 543
            Farkas, Philip
                Chicago Symphony Woodwind Quintet
                Audiophile Records AP 16
Haydn
    Presto
            Farkas, Philip
                Chicago Symphony Woodwind Quintet
                Audiophile Records AP 16
Haydn, Franz Joseph (1732-1809)
    Divertimento # 1 in Bb
                Wind Group of VSO
                Music Guild 118
                    1-AR 12-64 P. 359
                    2-AR 8-65 P. 1178
                    1-HF 10-64 P. 158
                    2-NR 7-64 P. 6
            Jones, Mason
                Philadelphia Woodwind Quintet
                Columbia ML 5093
                    1-AR 7-56 P. 179
                    1-HA 11-56 P. 110

212

Haydn, Franz Joseph (Cont'd)
    (3) Divertimentos for 2 Oboes, 2 Horns & 2 Bassoons
            Eichendorff Wind Group
            MHS 620
                    2-AR 11-65 P. 241
    (7) Divertimentos for 2 Oboes, 2 Horns & 2 Bassoons
        Civil/Harper
            London Wind Soloists
            London STS 15078
                    1-GR 3-68 P. 485
                    1-HF 4-72 P. 104
                    1-ML 3-68 P. 3
    (5) Divertimentos for 2 Oboes, 2 Horns & 2 Bassoons
        Medvecky/Mesterhazy
            Hungaroton SLPX 11719
                    1-NR 11-75 P. 8
    12 Nocturnes (2 Hn/2 Fl)
        Baumann/ ?
            Intercord 944-09 K
    Octet in F (2 Ob/2 Cl/2 Hn/2 Bsn)
        Von Freiburg
            Westminister WL 5002
Haydn/Kesztler
    Wind Quintet from Piano Trio in A
            Hungarian Wind Quintet
            Qualiton SLPX
                    1-GR 6-69 P. 51
                    1-ML 5-69 P. 8
                    1-NR 6-70 P. 6
    Wind Quintet from Piano Trio in F
            Hungarian Wind Quintet
            Qualiton SLPX 11379
                    1-GR 6-69 P. 51
                    1-ML 5-69 P. 8
                    1-NR 6-70 P. 6
Haydn, Michael (1737-1806)
    Divertimento in D for Horn, Flute, Oboe, & Bassoon
        Freund
            MHS 0528
                    1-AR 3-64 P. 627
Heiden, Bernhard (1910-    )
    Intrada for Saxophone & Wind Quintet
            Westwood Wind Quintet
            CRYS S 353
    Quintet for Woodwinds (1965)
            Clarion Wind Quintet
            Golden Crest GC 4125
                    1-MJ 3-74 P. 10
    Sinfonia (1949)
            Now 9632
Henze, Hans Werner (1926-    )
    Quintet (1952)
            Dorian Quintet
            Candide CE 31016
                    1-NR 9-69 P. 7
            Philips 6500 261

Hertel, Johann Wilhelm (1727-1789)
    Sonata a Quattro in Eb (2 Hn/2 Bsn)
        Werne/ ?
            Musica Rara MUS 16
Hidas, Frigyas (1928-    )
    Wind Quintet # 2 (1969)
        Tarjani, Ferenc
            Hungarian Wind Quintet
            Hungariton LPX 11 630
                1-ML 3-75 P. 7
                2-NR 5-75 P. 9
Hindemith, Paul (1895-1963)
    Kleine Kammermusik, Op. 24 # 2 (1922)
            Boston Symphony Chamber Players
            RCA LSC 3166
                1-HF 2-71 P. 88
                1-NR 10-70 P. 7
                1-ST 12-70 P. 100
            Fairfield Wind Ensemble
            Stradivari 606
                1-AR 8-51 P. 406
                1-CR 6-51 P. 31
                2-GS 6-51 P. 3
                1-SR 7-28-51 P. 40
            Fine Arts Wind Players
            Capitol P 8258
                1-AR 7-54 P. 374
                1-CR 11-54 P. 73
                1-GR 1-55 P. 354
                2-HA 9-54 P. 110
                1-HF 8-54 P. 44
                2-MA 11-1-54 P. 16
            French Wind Quintet
            L'Oiseau Lyre-London 53007
                1-AR 4-56 P. 139
                3-GR 9-55 P. 140
                1-HF 4-56 P. 76
                3-NYT 2-19-56 P. X13
            Haifa Wind Quintet
            Mace MCM 9053
                1-GR 8-65 P. 112
                3-ML 8-65 P. 7
                2-NR 3-67 P. 8
            Haifa Wind Quintet
            PYE GSGC 14034
            Netherlands Philharmonic Wind Quintet
                Concert Hall H 15
            Oberlin Faculty Woodwind Quintet
            Coronet S 1408
                1-HF 1-70 P. 126
                1-NR 10-69 P. 7
            Taffanel Wind Quintet
            Denon & Denon/PCM OX 7217-ND
                2-FF 11/12-81 P. 295
            Wind Ensemble of Orchestra National
            de la Radio Francaise
                Angel 35079

Hindemith, Paul (1895-1963) (Cont'd)
    Kleine Kammermusik, Op. 24 # 2 (1922) (Cont'd)
                          1-AR 2-55 P. 202
                          4-HF 2-44 P. 71
                          1-NYT 1-2-55 P. X10
                          1-SR 12-25-54 P. 50


        Barrows, John
            New York Woodwind Quintet
            Concert Disc CS 205
                          1-HF 6-59 P. 64
                          1-HMR 7-59 P. 45
                          4-NR 7-59 P. 7
                          1-NYT 4-19-59 P. X1
                          1-SR 7-25-59 P. 43
        Bujanovski, Vitali
            Melodiya D 10611-12/C 359-60
        Guse, Allen
            Westwood Wind Quintet
            CRYS S 601
                          4-NR 3-69 P. 5
                          1-ST 4-69 P. 97
        Jones, Mason
            Philadelphia Woodwind Quintet
            Columbia ML 5093
                          1-AR 7-56 P. 179
                          1-HA 11-56 P. 110
                          2-HF 12-56 P. 104
                          1-NR 10-56 P. 8
Holmboe, Vagn (1909-    )
    Notturno, Op. 19 (1940)
        Linder, Albert
            Gothenburg Quintet
            BIS LP 24
                          4-GR 3-77 P. 1457
Hovland, Egil
    Quintett fur Blaser, Op. 50
            Philips 839 248 AY
Hummel
    Octet-Partita in Eb (2 Ob/2 Cl/2 Hn/2 Bsn)
            Monadnock Wind Ensemble
            MHS 1733 W
Iannacone, Anthony (1943-    )
    Parodies (1975)
            Clarion Woodwind Quintet
            Golden Crest CRS 4191
                          1-AR 11-80 P. 49
                          2-FF 9/10-81 P. 278
                          1-NYT 4-27-80 P. D27
Ibert, Jacques (1890-1962)
    (3) Pieces breves
            Copenhagen Wind Quintet
            London LLP 734
                          3-AR 9-53 P. 22
                          1-CR 8-53 P. 20
                          3-GR 10-53 P. 133
                          1-GS 7-53 P. 8

Ibert, Jacques (Cont'd)
    (3) Pieces breves (Cont'd)
                Dennis Brain Ensemble
                Seraphim M 60169
                      1-HF 7-71 P. 94
                      1-NR 7-71 P. 4
                      1-ST 9-71 P. 103
                Dorian Wind Quintet
                Turnabout TVS 34507
                      1-HF 9-73 P. 120
                      1-NR 9-73 P. 9
                Fairfield Wind Ensemble
                Stradivari 606
                      1-AR 8-51 P. 406
                      1-CR 6-51 P. 31
                      2-GS 6-51 P. 3
                      1-SR 7-28-51 P. 40
                French Wind Quintet
                L'Oiseau Lyre 50122
                      4-AR 1/2-57 P. 77
                      1-GR 9-56 P. 128
                      1-ML 9-56 P. 8
                      1-SR 12-29-56 P. 42
                Frosunda Quintet
                BIS 136
                      2-ML 2-80 P. 9
                      1-NR 3-80 P. 8
                      1-ST 4-80 P. 136
                Haifa Wind Quintet
                Mace MCM 9053
                      1-GR 8-65 P. 112
                      3-ML 8-65 P. 7
                      2-NR 3-67 P. 8
                Haifa Wind Quintet
                PYE GSGC 14034
                New York Woodwind Quintet
                Counterpoint 505
                      1-HSR 10-65 P. 109
                New York Woodwind Quintet
                Esoteric 505
                      1-AR 12-51 P. 118
                      4-GS 10-51 P. 9
                      1-SR 8-25-51 P. 50
                Paris Wind Quintet
                4 Ades 7084/7
                Vienna Symphony Woodwinds
                Westminister XWN 19097
                      2-HF 8-63 P. 83
                      1-HSR 10-65 P. 100
                      2-SR 5-29-65 P. 56
                Vienna Wind Soloists
                London STS 15419
                Wind Ensemble of Orchestra National
              de la Radio Francaise
                Angel 35079
                      1-AR 2-55 P. 202
                      4-HF 2-55 P. 71

Ibert, Jacques (Cont'd)
    (3) Pieces breves (Cont'd)
        Barrows, John
            New York Woodwind Quintet
                Everest EV 3092
        Hennigar, Harcus
            York Winds
                Era 105
        Jones, Mason
            Philadelphia Woodwind Quintet
                Columbia ML 5093
                      1-AR 7-56 P. 179
                      1-HA 11-56 P. 110
                      2-HF 12-56 P. 104
                      1-NR 10-56 P. 8
        Tuckwell, Barry
            Tuckwell Wind Quintet
                Nonesuch 78022-1
                      1-AR 7-84 P. 53
                      1-FF 5/6-84 P. 351
                      1-HF 5-84 P. 72
                      1-NR 5-84 P. 7
                      3-OV 8-84 P. 59
Jacob, Gordon (1895-    )
    Sextet (1956)  (Pf/Fl/Ob/Cl/Hn/Bsn)
            Brain Ensemble
                Seraphim M 60169
                      1-HF 7-71 P. 94
                      1-NR 7-71 P. 4
                      1-ST 9-71 P. 103
Janacek, Leos (1854-1928)
    Sextet for Wind Instruments (Fl/Ob/Cl/B Cl/Hn/Bsn)
            Los Angeles Chamber Orchestra
                Nonesuch 79033
            Wingra Quintet
                Spectrum 142
            Vienna Wind Soloists
                London STS 15419
        Arnold, Karl
            Southwest German Radio Wind Quintet
                Mace M9034
        Bujanovski, Vitali
                Melodiya D 10611-12
        Kopecky, Otto
                Panton 11 0214
        Sanders, Neill
                HMV ASD 2344
Johnson, Roger (1941-    )
    Woodwind Quintet
            Dorian Wind Quintet
                CRI S 293
                      1-NR 9-72 P. 6

Jongen, Joseph (1873-1953)
     Concerto for Wind Quintet, Op. 123 (1942)
          Meek, Harold
                    Unicorn LP 1029
                         4-HF 12-56 P. 104
                         1-MH 9/10-56 P. 35
Kalabis, Victor (1923-    )
     Little Chamber Music for Wind Quintet, Op. 27 (1967)
                    Prague Wind Quintet
                    Supraphon 111 1426
                         2-NR 7-76 P. 5
Kasemets, Udo (1919-    )
     Woodwind Quintet, Op. 48 (1957)
          Rittich, Eugene
                    CBC SM 218
Kauffman, Leo (1901-1944)
     Quintet (1943)
                    Clarion Wind Quintet
                    Golden Cres⁺ GC 4076
                         1-NR 7-67 P. 7
Kaufmann, Walter (1907-    )
     Partita
          Farkas, Philip
                    American Woodwind Quintet
                    Golden Crest GC 4075
                         4-NR 8-66 P. 5
Kay, Norman Forber (1929-    )
     Miniature Quartet (1950) (Hn/Fl/Cl/Bsn)
          Brain, Dennis
                    PYE GSGC 14040
Kingman, Daniel
     Quintet for Winds
          Watt, Robert
                    Los Angeles Philharmonic Wind Quintet
                    WIM 9
                         1-NR 6-73 P. 6
Klughardt, August (1847-1902)
     Quintet, Op. 79
                    Boehm Quintette
                    Orion ORS 76254
                    Norwegian Chamber Soloists
                    Var/Sara 81002
          Smith, Calvin
                    Westwood Wind Quintet
                    CRYS S 250
                         1-CR 3-82 P. 43
                         1-FF 1/2-82 P. 257
                         1-NR 12-81 P. 11
Kohn, Karl (1926-    )
     Little Suite for Wind Quintet
                    Los Angeles Wind Quintet
                    Orion 7263
                         1-AR 4-72 P. 374
                         2-NR 3-72 P. 7

Kokkonen, Joonas (1921-     )
    Wind Quintet (1973)
                    Helsinki Quintet
                        BIS LP 11
                        1-ML 4-76 P. 8
Korte, Karl (1928-    )
    Matrix
                    New York Woodwind Quintet
                        CRI S 249
                        4-NR 3-70 P. 6
                        1-ST 6-70 P. 84
Kotonski, W.
    Quintett (1964)
                    MUZA XW 572
Kraft, Leo (1922-    )
    Partita # 3 for Wind Quintet (1964)
                    New Wind Quintet
                        Serenus SRE 12037
                            2-AR 8-72 P. 609
                            4-NR 10-72 P. 5
                            1-ST 1-73 P. 109
Krenek, Ernst (1900-      )
    Pentagram for Winds (1957)
            Bonnevie, Robert
                    Soni Ventorum Wind Quintet
                        Lyrichord LYR S 158
                            1-HF 10-66 P. 140
                            2-HSR 12-66 P. 88
                            2-NR 11-66 P. 9
                            1-SR 9-24-66 P. 76
Krommer, Franz (1759-1831)
        Partita for 2 Oboes, 2 Clarinets, 2 Horns & 2 Bsns.
                    Nash Ensemble
                        CRD 1110; 4110
                    Prague Collegium Musicum
                        Supraphon 111 0614
                            1-GR 4-74 P. 1862
                            1-HFN 3-74 P. 119
                            1-NR 8-72 P. 15
                            1-R&R 2-74 P. 29
            Soeteman/Meyers
                    Philips 9500 437
Kunad, Rainer (1936-    )
    Music for Winds in drei Satzen (1965)
                    Eterna 8 25 741
Kupferman, Meyer (1926-    )
    Woodwind Quintet
                    Ariel Quintet
                        Serenus SRS 12044
                            1-NR 11-73 P. 6
Kurz, Siegfried (1930-    )
    Woodwind Quintet, Op. 12 (1950)
                    Eterna 825741
Lachner
    Octet in Bb,   Op. 156 (Fl/Ob/2 Cl/2 Hn/2 Bsn)
                    Monadnock Wind Ensemble
                        MHS 1733

Lang, Istvan (1933-     )
    Fuvosotos
                        Cambini Wind Quintet
                            Coronet 3060
        Woodwind Quintet # 1
                        Hungarian Woodwind Quintet
                            Hungariton LPX  1246
                                1-HSR 12-66 P. 114
                                4-NR 8-66 P. 6
                Tarjani, Ferenc
                        Hungarian Woodwind Quintet
                            Hungariton LPX 11 630
                                1-ML 3-75 P. 7
                                2-NR 5-75 P. 9
Lefebvre, Charles (1843-1917)
    Suite for Woodwinds, Op. 57
                        Wisconsin Arts Quintet
                            Redwood ES 16
                Farkas, Philip
                        Chicago Symphony Woodwind Quintet
                            Audiophile Records AP 16
                Hennigar, Harcus
                        York Winds
                            Era 105
Lessard, John (1920-     )
    Partita for Wind Quintet (1952)
                    Flagello
                        Sinfonia Roma
                            Serenus SRS 12008
                                2-HSR 10-65 P. 96
        Wind Quintet II
                        New York Woodwind Quintet
                            Serenus SRS 12032
Ligeti, Gyorgy (1923-     )
    Six Bagatelles for Wind Quintet (1953)
                    Tuckwell, Barry
                        Tuckwell Wind Quintet
                            Nonesuch 78022-1
                                1-AR 7-84 P. 53
                                1-FF 5/6-84 P. 351
                                1-HF 5-84 P. 72
                                1-NR 5-84 P. 7
                                1-OV 8-84 P. 59
        Ten Pieces for Wind Quintet (1969)
                        Vienna Wind Soloists
                            London STS 15419
Linn, Robert (1925-     )
    Woodwind Quintet
                        Westwood Wind Quintet
                            CRYS S 811
                                1-NR 7-71 P. 13
Malipiero, G. F. (1882-1973)
    Dialogue # 4 for Wind Quintet (1956)
                Brain
                        Arabesque 8071
                                4-HF 5-81 P. 64
                                1-NR 11-80 P. 8

Martino, Donald (1931-    )
    Concerto for Wind Quintet (1964)
                    Contemporary Chamber Ensemble
                        CRI USD 230
                            2-HF 2-69 P. 114
                            4-NR 1-69 P. 4
                            1-ST 6-69 P. 102
Martinon, Jean (1910-1976)
    Domenon, Op. 21
                    Soni Ventorum Wind Quintet
                        CRYS S 253
                            1-CR 1-79 P. 43
                            1-FF 1/2-79 P. 109
                            1-NR 9-78 P. 7
Mathias, William (1934-    )
    Quintet, Op. 22
            Smith, Calvin
                    Westwood Wind Quintet
                        CRYS S 250
                            1-CR 3-82 P. 43
                            1-FF 1/2-82 P. 257
                            1-NR 12-81 P. 11
Milhaud, Darius (1892-1974)
    La Cheminee du Roi Rene Op. 205 (1939)
                    Athena Ensemble
                    Chandos 1012
                    Camerata Woodwind Quintet
                    Coronet 3040
                    Fairfield Wind Ensemble
                    Stradivari 606
                            1-AR 8-51 P. 406
                            1-CR 6-51 P. 31
                            2-GS 6-51 P. 3
                            1-SR 7-28-51 P. 40
                    French Wind Quintet
                    L'Oiseau Lyre-London 53002
                            1-CR 12-54 P. 87
                            2-GR 1-55 P. 355
                            4-HF 6-55 P. 62
                            2-ML 12-54 P. 11
                            1-SR 3-26-55 P. 59
                    Paris Wind Quintet
                    4-Ades 708417
                    Philadelphia Woodwind Quintet
                    Columbia ML 5613
                            1-AU 8-61 P. 69
                            1-HSR 6-61 P. 68
                            1-NR 4-61 P. 3
                            1-NYT 4-9-61 P. X18
                            1-SR 3-25-61 P. 50
                    Wind Ensemble of Orchestra National
                    de la Radio Francaise
                    Angel 35079
                            1-AR 2-55 P. 202
                            4-HF 2-55 P. 71
                            1-NYT 1-2-55 P. X10
                            1-SR 12-25-54 P. 50

Milhaud, Darius (Cont'd)
    La Cheminee du Roi Rene (Cont'd)
        Alonge, Ray
                Elaine Music Shop 6
                    1-CR 10-51 P. 31
                    2-CU 10-51 P. 478
                    1-LJ 2-1-52 P. 204
                    1-SR 8-25-51 P. 50
                    2-SR 9-15-51 P. 30
        Barrows, John
                New York Woodwind Quintet
                Everest EV 3092
        Brain, Dennis
                Dennis Brain Wind Quintet
                Bruno Walter Society I GI 370
                    4-HF 5-81 P. 64
                    1-NR 4-81 P. 7
        Bujanovski, Vitali
                Melodiya D 13179-80
        Tuckwell, Barry
                Tuckwell Wind Quintet
                Nonesuch 78022-1
                    1-AR 7-84 P. 53
                    1-FF 5/6-84 P. 351
                    1-HF 5-84 P. 72
                    1-NR 5-84 P. 7
                    1-OV 8-84 P. 59
    (2) Sketches, Op. 227b (1941)
                Columbia MS 6584
                    1-HF 9-64 P. 90
                    1-NYT 7-12-64 P. X17
                    1-SR 6-27-64 P. 62
                Athena Ensemble
                Chandos 1012
                New Art Wind Quintet
                Classic Edition 1003
                    2-NR 2-52 P. 7
                    4-SR 9-15-51 P. 30
                    4-SR 7-28-51 P. 40
                New York Woodwind Quintet
                Counterpoint 505
                    1-HSR 10-65 P. 109
                New York Woodwind Quintet
                Esoteric 505
                    1-AR 12-51 P. 118
                    4-GS 10-51 P. 9
                    1-SR 8-25-51 P. 50
                Wind Ensemble of Orchestra National
                de la Radio Francaise
                Angel 35079
                    1-AR 2-55 P. 202
                    4-HF 2-55 P. 71
                    1-NYT 1-2-55 P. X10
                    1-SR 12-25-54 P. 50
Moross, Jerome (1913-    )
    Woodwind Quintet
            London Pro Musica
            Desto 6469

Morris, Franklin (1920-    )
    Five Esoteric Pieces for Woodwind Quintet (1941;1955)
                Soni Ventorum Wind Quintet
                Desto 6401
Mortensen, Otto (1922-    )
    Quintet
            Bujanovski, Vitali
                Melodiya D 025233-34/ CM 02313-14
    Wind Quintet, Op. 4 (1951)
                Gothenburg Quintet
                BIS LP 24
                    4-GR 3-77 P. 1457
                Philips 6507 008
Moss, Lawrence (1927-    )
    Auditions for Wind Quintet (1973)
                Dorian Woodwind Quintet
                CRI SD 318
                    4-NR 8-74 P. 6
Mozart, W. A. (1756-1791)
    Adagio & Allegro
                Soni Ventorum Wind Quintet
                Lyr LLST 7168
    Andante
                Oberlin Faculty Woodwind Quintet
                Coronet S 1408
                    1-HF 1-70 P. 126
                    1-NR 10-69 P. 7
    Andante in F, K 616
                Soni Ventorum Wind Quintet
                Lyr LLST 7168
    Cassation in Eb
                New Art Wind Quintet
                Classic Edition 2010
                    2-AR 3-53 P. 229
                    1-GS 12-52 P. 5
                    1-NR 7-53 P. 8
                    1-NYT 1-18-53 P. X19
    Cassation for Horn, Oboe, Clarinet & Bassoon
            Coursier, Gilbert
                L'Oiseau Lyre 50016
                    3-AR 5-54 P. 293
                    1-CR 1-54 P. 74
                    1-GR 2-54 P. 343
                    2-HF 5-54 P. 50
                    2-ML 1-54 P. 16
                    2-NA 3-27-54 P. 267
    Divertimento # 3 in Eb, K 166
    (2 Ob/2 Cl/2 Eng Hn/2 Hn/2 Bsn)
                Philips 6500 002
                    1-GR 5-70 P. 1775
                    1-GR 10-71 P. 651
                    1-HF 8-71 P. 86
                    1-ML 5-70 P. 2
                    1-ML 10-71 P. 9
                    1-ST 4-71 P. 78

Mozart, W. A. (Cont'd)
    Divertimento # 3 in Eb, K 166 (Cont'd)
        Afanasev/ ?
                Westminister WGS 8338
                    1-NR 5-77 P. 5
    Divertimento in Bb for 2 Oboes, 2 Horns & 2 Bassoons,
    K 186
                Philips 6500 003
                    1-GR 7-70 P. 180
                    1-GR 10-71 P. 651
                    1-ML 6-70 P. 3
                    1-ML 10-71 P. 9
        Civil/Beers
                London Wind Soloists
                London CM 9348
                    1-GR 10-63 P. 186
                    2-ML 10-63 P. 3
                    1-NRE 3-7-64 P. 33
    Divertimento in Bb, K 196f
                Detmold Wind Sextet
                  DG 198023
                Soeteman/Soeteman
                Philips 6500 004
                    1-GR 7-70 P. 180
                    1-GR 10-71 P. 651
                    1-HF 10-71 P. 116
                    1-ML 7-70 P. 2
                    1-ML 10-71 P. 9
                    1-NR 10-71 P. 9
    Divertimento in F for 2 Oboes, 2 Horns & 2 Bassoons,
    K 213
                Danzi Quintett
                ABC 67028
                Philadelphia Woodwind Quintet
                Columbia MS 6315
                    1-AR 8-62 P. 943
                    1-HF 7-62 P. 62
                    1-NR 7-62 P. 8
                    1-NYT 8-19-62 P. X10
                    2-SR 3-31-62 P. 44
        Soeteman/Soeteman
                Philips 6500 002
                    1-GR 5-70 P. 1775
                    1-GR 10-71 P. 651
                    1-HF 8-71 P. 86
                    1-ML 5-70 P. 2
                    1-ML 10-71 P. 9
                    1-ST 4-71 P. 78
    Divertimento in Bb for 2 Oboes, 2 Horns & 2 Bassoons,
    K 240
        Soeteman/Soeteman
                Philips 6500 002
                    1-GR 5-70 P. 1775
                    1-GR 10-71 P. 651
                    1-HF 8-71 P. 86
                    1-ML 5-70 P. 2
                    1-ML 10-71 P. 9
                    1-ST 4-71 P. 78

Mozart, W. A. (Cont'd)
    Divertimento in Eb for 2 Oboes, 2 Horns & 2 Bassoons,
    K 252
            Soeteman/Soeteman
                    Philips 6500 002
                        1-GR 5-70 P. 1775
                        1-GR 10-71 P. 651
                        1-HF 8-71 P. 86
                        1-ML 5-70 P. 2
                        1-ML 10-71 P. 9
                        1-ST 4-71 P. 78
    Divertimento for 2 Oboes, 2 Horns & 2 Bassoons, K 253
                    Danzi Quintett
                    ABC 67028
                    London CM 9348
                        1-GR 10-63 P. 186
                        2-ML 10-63 P. 3
                    Philips 6500 003
                        1-GR 7-70 P. 180
                        1-GR 10-71 P. 651
                        1-ML 6-70 P. 3
                        1-ML 10-71 P. 9
    Divertimento in Bb for 2 Oboes, 2 Horns & 2 Bassoons,
    K 270
                    Danzi Quintett
                    ABC 67028
                    Hungarian Wind Quintet
                    Qualiton SLPX 11379
                        1-GR 6-69 P. 51
                        1-ML 5-69 P. 8
                        1-NR 6-70 P. 6
                    Philadelphia Woodwind Quintet
                    Columbia MS 6315
                        1-AR 8-62 P. 943
                        1-HF 7-62 P. 62
                        1-NR 7-62 P. 8
                        1-NYT 8-19-62 P. X10
                        2-SR 3-31-62 P. 44
            Brain, Dennis
                    Dennis Brain Wind Quintet
                    Bruno Walter Society IGI 370
                        4-HF 5-81 P. 64
                        1-NR 4-81 P. 7
                    Dennis Brain Wind Quintet
                    Seraphim M  60169
                        1-HF 7-71 P. 94
                        1-NR 7-71 P. 4
                        1-ST 9-71 P. 103
            Soeteman/Soeteman
                    Philips 6500 004
                        1-GR 7-70 P. 180
                        1-GR 10-71 P. 651
                        1-HF 10-71 P. 116
                        1-ML 7-70 P. 2
                        1-ML 10-71 P. 9
                        1-NR 10-71 P. 9

Mozart, W. A. (Cont'd)
    Divertimento for 2 Oboes, 2 Horns & 2 Bassoons,
    K 189
                    Danzi Quintett
                    ABC 67028
                    Philips 6500 003
                        1-GR 7-70 P. 180
                        1-GR 10-71 P. 651
                        1-ML 6-70 P. 3
                        1-ML 10-71 P. 9
    Fantasy, K 594
            Bonnevie, Robert
                    Soni Ventorum Wind Quintet
                    Lyrichord LLST 7168
    Fantasy in f, K 608
            Bonnevie, Robert
                    Soni Ventorum Wind Quintet
                    Lyrichord LLST 7168
    Fantasy, K 616
            Bonnevie, Robert
                    Soni Ventorum Wind Quintet
                    Lyrichord LLST 7168
    Minuet in D, K 594a = 355
                    Clarion Wind Quintet
                    Golden Crest CRS 4146
    Music from Die Entfuhrung aus dem Serail
            Soeteman/Peeters
                    Philips 6500 783
                        1-GR 1-75 P. 1349
                        1-HF 6-75 P. 100
                        1-ML 1-75 P. 6
                        1-NR 1-75 P. 8
                        1-ST 5-75 P. 97
    Music from Don Giovanni
            Soeteman/Peeters
                    Philips 6500 783
                        1-GR 1-75 P. 1349
                        1-HF 6-75 P. 100
                        1-ML 1-75 P. 6
                        1-NR 1-75 P. 8
                        1-ST 5-75 P. 97
    Quintet in Eb for Piano & Winds, K 452
    (Ob/Cl/Hn/Bsn/Pf)
                    Philadelphia Wind Quintet
                    CBS MP 38764
                    Berlin Philharmonic Ensemble
                    Denon 7009
                    Vienna Octet
                    London LLP 1609
                        3-AR 11-57 P. 110
                        1-GR 5-57 P. 451
                        2-MH 11/12-57 P. 53
                        1-ML 4-57 P. 8
                        2-NYT 2-16-58 P. X15
                    London STS 15059
                        1-AR 10-69 P. 133
                        1-LJ 1-70 P. 55

Mozart, W. A. (Cont'd)
    Quintet in Eb for Piano & Winds, K 452 (Cont'd)
            Seraphim M. 60368
                1-FF 7/8-82 P. 156
            Vienna Philharmonic Wind Group
            Westminister 50-07
                3-AR 8-50 P. 405
                2-GS 8-50 P. 7
                3-JR 7/8-50 P. 20
                2-LJ 9-1-50 P. 1421
                2-NA 3-31-51 P. 56
                3-SR 8-26-50 P. 56
        Barrows, John
            Orion 7281
                4-NR 10-72 P. 6
        Brain, Dennis
            Angel 35303
                1-AR 4-56 P. 137
                1-GR 1-56 P. 316
                1-HF 3-56 P. 67
                2-ML 1-56 P. 7
                1-MQ 4-56 P. 275
            Capitol G 7175
                1-AR 12-59 P. 265
                1-GR 2-55 P. 399
                1-HF 7-59 P. 53
                2-ML 2-55 P. 10
                1-NR 11-23-59 P. 22
                1-NYT 9-13-59 P. X21
            Seraphim 60073
                1-AU 10-68 P. 98
                2-HF 10-68 P. 140
                1-HSR 9-68 P. 102
                1-NR 9-68 P. 8
        Bujanovski, Vitali
            Melodiya D 016087-8
        Clevenger, Dale
            RCA ARL 1-3376
                2-NR 11-79 P. 7
                1-NYT 10-14-79 P. D27
        Coursier, Gilbert
            L'Oiseau Lyre LON 50016
                3-AR 5-54 P. 293
                3-CR 1-54 P. 74
                1-GR 2-54 P. 343
                2-HF 5-54 P. 50
                2-ML 1-54 P. 16
                2-NA 3-27-54 P. 267
        Devemy, Jean
            Mercury MG 10031
                2-AR 8-50 P. 405
                3-GR 3-53 P. 258
                1-GS 8-50 P. 7
                3-LJ 9-1-50
                3-NA 8-5-50 P. 134
                2-NR 12-50 P. 8

Mozart, W. A. (Cont'd)
    Quintet in Eb for Piano & Winds, K 452 (Cont'd)
        Huber, Sebastian
                Vox SVBX 548
                        2-NYT 4-3-66 P. X18
        Jones, Mason
                Columbia ML 4834
                        1-AR 4-54 P. 268
                        1-HF 6-54 P. 47
                        1-MA 4-54 P. 17
                        3-NA 3-27-54 P. 267
                        1-NYT 3-28-54 P. X8
        Kappy, David
                MHS 4375K
        Klein, Claus
                Cambridge CRM 817
                        2-AR 3-66 P. 638
                        2-CR 5-66 P. 18
                        2-HF 7-65 P. 76
                        1-NR 3-66 P. 6
                CCC 30
                Philips 6500 326
        Pandolfi
                Turnabout TVC 37013
                        1-AR 11-80 P. 27
                        2-FF 7/8-80 P. 115
                        1-NYT 5-4-80 P. D24
                        1-ST 9-80 P. 81
        Routch, Robert
                RCA A GL 1-4704
                        1-FF 9/10-83 P. 219
                        2-HF 2-84 P. 63
                RCA RL 1 2863
        Tarjani, Ferenc
                Hungaroton SLPX 11637
                        1-ML 10-74 P. 8
                Fidelio 3347
    Serenade # 10 in Bb,  K361
    (2 Ob/2 Cl/2 Bst Hn/4 Hn/2 Bsn/CBsn)
                Collegium Aureum Wind Ensemble
                BASF KHB 21414
                        1-MQ 4-74 P. 312
                        1-NR 9-73 P. 2
                        1-NYT 11-14-73 P. D33
                        1-ST 11-73 P. 122
        Routch/Rimon/ ? / ?
                Marlboro Recording Society MRS 11
        Soeteman/Soeteman/Meijer/Peeters
                Philips 6799 003
                Philips 839 734
                        1-HF 6-74 P. 90
                        1-HFN 12-72 P. 2443
                        2-NR 1-74 P. 5
                        1-NYT 1-27-74 P. D24
                        1-R&R 12-72 P. 70
        Wilson/Hearn/Jeffrey/Pattison
                Toronto Chamber Winds
                CRYS S 646

Mozart, W. A. (Cont'd)
      Serenade # 11 in Eb, K 375
            Brain/Sanders
                  PYE GSGC 14062
            Meijer/Peeters
                  Philips 802 907
      Serenade # 12 in c, K 388
            Brain/Sanders
                  PYE GSGC 14062
            Civil/Beers
                  London Wind Soloists
                  London CM 9348
                        1-GR 10-63 P. 186
                        2-ML 10-63 P. 3
            Meijers/Peeters
                  Philips 802 907
      Variations on "Ah, vous dirai je Maman"
            Clarion Wind Quintet
            Golden Crest CRS 4146
Muller, Peter (1791-1877)
      (3) Quintets for Winds
                  Richards Wind Quintet
                  CRYS S 252
                        2-NR 6-77 P. 7
Myslivecek, Josef (1737-1791)
      Octets # 1 & # 2
            Chavat/Brazda
                  Supraphon SUA 59763
Nielsen, Carl (1865-1931)
      Quintet in A for Winds, Op. 43 (1922)
                  Athena Ensemble
                  Chandos 1003
                  Copenhagen Wind Quintet
                  London LLP 734
                        3-AR 9-53 P. 22
                        1-CR 8-53 P. 20
                        3-GR 10-53 P. 133
                        1-GS 7-53 P. 8
                        2-ML 8-53 P. 5
                  Copenhagen Chamber Wind Quintet
                  Mercury MG 15046
                        4-SR 3-28-53 P. 48
                  Frosunda Quintet
                  BIS 136
                        2-ML 2-80 P. 9
                        1-NR 3-80 P. 8
                        1-ST 4-80 P. 136
                  Lark Woodwind Quintet
                  MHS 1004 Y
                  New Art Wind Quintet
                  Classic Edition 2001
                        4-GS 5-53 P. 1
                        4-HF 1/2-54 P. 58
                        1-LJ 8-54 P. 1392
                        1-MA 11-15-53 P. 18
                        1-NR 7-53 P. 8
                        1-NYT 4-19-53 P. X10

Nielsen, Carl (Cont'd)
    Quintet in A for Winds, Op. 43 (1922) (Cont'd)
             New York Woodwind Quintet
                CRI CS 254
                    2-AR 3-66 P. 638
                    1-HF 2-66 P. 91
                    2-NR 1-66 P. 7
             Philadelphia Woodwind Quintet
                Columbia ML 5441
                    1-AR 5-60 P. 714
                    1-HSR 5-60 P. 65
                    2-NR 4-60 P. 7
                    1-SR 3-26-60 P. 52
             Norwegian Wind Quintet
                Simax PS 1003
             Wind Quintet of 1932, Copenhagen
                Odeon MOAK 3 0004
        Brown, William
             Lark Woodwind Quintet
                Lyrichord LLST 7155
                    1-GR 11-66 P. 282
                    1-HF 8-66 P. 90
                    1-HSR 1-67 P. 86
                    1-NR 6-66 P. 2
        Creech, Robert
             CBC SM 139
        Guse, Allen
             Westwood Wind Quintet
                CRYS S 601
                    4-NR 3-69 P. 5
                    1-ST 4-69 P. 97
        Sanders, Neill
             Melos Ensemble
                Angel S 36538
                    1-GR 1-69 P. 1013
                    4-HA 6-69 P. 101
                    1-HF 5-69 P. 94
                    1-ML 2-69 P. 12
                    1-NR 4-69 P. 8
                    1-SR 2-22-69 P. 70
        Solis, Richard
             Mark MRS 5
                    1-HF 6-72 P. 88
                    1-ST 6-72 P. 86
                    1-HF 5-69 P. 94
                    1-ML 2-69 P. 12
                    1-NR 4-69 P. 8
                    1-SR 2-22-69 P. 70
Olsen, Sparre
    Quintett, Op. 35
             Philips 6507 011
Onslow, George (1784-1853)
    Quintet for Winds, Op. 81
             French Wind Quintet
                L'Oiseau Lyre-London 50049
                    1-CR 3-55 P. 137
                    2-GR 3-55 P. 446
                    4-HA 12-55 P. 111

Paganini, Niccolo (1782-1840)
    La Chasse
            Farkas, Philip
                    Chicago Symphony Woodwind Quintet
                    Audiophile Records AP 16
Pauer, Jiri (1919-    )
    Quintet (1961)
                    Pacific Arts Woodwind Quintet
                    Orion 79345
                        2-FF 7/8-80 P. 182
                        2-NR 6-80 P. 8
Perle, George (1915-    )
    Quintet # 3 (1967)
                    Clarion Woodwind Quintet
                    Golden Crest CRS 4191
                        1-AR 11-80 P. 49
                        2-FF 9/10-81 P. 278
                        1-NYT 4-27-80 P. D27
Persichetti, Vincent (1915-    )
    Pastoral for Winds, Op. 31 (1945)
                    New Art Wind Quintet
                    Classic Edition 2003
                        2-AR 5-54 P. 302
                        1-HF 7-54 P. 57
                        4-NYT 3-14-54 P. X8
                        4-SR 2-27-54 p. 71
Petrovics, Emil (1930-    )
    Wind Quintet (1964)
            Tarjani, Ferenc
                    Hungarian Wind Ensemble
                    Hungariton SLPX 11 630
                        1-ML 3-75 P. 7
                        2-NR 5-75 P. 9
Pierne, Gabriel (1863-1937)
    Pastorale, Op. 14 # 1
            Barrows, John
                    New York Woodwind Quintet
                    Everest EV 3092
Pierne, Paul (1874-1952)
    Suite Pittoresque, Op. 14
            Bujanovski, Vitali
                    Melodiya D 018529-30
Pijper, Willem (1894-1947)
    Quintet for Woodwinds (1929)
            Kittich, Eugene
                    CBC SM 186
Pillin, Boris (1940-    )
    Scherzo for Woodwind Quintet
                    Westwood Wind Quintet
                    CRYS S 811
                        1-NR 7-71 P. 13
    Serenade for Piano & Quintet
                    Westwood Wind Quintet
                    WIM R 11
                        2-NR 2-77 P. 6

Piston, Walter (1894-1976)
    Quintet (1956)
                    Boehm Quintette
                        Orion ORS 75206
                            1-NR 4-76 P. 7
                    Boston Woodwind Quintet
                        Boston 407
                            1-AR 10-58 P. 132
                            1-HF 11-58 P. 84
                            4-MA 12-1-58 P. 36
                            2-NYT 10-5-18 P. X21
Pleyel, Ignace (1757-1831)
    Serenade # 1 in F (2 Ob/2 Cl/2 Hn/2 Bsn)
                        MHS 42€9H
    Sextet in Eb for 2 Clarinets, 2 Horns & 2 Bassoons
                        MHS 4269H
    (3) Sextets for 2 Clarinets, 2 Horns & 2 Bassoons
                        Consortium Classicum
                        MHS 3024
Poot, Marcel (1901-    )
    Concertino for Wind Quintet (1958)
                    Leningrad State Philharmonic
                    Wind Quintet
                        WGS 8322
                            1-NR 10-76 P. 7
Poulenc, Francis (1899-1963)
    Sextet for Piano & Winds (Pf/Fl/Ob/Cl/Hn/Bsn)
                        BIS 61
                        RCA LSC 6189
                        TVS 34507
                            1-HF 9-73 P. 120
                            1-NR 9-73 P. 9
                    Fine Arts Wind Players
                        Capitol P 8258
                            1-AR 7-54 P. 374
                            1-CR 11-54 P. 73
                            1-GR 1-55 P. 354
                            2-HA 9-54 P. 110
                            1-HF 8-54 P. 44
                    Netherlands Philharmonic Wind Quintet
                        Concert Hall H 15
                    New York Woodwind Quintet
                        Nonesuch D 79045
                            1-AR 1-84 P. 70
                            1-FF 9/10-83 P. 235
                            2-NR 8-83 P. 4
                            3-NYT 1-15-84 P. 1126
                            1-ST 11-83 P. 85
                    Paris Wind Quintet
                        Angel 36261
                            1-HF 8-65 P. 77
                            2-HSR 10-65 P. 102
                            1-NR 8-65 P. 9
                            1-SR 6-26-65 P. 60

Poulenc, Francis (Cont'd)
    Sextet for Piano & Winds (Cont'd)
                    Philadelphia Woodwind Quintet
                        Columbia ML 5918
                            1-AR 3-64 P. 622
                            1-HF 2-64 P. 75
                            1-HSR 2-64 P. 82
                            1-MA 1-64 P. 61
                            1-NYT 11-10-63 P. X14
                Barrows, John
                    New York Woodwind Quintet
                        Concert Disc CS 221
                            1-HF 9-61 P. 99
                            1-HSR 10-61 P. 90
                            1-NR 7-61 P. 9
                Buddle, Anthony
                    Sydney Wind Quintet
                        Cherry Pie LA 07899
                Bujanovski, Vitali
                        Melodiya C 0751
                Klein
                        Robert E. Blake 7
                            1-AR 12-51 P. 120
                            2-GS 11-51 P. 7
                            4-LJ 2-21-52 P. 205
                            2-NR 9-52 P. 10
                            1-NYT 2-17-52 P. X10
Powell, Mel (1923-    )
    Divertimento for 5 Winds (1956)
                    Fairfield Wind Ensemble
                    CRI 121
                            4-AR 8-58 P. 496
                            1-HF 5-58 P. 54
                            1-MH 7/8-58 P. 28
                            4-MQ 7-58 P. 408
                            4-NYT 5-18-58 P. X15
                            2-SR 3-29-58 P. 46
Purcell/Wilder
    Pavane
                    New York Woodwind Quintet
                    Golden Crest GC 3019
                            2-HF 11-57 P. 82
                            4-LJ 8-58 P. 2149
Ravel, Maurice (1875-1937)
    Le Tombeau de Couperin
                    Camerata Woodwind Quintet
                    Coronet 3040
    Piece en Forme de Habanera
                Farkas, Philip
                    Chicago Symphony Woodwind Quintet
                    Audiophile Records AP 16
Reicha, Anton (1770-1836)
    Three Andantes
                Van Woudenberg, Adriaan
                    Danzi Quintet
                        Philips 839 703 Ly

Reicha, Anton (1770-1836) (Cont'd)
 Quintet in Ab, Op. 2
     Southwest German Radio Wind Quintet
      Mace M 9034
       1-NR 3-67 P. 8
 Quintet in e, Op. 88 # 1
     Ars Nova Woodwind Quintet
      MHS 4120
       2-FF 5/6-80 P. 137
     Soni Ventorum Wind Quintet
      MHS 3247
   Berenek, Rudolph
     Reicha Wind Quintet
      Supraphon 59663
       1-AR 11-67 P. 236
       1-NR 7-67 P. 9
 Quintet in Eb, Op. 88 # 1
     Eichendorff Wind Quintet
      Baroque (Canada) 2869
       2-NR 12-67 P. 10
 Quintet in Eb, Op. 88 # 2
     Ars Nova Woodwind Quintet
      MHS 4120
       2-FF 5/6-80 P. 137
     Boston Woodwind Quintet
      Boston 407
       1-AR 10-58 P. 132
       1-HF 11-58 P. 84
       4-MA 12-1-58 P. 36
       2-NYT 10-5-58 P. X21
     French Wind Quintet
      L'Oiseau Lyre-London 50019
       1-CR 2-54 P. 89
       1-GR 2-54 P. 343
       1-ML 2-54 P. 15
       4-SR 7-28-56 P. 42
     New Art Wind Quintet
      Classic Edition 2010
       2-AR 3-53 P. 229
       1-GS 12-52 P. 5
       1-NR 7-53 P. 8
       1-NYT 1-18-53 P. X19
     Philadelphia Woodwind Quintet
      Columbia MS 6315
       1-AR 8-62 P. 943
       1-HF 7-62 P. 62
       1-NR 7-62 P. 8
       1-NYT 8-19-62 P. X10
       2-SR 3-31-62 P. 44
     Wind Group of VSO
      Music Guild 118
       1-AR 12-64 P. 359
       2-AR 8-65 P. 1178
       1-HF 10-64 P. 158
       2-NR 7-64 P. 6

Reicha, Anton (Cont'd)
    Quintet in Eb, Op. 88 # 2 (Cont'd)
            Arnold, Karl
                    Southwest German Radio Wind Quintet
                    Mace M 9034
                            1-NR 3-67 P. 8
            Smith
                    Pasadena Chamber Orchestra Members
                    WIM 22
    Quintet in G, Op. 88 # 3
                    Ars Nova Woodwind Quintet
                    MHS 4448
                    Soni Ventorum Wind Quintet
                    MHS 3247
    Quintet in d, Op. 88 # 4
                    Ars Nova Woodwind Quintet
                    MHS 4448
                    Soni Ventorum Wind Quintet
                    MHS 3248
    Finale from Quintet for Winds in Eb
            Barrows, John
                    New York Woodwind Quintet
                    Everest EV 3092
    Quintet in C, Op. 91 # 1
                    Winds of Berlin Philharmonic Orchestra
                    DGG 2530 077
                            2-HF 4-71 P. 114
                            1-NR 3-71 P. 3
    Quintet in D, Op. 91 # 3
                    Czech Wind Quintet
                    Supraphon 111 1084
                            1-GR 3-74 P. 1712
                            2-ML 1-74 P. 7
                            1-NR 10-73 P. 7
                    French Wind Quintet
                    L'Oiseau Lyre-London 50019
                            1-CR 2-54 P. 89
                            1-GR 2-54 P. 343
                            1-ML 2-54 P. 15
                            4-SR 7-28-56 P. 42
    Quintet in A, Op. 91 # 5
                    Academia Quintet
                    Supraphon 1111 3027
                            3-FF 7/8-83 P. 210
                            2-GR 2-83 P. 936
                            3-NR 6-83 P. 7
            Berenek, Rudolph
                    Reicha Wind Quintet
                    Supraphon 59663
                            1-AR 11-67 P. 236
                            1-NR 7-67 P. 9
    Quintet in Bb, Op. 91 # 5
                    Resident Munich Quintet
                    Claves D 611
    Quintet in c, Op. 91 # 6
                    Soni Ventorum Wind Quintet
                    MHS 3248

Reicha, Anton (Cont'd)
     Quintet in f, Op. 99 # 2
                         Richards Wind Quintet
                         MHS 3758
                             2-FF 9/10-78 P. 97
     Quintet in G, Op. 99 #6
                         Danzi Quintet
                         Philips World Series PHC 9136
                             1-NR 4-70 P. 8
     Quintet in e, Op. 100 # 4
                         Soni Ventorum Wind Quintet
                         Lyrichord LLST 7216
                             1-NR 5-70 P. 6
             Coursier, Gilbert
                         L'Oiseau Lyre OLLD 23 (10" LP)
     Quintet in Bb, Op. 100 # 6
                         Richards Wind Quintet
                         MHS 3758
                             2-FF 9/10-78 P. 97
Riegger, Wallingford (1885-1961)
     Concerto for Piano & Woodwing Quintet, Op. 53 (1952)
                         New Art Wind Quintet
                         CRI 130
                             4-SR 5-28-60 P. 66
             Barrows, John
                         New York Woodwind Quintet
                         Concert Disc 221
                             1-HF 9-61 P. 99
                             1-HSR 10-61 P. 90
                             1-NR 7-61 P. 9
     Woodwind Quintet, Op. 51
                         New Art Wind Quintet
                         Classic Edition 2003
                             2-AR 5-54 P. 302
                             1-HF 7-54 P. 57
                             4-NYT 3-14-54 P. X8
                             4-SR 2-27-54 P. 71
Rieti, Vittorio (1898-    )
     Silograffe for Wind Quintet
                         Ariel Wind Quintet
                         Serenus SRS 12063
                             1-NR 4-76 P. 15
Rimsky-Korsakov, Nikolai (1844-1908)
     Quintet in Bb (Fl/Cl/Hn/Bsn/Pf)
                         Everest 3466
                             2-FF 5/6-80 P. 138
                             2-NR 5-80 P. 6
             Afanasiev, Boris
                         Melodiya D 021321/32
             Freiberg, Gottfried von
                         Westminister 50-19
                             1-GS 12-50 P. 3
                             4-LJ 3-15-57 P. 542
             Linder, Albert
                         BIS 44
                             1-HFN 11-77 P. 167
                             2-MM 9-78 P. 28
                             1-R&R 11-77 P. 74

Rimsky-Korsakov, Nikolai (Cont'd)
    Quintet in Bb (Cont'd)
        Tombock, Wolfgang
            Decca SDD 389
                1-GR 12-73 P. 1218
                2-R&R 1-74 P. 52
Romanovsky, Erich
    Blaserquintet (1968)
        Nitch, Herwig
            Preiser Records Pr 3174
Ropartz, Guy (1864-1955)
    (2) Pieces (1920)
            Boehm Quintette
            Orion ORS 78291
                2-NR 12-78 P. 8
            Boston Woodwind Quintet
            Boston 407
                1-AR 10-58 P. 132
                1-HF 11-58 P. 84
                4-MA 12-1-58 P. 36
                2-NYT 10-5-58 P. X21
            Paris Wind Quintet
            4-Ades 7084/7
Rorich, Carl
    Finale aus dem Blaserquintett, Op. 58
Rosenberg, Hilding (1892-    )
    Quintet for Winds (1959)
        Bengtsson, Rolf
            Caprice Riks LP 21
Rosetti-Rossler
    Quintet in Eb
            Czech Wind Quintet
            Supraphon 111 1084
                1-GR 3-74 P. 1712
                2-ML 1-74 P. 7
                1-NR 10-73 P. 7
        Arnold, Karl
            Southwest German Radio Wind Quintet
            Mace M 9034
                1-NR 3-67 P. 8
Ross, Walter (1935-    )
    Divertimento for Woodwind Quintet (1974)
            Clarion Woodwind Quintet
            Golden Crest CRS 4191
                1-AR 11-80 P. 49
                2-FF 9/10-81 P. 278
                1-NYT 4-27-80 P. D27
Rossini, Gioacchino (1792-1868)
    (6) Quartets # 1, 2, 3, 4, 5, & 6 (Hn/Fl/Cl/Bsn)
            New Art Quintet
            Classic 1010
                2-AR 8-52 P. 369
                2-GS 7-52 P. 5
                2-HF 11/12-52 P. 55
                1-MA 12-1-53 P. 19

Rossini, Gioacchino (Cont'd)
    (6) Quartets # 1, 2, 3, 4, 5, & 6 (Cont'd)
            Barrows, John
                New York Wind Quintet
                Dover 5214
    Quartets # 1, 4, 5, & 6 (Hn/Fl/Cl/Bsn)
            Barrows, John
                Period 737
                    1-HF 4-58 P. 62
                    1-LJ 8-58 P. 2149
                    3-NRE 4-14-58 P. 22
            Coursier, Gilbert
                MHS 0618F
                    1-CR 9-66 P. 27
                    1-HF 4-66 P. 110
    Quartets # 2 & 5 (Hn/Fl/Cl/Bsn)
                Quattor a Vent de Paris
                Concert Hall D 13
    Quartet # 2 (Hn/Fl/Cl/Bsn)
            Van Woudenberg, Adriaan
                Philips 839 703 LY
    Quartet # 3 (Hn/Fl/Cl/Bsn)
            Bujanovski, Vitali
                Melodiya D 13770
    Quartet # 4 (Hn/Fl/Cl/Bsn)
            Philadelphia Wind Quintet
                CSP AMS 6799
    Quartet # 6 (Hn/Fl/Cl/Bsn)
                Philips World Series PHC 9136
Roussel, Albert (1869-1937)
    Divertimento, Op. 6 (1906)
                Vienna Symphony Woodwinds
                Westminister XWN 19097
                    2-HF 8-63 P. 83
                    1-HSR 10-65 P. 100
                    2-SR 5-29-65 P. 56
             Paris Wind Quintet
                4 Ades 7084/7
             Los Angeles Wind Quintet
                Orion 7263
                    1-AR 4-72 P. 374
                    2-NR 3-72 P. 7
            Bujanovski, Vitali
                Melodiya D 13019-20
Rubinstein, Anton (1829-1894)
    Quintet in F, Op. 55 (Fl/Cl/Hn/Bsn/Pf)
                Everest 3466
                    2-FF 5/6-80 P. 138
                    2-NR 5-80 P. 6
Russell, Armand (1932-    )
    Suite Concertante for Tuba & Woodwind Quintet
                CRYS S 120
                    4-AU 5-84 P. 103
                    4-FF 3/4-84 P. 320
                    4-NR 3-84 P. 6

Salmenhaara, Erkki (1941-    )
     Quintet for Winds
               Linder, Albert
                    Gothenburg Quintet
                         BIS LP 24
                              4-GR 3-77 P. 1457
Scherman, R. W. (1921-    )
     Quintessant (1963)
               Hennigar, Harcus
                    York Winds
                         Centrediscs CMC 0482
                    York Winds
                         Centrediscs WRC 1-2304 (Canadian)
Schmitt, Florent (1870-1958)
     Chants Alizes, Op. 125 for Wind Quintet
                    Paris Wind Quintet
                         4-Ades 7084/7
Schoenberg, Arnold (1874-1951)
     Quintet for Wind Instruments, Op. 26 (1924)
                    Columbia ML 5217
                         2-AR 2-58 P. 260
                         1-HF 2-58 P. 60
                         1-HMR 3-58 P. 67
                         4-NR 1-58 P. 10
                         1-NYT 12-15-57 P. X19
                         2-SR 11-30-57 P. 62
                    Wergo WER 60032
                    Metropolitan Wind Ensemble
                    Dial 13
                         2-SR 9-29-51 P. 61
                    Oberlin Woodwind Quintet
                         Gasparo 204 CX
               Berges, Michel
                    (French) CBS S 75 552
               Duke, David
                    Westwood Wind Quintet
                    Columbia M2S 762
                         2-HF 9-67 P. 92
                         1-HSR 10-67 P. 108
                         2-NR 8-67 P. 14
                         1-SR 8-26-67 P. 78
               Johns, Michael
                    New England Conserv. Chamber Players
                    Crest/NEC 102
                         1-NR 6-73 P. 8
               Van Woudenberg, Adriaan
                    Danzi Quintet
                    Philips PHC 9068
                         2-HF 9-67 P. 92
                         1-NR 12-67 P. 9
Schulhoff, Erwin (1894-1942)
     Divertissement (1926)
                    Westwood Wind Quintet
                    CRYS S 101

Schuller, Gunther (1925-    )
    Quintet (1958)
                    Dorian Quintet
                    3 Vox SVBX 5307
                        1-AR 12-77 P. 51
                        1-FF 1-78 P. 73
                        1-HF 12-77 P. 110
                        1-NR 11-77 P. 8
            Barrows, John
                New York Woodwind Quintet
                Concert Disc CS 229
                        1-HF 11-63 P. 83
                        1-HSR 12-63 P. 78
                        2-NR 10-63 P. 7
                        1-NYT 1-26-64 P. X18
    Suite (1945)
            Bujanovski, Vitali
                    Melodiya D 018529-30/CM 02321-22
    Suite (1957)
                    Pacific Arts Woodwind Quintet
                    Orion 79345
                        2-FF 7/8-80 P. 182
                        2-NR 6-80 P. 8
Schultz, Svend S. (1913-    )
    Little Serenade for Wind Quintet (1945)
                    Copenhagen Chamber Wind Quintet
                    Mercury MG 15046
                        4-SR 3-28-53 P. 48
Schwartz, Elliott (1936-    )
    Interruptions (1964)
                    University of Oregon Woodwind Quintet
                    Advent Adv 11
Seeger, Ruth Crawford (1901-1953)
    Suite for Wind Quintet (1952)
                    Lark Quintet
                    CRI USD 249
                        4-NR 3-70 P. 6
                        1-ST 6-70 P. 84
Seiber, Matyas (1904-1960)
    Permutazioni a cinque (1958)
                    Taffanel Wind Quintet
                    Denon & Denon/PCM OX 7217-ND
                        2-FF 11/12-81 P. 295
            Civil, Alan
                London Wind Quintet
                ARGO ZRG 5326
                        1-GR 2-63 P. 391
                        1-HF 8-64 P. 88
                        1-ML 1-63 P. 10
                        1-NR 8-64 P. 5
                        1-NYT 5-24-64 P. X18
Somis, Giovanni Battista (1686-1763)
    Adagio & Allegro
            Farkas, Philip
                    Chicago Symphony Woodwind Quintet
                    Audiophile Records AP 16

Sowerby, Leo (1895-1968)
    Pop Goes the Weasel (1927)
                    Westwood Wind Quintet
                    CRYS S 101
Spohr, Ludwig (1784-1859)
    Quintet in c for Flute, Clarinet, Horn, Bassoon
    & Piano
                    Nash Ensemble
                    CRD 1099; 4099
                    Resident Munich Quintet
                    Claves D 8101
                        1-GR 6-81 P. 48
            Howard, Howard
                    Turnabout 34506
                        1-HF 9-73 P. 109
                        2-NR 9-73 P. 9
                        1-ST 10-73 P. 87
Stamitz, Carl (1745-1800)
    Quartet in Eb for Horn, Oboe, Clarinet & Bassoon,
    Op. 8 # 2
                    Berlin Philharmonic Orchestra Winds
                    DG 2530 077
                        2-HF 4-71 P. 114
                        1-NR 3-71 P. 3
                    Czech Wind Quintet
                    Supraphon 111 1084
                        1-GR 3-74 P. 1712
                    Eichendorff Wind Group
                    MHS 0528H
                    Resident Munich Quintet
                    Claves D 611
                        1-HFN 5-77 P. 121
                        1-HFN 4-78 P. 129
                        3-R&R 4-77 P. 66
                        1-R&R 3-78 P. 49
            Van Woudenberg, Adriaan
                    Philips 839 703 LY
    Quintet in Eb, Op. 8 # 2
                    New Art Wind Quintet
                    Classic Edition 2010
                        2-AR 3-53 P. 229
                        1-GS 12-52 P. 5
                        1-NR 7-53 P. 8
                        1-NYT 1-18-53 P. X19
    7 Serenades for 2 Flutes,
    2 Horns & Bassoon
                    Eichendorff Wind Group
                    MHS 524
                        1-AR 1-64 P. 419
                        1-HF 5-64 P. 78
Stearns, Peter Pindar (1931-    )
    Quintet for Winds (1966)
                    Dorian Woodwind Quintet
                    CRI SD 318
                        4-NR 8-74 P. 6

241

Stein, Hermann (1915-     )
    Sour Suite for Woodwind Quintet
                        Westwood Wind Quintet
                        CRYS S 811
                            1-NR 7-71 P. 13
Stein, Leon (1910-     )
    Sextet for Alto Saxophone & Woodwind Quintet
                        Westwood Wind Quintet
                        CRYS S 154
Stockhausen, Karlheinz (1928-     )
    Adieu for Wind Quintet (1966)
                        DG 2530443 PSI
                            1-GR 6-75 P. 50
                            4-ML 4-75 P. 3
Strauss, Richard (1864-1949)
    Serenade, Op. 7 in Eb (1884)
    (2 Ob/2 Bst Hn/4 Hn/2 Bsn/C Bsn)
            Meijer/Peeters/Soeteman/Soeteman
                        Netherlands Wind Ensemble
                        Philips 6500 097
                            1-AU 12-72 P. 89
                            1-GR 12-71 P. 1049
                            1-HF 11-72 P. 96
                            1-ML 12-71 P. 10
                            1-ST 12-72 P. 138
        Sonatina # 1 in F (1943)
        (2Fl/2Ob/3Cl/Bst Hn/BCl/4 Hn/2Bsn/CBsn)
                Soeteman/Peeters/Meijer/van Vliet
                        Philips 6500 297
                            1-AU 12-73 P. 84
                            1-GR 10-72 P. 707
                            1-HF 1-74 P. 80
                            1-ML 10-72 P. 11
                            1-ST 11-73 P. 127
    Suite in Bb, Op. 4 (1884)
    (2 Ob/2 Cl/2 Bst Hn/2 Fl/4 Hn/2 Bsn/Cbsn)
                Soeteman/Peeters/Meijer/van Vliet
                        Philips 6500 297
                            1-AU 12-73 P. 84
                            1-GR 10-72 P. 707
                            1-HF 1-74 P. 80
                            1-ML 10-72 P. 11
                            1-ST 11-73 P. 127
Stravinsky, Igor (1882-1971)
    Pastorale (1908)
                        Oberlin Faculty Woodwind Quintet
                        Coronet S 1408
                            1-HF 1-70 P. 126
                            1-NR 10-69 P. 7
Sweelinck, J. P. (1562-1621)
    Variation on a Folksong
                        Cambini Wind Quintet
                        Coronet 3060
                Barrows, John
                        New York Woodwind Quintet
                        Everest EV 3092

242

Sydeman, William (1928-    )
    Quintet # 2 (1959-61)
                 University of Oregon Woodwind Quintet
                 Advent Adv 11
Taffanel, Paul (1844-1908)
    Quintet pour Instruments au vent
                 Camerata Woodwind Quintet
                 Coronet 3040
                 New York Woodwind Quintet
                 Counterpoint 505
                     1-HSR 10-65 P. 109
                 New York Woodwind Quintet
                 Esoteric 505
                     1-AR 12-51 P. 118
                     4-GS 10-51 P. 9
                     1-SR 8-25-51 P. 50
                 Paris Wind Quintet
                 4 Ades 7084/7
    Quintet in g (1882)
                 New York Woodwind Quintet
                 CRI CS 222
                     1-AR 10-61 P. 114
                     4-HF 10-61 P. 102
                     1-HSR 10-61 P. 82
                     1-NR 7-61 P. 9
                 Soni Ventorum Wind Quintet
                 CRYS S 253
                     1-CR 1-79 P. 43
                     1-FF 1/2-79 P. 109
                     1-NR 9-78 P. 7
    Quintet (1880)
          Barrows, John
                 New York Woodwind Quintet
                 Everest EV 3080; 6080
                     1-CR 11-63 P. 27
                     1-HF 2-64 P. 89
                     1-HSR 12-63 P. 82
                     2-NR 10-63 P. 7
Tang, Jordon (1948-    )
    A Little Suite (1972)
                 Clarion Woodwind Quintet
                 Golden Crest CRS 4191
                     1-AR 11-80 P. 49
                     2-FF 9/19-81 P. 278
                     1-NYT 4-27-80 P. D27
Telemann/Hinnenthal (1681-1767)
    Overture from Suite in D
                 Boston Woodwind Quintet
                 Boston 407
                     1-AR 10-58 P. 132
                     1-HF 11-58 P. 84
                     4-MA 12-1-58 P. 36
                     2-NYT 10-5-58 P. X21

Telemann, Georg Philipp
        Overture Suite for 2 Oboes, 2 Horns & Bassoon (1733)
                Freund/Sungler
                        MHS 0528H
                                1-AR 3-64 P. 627
            Suite for Horns, Oboes & Bassoons
                        MHS 4505
                                1-FF 9/10-82 P. 232
Thomas, Andrew (1939-    )
        2 Studies for Woodwind Quintet
                        Opus One 8
Thuille, Ludwig (1861-1901)
        Sextet for Piano & Wind Instruments
                        Los Angeles Wind Quintet
                        Orion 7263
                                1-AR 4-72 P. 374
                                2-NR 3-72 P. 7
            Sextet in Bb, Op. 6 (1887)
            (WW Quintet & Piano)
                        Boston 410
                                1-AR 1-59 P. 343
                                1-HF 2-59 P. 74
                                1-HMR 12-58 P. 94
                                2-NYT 10-19-58 P. X19
Tomasi, H. (1901-    )
        Variations on a Corsican Theme
                        French Wind Quintet
                        L'Oiseau Lyre 50122
                                4-AR 1/2-57 P.77
                                1-GR 9-56 P. 128
                                1-ML 9-56 P. 8
                                1-SR 12-29-56 P. 42
Turner, Robert (1920-    )
        Serenade for Woodwind Quintet (1960)
                Creech, Robert
                        CBC SM 139
Valen, Olav Fartein
        Serenade, Op. 42
                        Philips 839 248 AY
Van Vactor, David (1906-    )
        Music for Woodwinds
                Neudecker/Vollman
                        Orion ORS 7025
                                2-NR 11-70 P. 7
        Scherzo
                Barrows, John
                        New York Woodwind Quintet
                        Everest EV 3092
Villa-Lobos, Heitor (1887-1959)
        Quintet en forme de Choros (1928; rev. 1953)
                        New Art Wind Quintet
                        Westminister 53 60
                                1-AR 5-55 P. 310
                                1-GR 7-55 P. 59
                                4-HF 4-55 P. 64
                                1-MH 3/4-55 P. 29
                                2-ML 8-55 P. 9
                                4-SR 5-14-55 P. 33

Villa-Lobos, Heitor (Cont'd)
 Quintet en forme de Choros
    New Art Wind Quintet
     Westminister W 9071
       1-AR 10-64 P. 148
       3-LJ 3-1-65 P. 1105
       4-NR 1-65 P. 6
    New York Woodwind Quintet
     CRI CS 254
       2-AR 3-66 P. 638
       1-HF 2-66 P. 91
       2-NR 1-66 P. 7
    New York Woodwind Quintet
     Philharmonia 110
       1-AR 12-55 P. 67
       4-AU 1-56 P. 45
       4-HF 12-55 P. 84
    Soni Ventorum Wind Quintet
     Lyrichord LLST 7168
    Woodwind Arts Quintet
     Orion 73123
       1-NR 11-73 P. 6
   Barrows, John
    New York Woodwind Quintet
     Nonesuch H 71030
       4-AR 2-65 P. 502
       1-GR 8-65 P. 105
       2-ML 5-65 P. 8
   Bonnevie, Robert
     Lyrichord Ll 168
       -1-AU 4-65 P. 8
       4-NR 3-65 P. 8
   Bujanovski, Vitali
     Melodiya CM 02249-50
Washburn, Robert (1928-    )
 Quintet for Winds (1971)
    Wisconsin Arts Quintet
     Redwood ES 16
Weait, Christopher (1939-    )
 The Jolly Raftsmen (1971)
   Hennigar, Harcus
    York Winds
    Era 105
Weber, Ben (1916-1979)
 Consort of Winds Op. 66 (1974)
    Boehm Quintette
     Orion ORS 75206
       1-NR 4-76 P. 7
Weber, Carl Maria Von (1786-1826)
 Adagio & Rondo in Eb for 2 Clarinets,
 2 Horns & 2 Bassoons
    Van Woudenberg/Soeteman
     MHS 834383
     Pro Arte PAL 1073
       2-FF 5/6-83 P. 250

Weinzweig, John (1913-    )
     Woodwood Quintet
          Rittich, Eugene
               CBC SM 218
White, Donald H. (1921-    )
     3 for 5
               American Woodwind Quintet
                    Golden Crest GC S 4075
                         4-NR 8-66 P. 5
Whittenberg, Charles (1927-1984)
     Games of 5, Op. 44 (1968)
               Connecticut University Wind Quintet
                    Serenus SRS 12028
               University of Oregon Woodwind Quintet
                    Advent Adv 11
Wilder, Alec (1907-1980)
     Quintet # 1 (Up Tempo)
          Barrows, John
               New York Woodwind Quintet
                    Everest EV 3092
     Quintet for Woodwinds
               New York Woodwind Quintet
                    Philharmonia 110
                         1-AR 12-55 P. 67
                         4-AU 1-56 P. 45
                         4-HF 12-55 P. 84
     Quintet # 2 (1956)
               New York Woodwind Quintet
                    Golden Crest GC 3019
                         2-HF 11-57 P. 82
                         4-LJ 8-58 P. 2149
          Barrows, John
               New York Woodwind Quintet
                    Golden Crest GC 4028
     Quintet # 3
          Barrows, John
               New York Woodwind Quintet
                    Concert Disc CS 223
                         4-HF 9-61 P. 104
                         4-NR 7-61 P. 9
                         1-SR 10-28-61 P. 48
     Quintet # 4 (1958)
          Barrows, John
               New York Woodwind Quintet
                    Concert Disc CS 223
                         4-HF 9-61 P. 104
                         4-NR 7-61 P. 9
                         1-SR 10-28-61 P. 48
     Quintet # 6 (1960)
          Barrows, John
               New York Woodwind Quintet
                    Concert Disc CS 223
                         4-HF 9-61 P. 104
                         4-NR 7-61 P. 9
                         1-SR 10-28-61 P. 48

Wilder, Alec (Cont'd)
    Quintet # 11
                    Wingra Quintet
                        Golden Crest GC 4150
    Sextet for Marimba & Wind Quintet (1977)
                    Clarion Wind Quintet
                        Golden Crest GC 4190
    Sketches of "The World's Most Beautiful Girls"
                    New York Woodwind Quintet
                        Golden Crest GC 4208
    Suite for Woodwinds (1956)
                    New York Woodwind Quintet
                        Golden Crest GC 3019
                            2-HF 11-57 P. 82
                            4-LJ 8-58 P. 2149
                Barrows, John
                    New York Woodwind Quintet
                        Golden Crest GC 4028
Witt, Friedrich (1770-1837)
    Quintet in Eb for Piano & Winds,
    Op. 6 (Ob/Cl/Hn/Bsn/Pf)
            Meyendorf, Werner
                            1-FF 11/12-83 P. 247
Zador, Eugene (1894-1977)
    Wind Quintet (1972)
                    Los Angeles Wind Quintet
                        Orion ORS 73126
                            1-CR 5-74 P. 36
                            2-NR 10-73 P. 6
Zaninelli, Luigi (1932-    )
    Dance Variations
                    American Woodwind Quintet
                        Golden Crest GC S 4075
                            4-NR 8-66 P. 5

# Mixed Ensemble

Amram, David (1930-    )
    Shakespearean Concerto (2 Hn/Ob/Stg) (1959)
        Barrows/Cowan
            Washington 470
                4-AM 5-67 P. 122
                1-NR 4-67 P. 6
        Miranda/Howard
            RCS VCS 7089
                1-HF 4-72 P. 78
                1-NR 2-72 P. 2
                4-NYT 3-12-72
                4-ST 5-72 P. 71
    Triple Concerto for Woodwind
    & Brass Jazz Quintets & Orchestra
        Amram, David
            Flying Fish GRO 751
            RCA RAL 1 0459
                2-AU 11-74 P. 92
                2-NR 5-74 P. 7
Andriessen, Juriaan
    Movementi for Hn, Tpt, Trb, Pc & Stg
        Donemus DAVS 6602
Anonymous
    Intradas in D (2 Tpt/2 Hn/Tmp/2 Org)
        Penzel/Seifert
            DG Privilege 2535 362
                4-FF 5/6-80 P. 195
                1-NR 4-80 P. 8
Babbitt, Milton
    Paraphrases for Winds, Brass & Piano (1979)
        CRI S 499
Bach, C. P. E. (1714-1788)
    Concerto for Harpsichord
    (Hammer Klavier/2 Fl/2 Hn/Stg)
        Holden/Holden
            Leonhardt Consort/
            Concentus Musicus
            Telefunken SAWT 9490
                1-AR 3-69 P. 554
                2-GR 6-67 P. 8
                1-ML 5-67 P. 5
                2-NR 2-69 P. 8

Bach, J. C. (1735-1782)
    Concerto for Oboes, 2 Horns & Strings in F
        Holden/Holden
                Leonhardt Consort/Concentus Musicus
                    Telefunken SAWT 9490
                        1-AR 3-69 P. 554
                        2-GR 6-67 P. 8
                        1-ML 5-67 P. 5
                        2-NR 2-69 P. 8
                        2-NYT 11-3-68 P. D25
    Sextet in C (Ob/2 Hn/Vn/Vc/Hpscd)
        Oheim /Wunder
                Music Guild S 14
                        2-HF 4-62 P. 63
                        1-HSR 10-62 P. 70
                        1-NR 6-62 P. 4
    Six Favourite Overtures in 7 Parts
    (Vns/Obs/Hns/Vc Hpsichd)
        Hogwood
                Academy of Ancient Music
                    L'Oiseau-Lyre DSLO 525
                        1-FF 11/12-78 P. 11
                        1-GR 5-78 P. 1851
                        1-ML 4-78 P. 2
Bach, W. F. (1710-1784)
    Concerto (2 Hpscd/2 Tpt/2 Hn/Tp/Stg)
        Holden/Holden
                 Leonhardt Consort/Concentus Musicus
                    Telefunken SAWT 9490
                        1-AR 3-69 P. 554
                        2-GR 6-67 P. 8
                        1-ML 5-67 P. 5
                        2-NR 2-69 P. 8
                        2-NYT 11-3-68 P. D25
Bach, W. F. E.
    Sextet in Eb (Cl/2 Hn/Vn/Va/Vc)
                    Melodiya CM 01901-02
                    Zimbler Sinfonietta
                    Boston B 405
                        1-AM 2-57 P. 91
                        2-HF 3-57 P. 61
                        1-MH 3/4-57 P. 41
                        2-NYT 2-19-57 P. X16
                        1-SR 1-26-57 P. 46
        Shapiro/Meek
                    Boston BST 1006
                        1-AR 8-59 P. 838
                        1-AU 5-59 P. 51
                        1-SR 8-29-59 P. 40
Beethoven, L. Van (1770-1837)
    Septet in Eb, Op. 20 (Cl/Bsn/Hn/Vn/Va/Vc/Db)
                    Barylli String Ensemble/
                    Vienna Philharmonic Wind Group
                    Westminister 18003
                        1-AR 8-55 P. 401
                        2-HF 11-55 P. 52
                        2-NR 2-56 P. 7

Beethoven, L. Van (Cont'd)
        Septet in Eb, Op. 20 (Cont'd)
                        Berlin Philharmonic Octet
                        Decca DL 9934
                                2-AR 11-57 P. 96
                                1-GR 4-57 P. 413
                                2-HA 1-58 P. 94
                                2-HF 2-58 P. 52
                                2-ML 4-57 P. 7
                                1-NR 12-57 P. 4
                        Berlin Philharmonic Octet
                        Philips 6500 543
                                2-GR 8-74 P. 370
                                1-RR 7-74 P. 49
                        Consortium Classicum
                        MHS 1062
                                1-GR 2-70 P. 1288
                                2-ML 1-70 P. 6
                        Fine Arts Quartet/
                        New York Woodwind Quintet
                        Concert Disc CS 214
                                1-AR 2-61 P. 474
                                1-NR 4-61 P. 6
                                1-SR 2-25-61 P. 58
                        Jilka Sextet
                        Remington 199-22
                                2-HF SPRING 1952 P. 45
                        Soloists/Leipzig Gewandhaus Orchestra
                        Philips World Series PHC 9013
                                1-HF 11-66 P. 101
                        Pro Musica Chamber Group
                        Vox PLP 6460
                                1-HF SPRING 1952 P. 45
                        St. James Ensemble
                        Classics for Pleasure CFP 40059
                                1-GR 1-74 P. 1388
                                3-RR 1-74 P. 51
                        Vienna Octet
                        London LLP 1191
                                2-HF 7-55 P. 44
                                1-MH 7/8-55 P. 30
                                1-NYT 8-14-55 P. X8
                                1-SR 5-28-55 P. 48
                Barrows, John
                        Odyssey Y 33309
                Sanders
                        Melos Ensemble of London
                        HMV HQS 1286
                        L'Oiseau Lyre 60015
                                2-AR 7-61 P. 858
                                1-CR 8-61 P. 34
                                2-GR 10-60 P. 220
                                2-HF 6-61 P. 53
                                1-ML 9-60 P. 6
                                1-NR 5-61 P. 14

Berger, Arthur (1912-    )
      Chamber Music
      (Fl/Ob/Cl/Bsn/Hn/Tpt/Hp/Ca/2 Vn/Va/Vc/Db)
                        CRI SD 290
Berkeley, Lennox (1903-    )
      Sextet for Clarinet, Horn & String Quartet, Op. 47
      (1955)
                        Nash Ensemble
                        Hyperion A 66086
              Civil, Alan
                        Argo ZRG 749
Berwald, Franz (1796-1868)
      Quartet in Eb, for Hn, Cl, Bsn, & Pf, Op. 1
              Linder, Albert
                        BIS 44
                        Septet in Bb
                        (Cl/Bsn/Hn/Vn/Va/Vc/Db)
                        Vanguard VSD 71260
                            1-AU 4-80 P. 95
                            2-FF 3/4-80 P. 105
                            1-GR 8-78 P. 348
                            1-ML 7-78 P. 8
                            1-NR 1-80 P. 5
                            1-ST 3-80 P. 96
              Sanders
                        Angel S 36538
                            1-GR 1-69 P. 1013
                            4-HA 6-69 P. 101
                            1-HF 5-69 P. 94
                            1-ML 2-69 P. 12
                            1-NR 4-69 P. 8
                            1-SR 2-22-69 P. 70
              Tomboeck, Walter
                        Decca SXL 6462
Birtwhistle, Harrison (1934-    )
      Tragoedia
      (Fl/Ob/Cl/Hn/Bsn/Hp/2 Vn/Va/Vc)
                        HMV ASD 2333
Boccherini, Luigi
      Sextet in Eb, Op. 41 (Ob/Hn/Bsn/Vn/Va/Db)
              Chapman, Edward
                        Westminister XWN 18052
Bodinus, Sebastian (1700-1760)
      Sonata a 4 in D (Hn/Fl/Vn/ B. C.)
                        Da Camera Magna SM 90149
                            2-FF 9/10-81 P. 83
Brown, Raynor (1912-    )
      Concerto for 2 Pianos, Brass & Percussion
                        WIM 8
                            1-NR 10-73 P. 14
      Five Pieces for Organ, Harp, Brass & Percussion
                        Avant AV 1001
                            2-HF 4-72 P. 104
                            1-NR 9-71 P. 14
                        CRYS S 110

251

Brun, Herbert (1918-    )
        Gestures for 11 Instruments
                Fairchild
                        CRI SD 321
Brunswick, Mark
        Septet in 7 Movements (Fl/Ob/Cl/Bsn/Hn/Va/Vc)
                Froelich
                        CRI 170
                                1-HF 11-63 P. 180
                                2-HSR 11-63 P. 84
                                2-LJ 10-15-63 P. 3830
                                1-MQ 1-64 P. 115
                                1-NR 7-63 P. 12
Buhler
        Grand Sonata in Eb for Piano,
        String Quartet & 2 Horns
                        Consortium Classicum
                        BASF KBF 21195
                                2-ST 1-74 P. 113
Chihara, Paul
        The Beauty of the Rose Is In Its Passing
        (Bsn/2 Hn/Hp/Perc)
                        CRYS S 352
Chou, Wen-Chung (1923-    )
        Pien (1966)
        (2 Fl/Ob/Cl/Bsn/Hn/2 Tpt/2 Trb/4 Perc/Pf)
                Benjamin, Barry
                        CRI SC 251
Danzi, Franz (1763-1826)
        Sinfonia Concertante in Eb (Fl/Ob/Hn/Bsn/Pf)
                Muhlbacher, Ernst
                        Westminister XWN 19100
                                2-HF 12-66 P. 91
                                1-NR 11-66 P. 4
                                1-SR 10-29-66 P. 58
Doppler, Albert Franz (1821-1883)
        L'Oiseau des Bois (4 Hn/Fl)
                Cerminaro, John
                        CRYS S 375
Dugger, Edwin (1940-    )
        Absences & Reunions (1971)
        (Fl/Cl/Hn/Tpt/Trb/2 Vn/Va/Vc/2 Perc)
                Dickow, Robert
                        CRI SD 378
Dvorak, Anton (1841-1904)
        Serenade in d, Op. 44
        (2 Ob/2 Cl/3 Hn/2 Bsn/C Bsn/Vc/Db)
                        Netherlands Wind Ensemble
                        Philips 6500 163
                        Members/Halle Orchestra
                        PYE GSGC 4082
                        Boston BST 1004
                                2-AR 11-58 P. 182
                                2-AU 1-59 P. 50
                                2-HF 2-59 P. 54
                                1-HMR 2-59 P. 74
                                2-NYT 10-26-58 P. X20

252

Dvorak,  Anton  (Cont'd)
     Serenade  in  d,  Op.  44  (Cont'd)
                    Members/Halle  Orchestra  (Cont'd)
                    Parlophone  Odeon  PMB  1001
          Bloom/Mackey/Ernst
                    Columbia  ML  5426
                         1-AR  6-60  P.  817
                         1-AU  7-60  P.  42
                         4-HF  6-60  P.  59
                         1-HSR  10-60  P.  76
                         2-LJ  2-15-61  P.  786
                         1-NR  5-60  P.  6
Endler
     Concerto  in  F
     (Tpt/2  Hn/Ob/Bsn/3  Vn/Tmp/Cont)
                    Pro  Arte  PAD  100
                         2-AR  10-81  P.  48
                         1-CR  9-81  P.  43
                         1-FF  7/8-81  P.  184
                         1-ST  9-81  P.  103
Erickson,  Robert  (1917-    )
     Chamber  Concerto  (1960)
                    Hartt  Chamber  Players
                    CRI  SD  218
Etler,  Alvin  (1913-1973)
     Concerto  for  Brass  Quintet,
     String  Orchestra  &  Percussion
               Birdwell,  Edward
                    American  Brass  Quintet
                    CRI  SD  229
                         1-HF  9-68  P.  84
                         1-HSR  9-68  P.  104
                         1-NR  8-68  P.  14
Fibich,  Zdenek  (1850-1900)
     Quintet  in  D,  Op.  42  (Vn/Vc/Cl/Hn/Pf)  (1892)
               Tylsar,  Zdenek
                    Supraphon  111  1617
                         2-AR  12-76  P.  29
                         1-GR  9-76  P.  437
                         2-ML  8-76  P.  7
                         2-NR  11-76  P.  6
                         1-ST  2-77  P.  117
Forsyth,  Malcolm
     Sagittarius  (Brass  Quintet  &  Orchestra)
               Page,  Graeme
                    Canadian  Brass  Quintet  +
                    National  Arts  Centre  Orchestra
                    CBC  ISM  328
Foss,  Lukas  (1922-    )
     Night  Music  for  Brass  Quintet  &  Orchestra  (1981)
                    Grama  7005
Gabrieli,  Giovanni  (1554-1612)
     Canzoni  for  Brass,  Winds,  Strings  &  Organ
               Tarr  Brass  Ensemble
                    Columbia  MS  7142
                         1-HF  12-68  P.  88
                         1-NR  10-68  P.  16
                         1-NYT  12-22-68  P.  D27

Hackbarth
    Double Concerto (Tpt/Fl/Hn/Ta/2 Fl/Cl/Sax/
Bsn/4 Hn/2 Vc/Pr/Pf)
                Contemporary Chamber Players of
                Illinois
                CRYS S 394
Haines, Edmund (1914-1974)
    Concertino for 7 Solo Instrument & Orchestra
(Fl/Cl/Hn/Tpt/Vn/Va/Vc)
        Garber, Harvey
                CRI SD 153
Handel, G. F. (1685-1759)
    Concerto (2 Ob/Bsn/2 Hn/Stg/Cont)
        Schollmeyer/Roth
                Cantate 047705
                    2-AR 1-65 P. 437
                    2-GR 3-65 P. 422
                    3-NYT 1-3-65 P. X21
    Concerto in F (2 Ob/Bsn/2 Hn/Stg/Cont)
        Spach/Roth
                Vox DL 1080
                    1-GR 9-64 P. 131
                    1-HF 9-64 P. 82
                    2-ML 8-64 P. 7
                    2-NR 6-64 P. 6
Haydn, Franz Joseph (1732-1809)
    (3) Concerti (# 1, 2, & 3)
    (2 Rec/2 Vn/2 Va/Vc/2 Hn)
        Schynol/Fischer
                MHS 1723
                MHS 1703
    Sonata in Eb (2 Hn/Vn/Vc/Pf)
        Baumann/ ?
                Intercord 944-09 K
    Sonata (Divertimento) in Eb (2 Fl/2 Hn/Vc/Pf)
                Eichendorff Wind Group
                MHS 524
                    1-AR 1-64 P. 419
                    1-HF 5-64 P. 78
Haydn, Michael (1737-1806)
    Concerto in D for Tpt, Hns & Stgs
                DG 413260-1 GMF
                Quin 7117
    Quintet in Eb (Vn/Va/Cl/Bsn/Hn)
        Freund, Robert
                Biedermeier Chamber Ensemble
                MHS 861 S
                    2-AR 3-69 P. 562
Heiss, John (1938-    )
    Inventions, Contours & Colors (1973)
        Clark, John
                CRI SD 363
Hindemith, Paul (1895-1963)
    Concert Music for Piano, Brass & 2 Harps, Op. 49
                Philip Jones Brass Ensemble
                London LDR 71053

Hindemith, Paul (Cont'd)
    Concert Music for Piano (Cont'd)
        Michalec, V.
                Prague Chamber Harmony Ensemble
                Supraphon SUA 10475
    Concert Music for Strings & Brass, Op. 50
                Angel SZ 37536
                Columbia MS 6579
                Seraphim 60005
                DG 2530 246
                    1-GR 11-72 P. 910
                    1-HF 12-72 P. 85
                    1-MJ 12-73 P. 64
                    1-NR 11-72 P. 4
                    2-R&R 11-72 P. 50
                Philip Jones Brass Ensemble
                London LDR 71053
    Octet (Cl/Bsn/Hn/Vn/2 Va/Vc/Db)
        Barrows, John
                Fine Arts Quartet/
                New York Woodwind Ensemble
                Concert Disc CS 218
                    1-HF 1-61 P. 68
                    1-NR 12-60 P. 11
                    1-SR 12-31-60 P. 40
    Septet for Wind Instruments
    (Fl/Ob/Cl/Bsn/B/Cl/Tpt/Hn
                Clarion Wind Ensemble
                Golden Crest GC 4188
        Stefek, Miraslav
                Supraphon 50582
Holmboe, Vagn (1909-    )
    Concerto II for 2 Horns, Trumpet & Strings (1948)
                MGM E 3375
Hummel (1778-1837)
    Septet in d, Op. 74 (Pf/Fl/Ob/Hn/Va/Vc/Db)
                Melos Ensemble of London
                L'Oiseau Lyre OL 290
                    1-GR 5-66 P. 562
                    1-ML 5-66 P. 7
                    1-NR 11-66 P. 8
                    1-NYT 10-30-66 P. D20
                    1-SR 10-29-66 P. 62
        Koch, Franz
                Westminister 50-18
                    1-AR 8-50 P. 404
                    2-CR 2-54 P. 89
                    4-GR 2-54 P. 342
                    1-GS 9-50 P. 4
                    2-LJ 10-1-50 P. 1683
                Westminister 9034
                    2-AR 3-64 P. 612
        Meyendorf, Werner
                MHS 1269

Hummel (Cont'd)
        Septet in d, Op. 74 (Cont'd)
                Sanders (Cont'd)
                        L'Oiseau Lyre OL 290
                                1-GR 5-66 P. 562
                                1-ML 5-66 P. 7
                                1-NR 11-66 P. 8
                                1-NYT 10-30-66 P. D20
                                1-SR 10-29-66 P. 62
Husa, Karl (1921-    )
        Serenade, Woodwind Quintet with
        Strings, Harp & Xylophone
                        CRI SD 261
                                1-AR 5-71 P. 562
                                1-NR 5-71 P. 2
                                2-ST 10-71 P. 106
Huszar
        Musica Concertante
        (Pi/Fl/Cl/B.Cl/Sax/Hn/Tpt/Trb/Ti/Perc/Pf)
                        Hungaroton SLPX 12178
                                2-FF 9/10-82 P. 462
                                2-NR 8-82 P. 15
Ireland
        Sextet (Cl/Hn/2 Vn/Va/Vc)
                        Sanders
                        Lyrita SRCS 59
Janacek (1854-1928)
        Concertino (1925)
        (Pf/Cl/Bsn/Hn/2 Vn/Va)
                        Sanders
                        HMV ASD 2344
                        Tillotson, Brooks
                        Desto D 427; DST 6427
Kalkbrenner, F. M. (1785-1849)
        Quintet in a for Clarinet, Horn, Cello,
        Double Bass & Piano
                        Howard, Howard
                        Turnabout 34506
                                1-HF 9-73 P. 109
                                2-NR 9-73 P. 9
                                1-ST 10-73 P. 87
Korf, Anthony (1951-    )
        A Farewell for Wind & Brass Instruments (1980)
                        CRI S 499
Kreutzer, Conradin (1780-1849)
        Grand Septet in Eb, Op. 62
                        Decca SXL 6462
                        Nash Ensemble
                        MHS 4521
                                1-GR 7-81 P. 167
                                2-MG 9-81 P. 12
Lachner
        Nonet in f
        (Fl/Ob/Cl/Bsn/Hn/Vn/Va/Vc/Db)
                        Harmonia Mundi EA 23 143

Laderman, Ezra
        Theme, Variations & Finale
        (Fl/Cl/Hn/Bsn/Vn/Va/Vc/Db)
                        CRI 130
                        4-SR 5-28-60 P. 66
Lambro
        Music for Wind, Brass, & Percussion
                        CRYS S 861
Martinu, Bohuslav
        Quartet for Clarinet, Horn, Cello & Drum in C
                Sturmann
                        Da Camera Magna SM 92421
                        1-FF 3/4-83 P. 200
Matej, Josef
        Triple Concerto for Trumpet, Horn,
        Trombone & Chamber Orchestra
                Petr, Milos
                        Panton 11 0456
Mayer, W.
        Essay for Brass & Winds (1954)
                        New York Brass & Woodwind Ensemble
                        CRI 185
                                1-AR 11-64 P. 255
                                1-HF 3-65 P. 96
                                2-LJ 2-1-64 P. 622
                                1-MA 9-64 P. 49
McCauley, William
        Concerto Grosso (Brass Quintet & Orchestra)
                Page, Graeme
                        Canadian Brass Quintet +
                        Hamilton Philharmonic Orchestra
                        CBC ISM 264
McPhee, Colin (1901-1964)
        Concerto for Piano
        (Pf/Pc/Fl/Ob/Cl/Bsn/Hn/Tpt/Trb)
                        CRI SD 315
Meale, Richard (1932-    )
        Las Alboradas for Hn, Vn, Fl & Pf (1963)
                        Australian World Record Club A 601
Mihalovici, Marcel
        Study in 2 Parts, Op. 64
        (Piano, Winds, Brass Celeste & Perc.)
                        MHS 1405 H
                        2-ML 2-73 P. 3
Moss, Lawrence (1927-    )
        Symphonies for Brass Quintet & Chamber Orchestra
                        Annapolis Brass Quintet
                        ORS 79362
                                1-AR 7/8-80 P. 27
                                1-FF 5/6-80 P. 95
                                2-NR 5-80 P. 15
Mozart, W. A. (1756-1791)
        Divertimento # 2 In D, K 131
        (Fl/Ob/Bsn/4 Hn/Strings)
                        Columbia D 3 M 33261

Mozart, W. A. (Cont'd)
        Divertimento # 2 In D, K 131 (Cont'd)
                Bloom/Waas/Morris/Angelucci
                        Columbia MS 6968
                                2-NR 6-67 P. 8
        Sinfonia Concertante in Eb, K 297b
        (Ob/Cl/Bsn/Hn/Strings)
                        4 DG 274 0231
                        Chamber Orchestra of Vienna State Opera
                        & Wind Group of VPO
                                Westminister 50-20
                                        2-AR 10-50 P. 51
                                        2-GR 11-54 P. 247
                                        1-GS 11-50 P. 6
                                        1-LJ 1-15-51 P. 132
                                        2-NR 3-51 P. 6
                                        2-SR 3-51-50 P. 76
                        English Chamber Orchestra
                                Angel RL 32119
                        Orpheus Chamber Orchestra
                                Nonesuch 79009
                        Pro Musica Orchestra, Stuttgart
                                Vox PLP 7320
                                        3-GR 5-53 P. 320
                                        1-GS 4-52 P. 6
                                        1-ML 5-53 P. 7
                                        2-NYT 2-24-52 P. X8
                                        2-SR 4-26-52 P. 55
                        Vienna Philharmonic Wind Group
                        & Chamber Orchestra of VSO
                                Westminister 18041
                                        1-MQ 4-56 P. 272
                Barboteu, Georges
                        Erato STU 70516
                        MHS 1041
                                1-AR 2-71 P. 378
                Baumann, Hermann
                        Vox PL 14180
                                2-AR 4-65 P. 732
                                2-HF 4-65 P. 86
                                2-NR 2-65 P. 3
                                1-SR 5-29-65 P. 56
                        Turnabout TVS 34416
                                2-GR 10-73 P. 686
                                2-ML 10-73 P. 3
                Brain, Dennis
                        Angel 35098
                                1-CR 11-54 P. 69
                                1-GR 11-54 P. 247
                                1-HF 12-54 P. 67
                                2-ML 12-54 P. 9
                                1-NR 2-55 P. 3
                                2-NYT 12-5-54 P. X14
                Civil, Alan
                        Philips 6500 380
                                1-AMR 2-74 P. 24

Mozart, W. A.   (Cont'd)
    Sinfonia Concertante in Eb, K 297b (Cont'd)
        Civil, Alan (Cont'd)
            Philips 6500 380 (Cont'd)
              1-GR 12-74 P. 1137
              1-HF 4-74 P. 100
              1-MJ 2-74 P. 42
              1-NR 1-74 P. 6
              1-R&R 10-74 P. 50
        Coursier, Gilbert
            L'Oiseau Lyre LON 50006
              3-AR 8-54 P. 400
              3-CR 2-54 P. 85
              1-HF 11-54 P. 54
              1-MA 10-54 P. 18
        Friedrich, Adam
            Hungaroton SLPX 12264
              1-FF 5/6-82 P. 177
        Fournier, Andre
            Nonesuch 71068
              1-AR 1-66 P. 456
              1-GR 12-65 P. 296
              1-HF 3-66 P. 88
              2-ML 11-65 P. 7
              2-NR 10-65 P. 2
              1-NYT 11-21-65 P. X19
        Hauptmann, Norbert
          Members/Berlin Philharmonic Orchestra
            3 Angel S 3783
              3-HF 10-72 P. 102
              2-ML 6-72 P. 6
              3-SR 7-15-72 P. 37
              1-ST 10-72 P. 133
        Hogner
            Deutsche Grammophon 2740 231
              2-FF 5/6-81 P. 111
              2-GR 12-80 P. 836
              3-MG 3-81 P. 30
        James, Ifor
          English Chamber Orchestra
            Angel S 36582
              3-NR 8-69 P. 5
              3-NYT 6-15-69 P. D29
              3-ST 9-69 P. 112
        Jones, Mason
            Camden 213
              2-NYT 6-19-55 P. X15
            Columbia MS 6061
              1-AR 2-60 P. 444
              1-HF 9-59 P. 68
              1-HMR 9-59 P. 68
              1-LJ 1-15-60 P. 228
              1-NR 8-59 P. 7
        Kasprzok, Alfred
            MHS 4739 H
        Klinko, Albert
            Pelca PSRL 40 007

Mozart, W. A.   (Cont'd)
        Sinfonia Concertante in Eb, K 297b (Cont'd)
            Lexutt
                        Harmonia Mundi 065 99801
                            2-FF 9/10-80 P. 64
                            1-ML 11-79 P. 6
                Molnar, Joseph
                        Westminminster XWN 19036
                            1-AM 8-63 P. 115
                            2-HF 9-63 P. 89
                            2-HSR 10-63 P. 86
                            2-NR 7-63 P. 4
                            2-SR 6-29-63 P. 46
                Muhlbacher, Ernst
                        Remington 199-54

                Seifert, Gerd
                        DGG LPM 39156
                            1-AR 2-67 P. 506
                            1-HF 11-66 P. 119
                            1-HSR 1-67 P. 86
                            1-ML 2-67 P. 5
                            2-NR 1-67 P. 3
                            1-SR 11-26-66 P. 72
                Stefek, Miroslav
                        Crossroads 22-16-0035
                            1-AU 12-66 P. 40
                            2-HF 11-66 P. 119
                            3-NR 11-66 P. 7
                            2-NYT 9-18-66 P. D20
                            2-SR 10-29-66 P. 60
                        Supraphon SUA 10709
                            1-AU 12-66 P. 40
                            2-HF 11-66 P. 119
                            3-NR 11-66 P. 7
                            2-NYT 9-18-66 P. D20
                            2-SR 10-29-66 P. 60
                Tarjani, Ferenc
                        Qualiton LPX 1265
                            2-GR 7-67 P. 64
                            2-ML 5-67 P. 3
                            2-NYT 9-10-67 P. D29
Nielson, Carl (1865-1931)
        Serenata in Vano (Cl/Bsn/Hn/Vc/Db) (1914)
                        Chandos ABR 1003
                        Lyrichord LYR 7156
                Sorensen, H. C.
                        Turnabout TV 34109 S
                            2-AR 7-67 P. 1031
                            2-HF 10-67 P. 150
                            2-HSR 11-67 P. 110
Nisle, Johann Georg (1731-1788)
        Septet in Ab
        (Fl/Cl/Bsn/Hn/Vn/Va/Vc)
                        BASF BAC 21189
                            2-GR 11-73 P. 942
                            2-NR 4-74 P. 4

Overton, Hall (1920-1972)
    Pulsations (Fl/Cl/Bsn/Hn/Tpt/Trb/
    Vn/Vc/Db/Hp/Pf/Perc)
        Jolley, David
               CRI SD 298
Perkins, John MacIvor (1935-    )
    Music for 13 Players (Fl/Ob/Cl/Bsn/Hn/
    Tpt/Vn/Va/Vc/Hp/Pf/2 Perc)
               CRI SD 232
Piston, Walter (1894-1976)
    Concerto for String Quartet, Wind Instru-
    ments & Percussion
               CRI SD 248 (78)
Ratner, Leonard (1916-    )
    Serenade (Ob/Hn/2 Vn/Va/Vc)
               Music Library 7023
Rheinberger, Josef
    Concerto for Organ, 2 Trumpets, 2 Horns,
    Timpani & Strings
               Columbia M 32297
                    2-GR 8-74 P. 364
                    1-HF 12-73 P. 109
                    2-MJ 11-73 P. 8
                    1-NR 11-73 P. 11
                    1-R&R 9-74 P. 60
                    1-ST 12-73 P. 136
Rochberg, George
    Chamber Symphony (Fl/Cl/Bsn/Tpt/Hn/Trb/Vn/Va/Vc)
        Hunt
               Desto DC 6444
                    1-HF 5-76 P. 90
                    2-ST 7-76 P. 111
Rodriguez, Robert Xavier (1946-    )
    Lyric Variations for Oboe, 2 Horns & Strings
               Orion 74138
                    2-NR 7-74 P. 9
                    1-ST 10-74 P. 132
Schobert, Johann (1740-1767)
    Sinfonie, F. Op. 9 # 3 (2 Hn/Vn/Pf)
        Oheim/Wunder
               MHS 1421
                    1-GR 5-68 P. 596
                    1-ML 5-68 P. 7
    Sinfonie, Eb, Op. 10 # 1 (2 Hn/Vn/Pf)
        Oheim/Wunder
               MHS 1421
                    1-GR 5-68 P. 596
                    1-ML 5-68 P. 7
Schubert, Franz (1797-1828)
    Minuet & Finale for Wind Octet
    (Cl/Bsn/Hn/2 Vn/Va/Vc/Db)
            Netherlands Wind Ensemble
             Philips 6500 163

Schubert, Franz (Cont'd)
    Octet in F, Op. 166
    (Cl/Bsn/Hn/2 Vn/Va/Vc/Db)
                    Berlin Philharmonic Chamber Music Ens.
                        Capitol EMI G 7112
                            2-GR 4-58 P. 454
                            1-HF 10-58 P. 76
                            1-HMR 12-58 P. 80
                            2-ML 4-58 P. 10
                            1-NYT 9-28-58 P. X21
                            2-SR 9-27-58 P. 55
                    Berlin Philharmonic Chamber Music Ens.
                        Decca DL 9669
                            2-AR 6-53 P. 327
                            2-HA 8-53 P. 104
                            2-HF 7/8-53 P. 52
                            2-NR 8-53 P. 7
                            2-NYT 6-14-53 P. X6
                            2-SR 6-27-53 P. 58
                    Berlin Philharmonic Octet
                        DG 139 102
                            2-AU 4-66 P. 54
                            1-HF 12-65 P. 104
                            1-HSR 2-66 P. 102
                            1-NR 2-66 P. 7
                            2-SR 11-27-65 P. 66
                    Fine Arts Quartet/
                    New York Woodwind Quintet
                        Everest 6082
                            1-AR 2-64 P. 525
                            2-HF 11-63 P. 102
                            2-NR 10-63 P. 7
                    Melos Ensemble
                        Angel S 36539
                            1-GR 11-68 P. 687
                            1-HF 12-68 P. 96
                            1-ML 12-68 P. 9
                            3-NR 12-68 P. 9
                            1-NYT 2-23-69 P. D26
                            1-ST 1-69 P. 106
                    Munich Octet
                        Turnabout TV 34152
                            3-AR 8-68 P. 1123
                            2-GR 2-69 P. 1172
                    Stradivari Records Chamber Society
                        Stradivari 603
                            2-AR 9-51 P. 22
                            2-GS 12-51 P. 4
                            3-LJ 2-1-52 P. 205
                            3-OR 11-51 P. 9
                    Vienna Octet
                        London CS 6051
                            1-AM 2-59 P. 113
                            4-AR 2-59 P. 410
                            1-DI 2-59 P. 140
                            2-GR 12-58 P. 308
                            3-ML 12-58 P. 11
                            2-SR 12-27-58 P. 40

Schubert, Franz (Cont'd)
    Octet in F, Op. 166 (Cont'd)
                Vienna Octet
                    London LLP 1049
                        1-AR 2-55 P. 204
                        2-CR 1-55 P. 106
                        1-ET 2-55 P. 61
                        1-GR 2-55 P. 400
                        2-HF 1-55 P. 60
                Octet/Vienna Symphony Orchestra
                    Vox PLP 6970
                        1-CR 12-51 P. 31
                        2-GS 12-51 P. 4
                        4-NR 4-52 P. 8
                        3-OR 11-51 P. 9
        Barrows, John
            Fine Arts Quartet/
            New York Woodwind Quintet
                    Concert Disc CS 220
                        1-AR 8-61 P. 956
                        1-HF 9-61 P. 101
                        1-HSR 9-61 P. 76
                        1-NR 6-61 P. 7
                        1-SR 10-28-61 P. 45
        Coursier, Gilbert
                    Monitor 2110
                        2-AR 7-67 P. 1036
                        1-HSR 7-67 P. 83
                        1-NR 5-67 P. 4
        Freidberg, Gottfried von
                    Westminister 50-94
                        1-CR 1-52 P. 31
                        2-GR 1-54 P. 292
                        2-GS 12-51 P. 4
                        2-LJ 2-1-52 P. 205
                        3-ML 1-54 P. 17
        Meyendorf, Werner
                    BASF BAC 3099
        Palm, Kurt
                Berlin Octet
                    Eterna 826 443
        Routch, Robert
                    MHS 4467 Y
        Shapiro, Jacob
                    Angel 35362
                        3-HF 2-57 P. 73
                        3-MH 11/12-56 P. 45
                        1-NYT 11-25-56 P. X15
                        2-SR 11-24-56 P. 52
        Tuckwell, Barry
                    RCA ARL 1 1047
                        2-CR 11-75 P. 36
                        2-GR 2-76 P. 1356
                        3-HF 11-75 P. 120
                        1-NR 11-75 P. 7

Schumann, Robert (1810-1856)
Andante & Variations for 2 Pianos,
2 Cellos & Horn, Op. 46
Barrows, John
Music Masters MM 20007
2-NR 12-81 P. 14
1-ST 4-82 P. 97
Vox VLP 6050
2-GS 9-50 P. 5
1-LJ 10-15-50 P. 1849
1-NR 5-51 P. 7
1-SR 7-8-50 P. 38
Vox PL 7740
2-AR 9-53 P. 19
2-GS 1-53 P. 8
4-NR 5-54 P. 6
Tombock, Walter
Turnabout TV 34204 S
1-HF 9-68 P. 86
2-NR 4-68 P. 7
4-NYT 6-30-68 P. D22
Tuckwell, Barry
London CS 6411
1-AR 5-65 P1 815
1-GR 11-64 P. 233
1-HF 4-65 P. 90
1-HSR 5-65 P. 68
1-ML 11-64 P. 10
1-NR 6-65 P. 13
Shifrin, Seymour (1926-      )
Serenade for 5 Instruments (Ob/Cl/Hn/Va/Pf)
Cecil, Robert
CRI 123
2-AR 11-58 P. 182
4-HF 9-58 P. 72
2-NR 9-58 P. 9
4-NYT 9-14-58 P. X19
1-SR 7-26-58 P. 42
Spohr, Ludwig (1784-1859)
Nonette in F, Op. 31
Stradivari Records Chamber Ensemble
Stradivari 609
2-AR 8-52 P. 378
1-CU 9-52 P. 446
1-GS 7-52 P. 6
1-HF 11/12-52 P. 56
2-NYT 7-13-52 P. X6
1-SR 8-9-52 P. 45
Members/Vienna Octet
London LLP 710
1-AR 9-53 P. 23
1-CR 5-53 P. 94
1-GR 5-53 P. 322
1-GS 7-53 P. 5
1-ML 5-53 P. 8

Spohr, Ludwig (Cont'd)
    Nonette in F, Op. 31 (Cont'd)
        Barrows, John
            Fine Arts Quartet/
            New York Woodwind Quintet
                Concert Disc CS 201
                    2-AR 5-59 P. 630
                    4-HF 6-59 P. 74
                    2-HMR 7-59 P. 54
                    4-NR 7-59 P. 7
                    4-NYT 4-19-59 P. X15
                    2-SR 4-25-59 P. 50
          Pigneguy/Halstead   ?
            Nash Ensemble
                CRD 1054
          Seiffert/Klier    ?
                Philips SAL 3709
          Veleba
                Decca SDD 416
                    1-GR 7-74 P. 224
                    1-R&R 7-74 P. 50
    Octet in E, Op. 32
    (Cl/2 Hn/2 Vn/Va/Vc/Db)
            Soloists/Berlin Philharmonic Orchestra
                Philips 657 0884; 731 0884
                    1-GR 10-82 P. 450
                    1-HFN 12-82 P. 103
          Pigneguy/Halstead
            Nash Ensemble
                CRD 1054
          Veleba/Nitsch
                Decca SDD 256
    Septet in a (Pf/Fl/Cl/Bsn/Hn/Vn/Vc)
            Nash Ensemble
                CRD 1099; 4099
Stamitz, Carl (1745-1801)
    Horn Quartet in D, Op. 8/1
    (Hn/Fl or Ob/Vn/Vc)
          Coursier, Gilbert
                Nonesuch 71125
                    2-HF 11-66 P. 162
                    1-NR 9-66 P. 6
                    1-SR 9-26-66 P. 76
    Horn Quartet in F, Op. 8/3
    (Hn/Fl or Ob/Vn/Vc)
          Coursier, Gilbert
                Nonesuch 71125
                    2-HF 11-66 P. 162
                    1-NR  9-66 P. 6
                    1-SR  9-26-66 P. 76
Stoelzel, G. H.
    Sonata in F (Vn/Vc or Bsn/Ob/Hn/Pf)
          Baumann, Hermann
                Intercord 944-09 K

Stravinsky, Igor (1882-1971)
    Septet (Pf/Cl/Bsn/Hn/Vn/Va/Vc)
        Barrows, John
            Columbia CML 5107
                1-AR 9-56 P. 2
                1-CR 10-56 P. 35
                1-HF 12-56 P. 96
                2-LJ 9-1-56 P. 1888
                1-MH 7/8-56 P. 31
                1-SR 9-29-56 P. 44
        Creech, Robert
            (Canadian) Ace of Diamonds SDD 2162
Telemann, Georg Philipp (1681-1767)
    Concerto in D for 3 Horns, Violin, Strings &
    Continuo
            Da Camera Magna SM 91039
                3-FF 1/2-80 P. 155
                3-FF 55/6-80 P. 164
        Stagliano/Berv/  ?
            Westminister MCA 1422
                2-FF 5/6-81 P. 170
                1-NR 12-80 P. 6
    Concerto in F for Horn, Flute, Bassoon, & Harpsichord
        Pottle, Ralph
            Boston Baroque Ensemble
            Cambridge CRS 3825
                2-AMR 8-73 P. 102
                1-HF 9-73 P. 5
                1-NR 7-73 P. 5
                2-ST 8-73 P. 98
    Concerto, Vn Concertino,
    Fls, Obs, Tpts, Hns, Strings & Cont.
            DGG Archive 198 467
    Ouverture in D (2 Hn/2 Ob/Stg)
            Argo ZRG 836
                1-GR 2-76 P. 1350
                1-HF 10-76 P. 122
                1-ML 2-76 P. 4
                2-NR 6-76 P. 5
    Ouverture in D (2 Hn/2 Ob/Bsn/Stg/Cont)
        Barboteu/Coursier
            Nonesuch H 71124
                1-AR 1-67 P. 424
                1-CR 10-66 P. 17
                2-GR 4-67 P. 526
                3-HF 12-66 P. 110
                1-ML 2-67 P. 4
                1-NR 9-66 P. 6
    Ouverturensuite in F
    (Fls/Obs/4 Hn/Strings/Cont)
            Eterna 8 27 450
    Suite for 2 Horns, 2 Oboes, Bassoon, Strings & Cont
            Da Camera Magna SM 91039
                3-FF 1/2-80 P. 155
                3-FF 5/6-80 P. 164

Telemann, Georg Philipp (Cont'd)
        Suite for 4 Horns, 2 Oboes & Strings in F
                Spach/Roth/Schollmeyer/Balser
                        Vox DL 1080
                                1-GR 9-64 P. 131
                                1-HF 9-64 P. 82
                                2-ML 8-64 P. 7
                                2-NR 6-64 P. 6
                        Turnabout TV 34078
                                2-LJ 5-1-67 P. 1817
                                1-SR 1-28-67 P. 66
                                2-ML 8-64 P. 7
                                2-NR 6-64 P. 6
        Suite for 4 Horns, 2 Oboes, Bassoon,
        Strings & Continuo
                Klecha/Machata/Kunth/Roth
                        Da Camera Magna SM 91039
                                3-FF 1/2-80 P. 155
                                3-FF 5/6-80 P. 164
Thiele, Siegfried
        Octet (Cl/Bsn/Hn/2 Hn/2 Vn/Va/Vc/Db)
                        Eterna 8 25 741
Thomson, Virgil (1896-    )
        Sonata da Chiesa (Va/Cl/Tpt/Hn/Trb) (1926)
                Ingraham, Paul
                        CRI 207
                                4-AM 10-67 P. 134
                                1-AR 8-67 P. 1104
                                1-NYT 4-30-67 P. D26
Thorne, Francis
        Simultaneities for Brass Quintet,
        Amplified Guitar & Perc.
                        American Brass Quintet
                        Serenus SRS 12035
                                3-NR 11-74 P. 6
Townsend, Douglas
        Chamber Concerto # 3 for Flute, Horn,
        Piano & Strings
                        MHS 4223 L
Varese, Edgard
        Octandre (Fl/Cl/Ob/Bsn/Tpt/Hn/Trb/Db)
                        Die Reihe Ensemble
                        Candide CE 31028
                                1-GR 6-71 P. 46
                                3-HF 12-71 P. 110
                                2-ML 8-71 P. 3
Villa-Lobos (1887-1959)
        Fantasy for Saxophone, 3 Horns & String Orchestra
                        DG 2530209
                                1-GR 11-82 P. 580
Vivaldi, Antonio (1878-1741)
        Concerto in F (2 Ob/Bsn/2 Hn/Vn)
                Brown/Davis
                        Argo ZRG 839
                                1-GR 11-77 P. 853
                                1-HF 8-78 P. 90
                                1-ML 11-77 P. 5
                                1-ST 10-78 P. 169

Vivaldi, Antonio (Cont'd)
    Concerto in F, P. 267
    (2 Ob/Bsn/2 Hn/Vn + Strings & Cont.)
                    MHS 3312
    Concerto in g, P. 359
    (3 Ob/Bsn/2 Hn/Vn + Strings & Cont.)
                    MHS 3312
    Concerto in F for Viola d'Amore,
    2 Oboes, Bassoon & 2 Horns
                    RCA LSC 7065
            Eger/Corrado
                    Odyssey 32-16-0137
                        2-AR 5-68 P. 839
                        1-NR 2-68 P. 6
Vogel, Johann Cristoph
    Symphonie Concertante # 1 in Bb
    (Cl/Bsn/2 Ob/2 Hn/Strings)
                    Acanta 40 23140
                        2-FF 11/12-83 P. 336
Weigl, Vally (1899-1983)
    Echoes from Poems (Hn/Cl/Vn/Pf)
            Gordon
                    MHS 3880
                        4-AR 4-79 P. 46
Weinberg, Henry (1931-    )
    Cantus Commemorabilis (2 Fl/2 Ob/2 Cl/
    Hn/Tpt/Trb/Vn/Vc/Db/Pf/Perc)
            Ondracek, Paul
                Contemporary Chamber Players
                of the University of Chicago
                CRI SD 245
Werder, Felix (1922-    )
    Music for Horn, Clarinet & String Trio (1959)
            White, Roy
                (Australian) W & G WGA 1
Wilson, George Balch (1927-    )
    Concatenations (Fl/Cl/B.Cl/Hn/Tpt/Trb/
    Va/Vc/Db/Perc/Acc/E.Gui)
            Holden, Thomas
                University of Illinois
                Contemporary Chamber Players
                CRI SD 271
Wolf-Ferrari, Ermanno (1876-1948)
    Idillio-Concertino for Oboe, 2 Horns
    & String Orchestra (1932)
                    Coronet S 1510
                        4-NR 2-70 P. 8
Wolpe, Stephan
    Piece for Trumpet & 7 Instruments
    (Cl/Bsn/Hn/2 Vn/Vc/Db)
                    CRYS S 352
Wyner
    Serenade for 7 Instruments (Pf/Fl/Hn/Tpt/Trb/Va/Vc)
            Froelich, Ralph
                    CRI 141
                        4-HF 10-61 P. 101
                        2-HSR 8-61 P. 67

Ytterhus, Rolv
      Sextet (Tpt/Hn/Vn/Db/Pf/Perc)
            Benjamin, Barry
                  CRI SD 321
                     2-HF 2-75 P. 108
                     1-NR 9-74 P. 6

# Composer Index

CO

### COMPOSER INDEX

Berlioz, Hector pp. 82, 102
Bernstein, Leonard pp. 7,102
Bertali, Antonio p. 102
Berwald, Franz p. 251
Besozzi, Carlo p. 199
Beversdorf, Thomas p. 7
Beyer, Frederick p. 67
Bialosky p. 199
Bibalo, Antonio p. 199
Birtwhistle, Harrison p. 251
Blanc, Allan p. 7
Blank, Allan p. 102
Blanton p. 102
Bliss p. 102
Blumenfeld, Harold p. 199
Boccherini, Luigi pp. 76,251
Boda, John p. 102
Bodinus, Sebastian pp.50,251
Boehner, Johann Ludwig p. 76
Bogar p. 102
Boismortier, Joseph p. 58
Bonelli, A. p. 103
Borodin p. 7
Borowski, Felix p. 199
Boyce p. 103
Bozay, Attila p. 199
Bozza, Eugene pp.7,103-104,
199-200
Brade, W. p. 104
Bradford p. 7
Brahms, Johannes pp.7, 67-70
82, 104, 200
Brant, Henry p. 104
Braun, Yeheztel p. 7
Brehm, Alvin p. 105
Bright, Houston p. 200
Britten, Benjamin pp.82-84
Brown, Rayner pp. 105, 251
Brubeck, Dave p. 105
Bruckner, Anton p. 59
Brun, Herbert p. 252
Brunswick, Mark p. 252
Bubalo, Rudolf p. 105
Bucchi, Annibale p. 7
Bucchi, Valentino p. 7
Buhler p. 252
Bujanovski, V. pp.8,59,84
Buonamente, Giovanni p. 106
Busser, Henri p. 8
Buxtehude, Dietrich pp.106,
200
Byrd, William p. 106

Cabezon,Antonio de pp.106-7
Cable p. 107
Cabus, P. p. 107
Calvert, Morley p. 107
Cambini, Giovanni pp.200-201

Campo, Frank pp.107,201
Cantin, Jules p. 59
Cantrell p. 201
Capuzzi p. 107
Carlstedt, Jan p. 201
Carr, Gordon p. 108
Carter, Elliott pp. 108,
201-202
Casadeus, Robert p. 202
Ceccavossi, Domenico p. 8
Chabrier, Emmanuel pp.8,108
Chailly, Luciano p. 8
Chance, Nancy p. 108
Charpentier, Jacques p. 8
Chase, Allen p. 108
Chavez, Carlos pp. 70,202
Cherney, Brian p. 202
Cheetham, John p. 108
Cherubini, Luigi pp.8-9,
108,109
Chevreuille, Raymond p. 9
Chihara, Paul p. 252
Childs, Barney p. 109
Chou, Wen-Chung pp. 202,252
Civil, Alan p. 109
Clarke, Jeremiah p. 109
Clerisse, Robert p. 9
Coleman, Ornette p. 202
Colomer, B. M. p. 202
Cooke, Arnold p. 9
Cooper, John p. 109
Copland, Aaron p. 110
Corelli, Arcangelo p. 9
Corette, Michel p. 10
Cortes, Ramiro p. 203
Cortese, Luigi p. 10
Couperin, Francois p. 110
Cowell, Henry p. 203
Crosley p. 110
Crusell, Bernhard p. 70
Cui, Cesar p. 10
Custer, Arthur pp. 110, 213
Czerny, Carl p. 10
Daetwyler, Jean p. 10
Dahl, Ingolf pp. 10, 110-1,
203
Damase, Jean-Michel pp. 10,
203
Danzi, Franz pp.10-11, 71,
204-206, 252
Dauprat, Louis Francois pp.
59, 65
David, Gyula p. 11
Davidovsky, Mario p. 206
Debussy, Claude pp. 111-
112, 206
Deisenroth, Friedrich p. 59
De Jong p. 112

271

COMPOSER INDEX

# Hornist Index

Abraham, Rober    p. 35
Afanasiev, Boris pp.16,31,
    39,40-42,62,224,236
Albrecht, Kenneth    p. 39
Alfing, Heinrich    p. 55
Alfing, Konrad    p. 55
Alonge, Raymond pp.176,222
Altmann    p. 76
Amram, David    p. 248
Anderson, Paul pp.91,96,103,
    139,147,151-152,155,
    177,186
Andrus, Brice pp.88,95,106,
    157,159
Angelucci, Ernani    p. 258
Angus, David    p. 40
Arnold, Karl pp.17,18,217,
    235,237
Auerbach    p. 51

Baar, Roland    p. 59
Baccelli, Umberto    pp.51,56
Baker, Julian pp.93,130,138,
    152,199
Bakkegard    p. 73
Balser, Alfred    p. 267
Barboteu, Georges pp.4,19,
    22,25,31,40,45-46,48,51,
    54,56,61,65,72,100,150,
    159,161,166,170,176,198,
    258,266
Barnett, George pp.73,95,
    127,145,149
Barrington, Wayne pp. 58-59,
    60,63
Barrows, John pp.20,34,41,
    49,67,73-74,77,192,194,
    197-198,201,203,205,207,
    215,217,222,227,231,233,
    235-236,238,240,242-248,
    250,255,263-266

Battey, David pp.109,131,
    139,158,169
Baumann, Hermann pp.5,7,9-
    11,13,16,18,19,22-26,29,
    34-40,42-44,46-49,52-53,
    55-58,60-61,65,67,73,75-
    77,196-197,213,254,258,
    265
Becknell, Nancy pp.98,150
Beers    pp.197,224,229
Belfrage, Bengt pp.6,14,22-
    23,48
Bengtsson, Rolf    p. 237
Benjamin, Barry pp.66,115,
    116,252,269
Bentley    pp.130,155
Berenek, Rudolf pp.52,61,
    234-235
Berger, Hans    pp.52,80
Berger, Michael pp.90,119,
    166
Berger, Othmar    p. 52
Berger, Roland pp.31,55,59
Berges, Michel pp.61,198,
    239
Bernard, (Paul)    p.29
Berv, Arthur pp.46,50,51,
    55,63,72,81,266
Beversdorf, Thomas    p.7
Binstock, Paul pp.52-53,58-
    60,63,75
Birdwell, Edward pp.72,84,
    100,105,110,113-115,129,
    151, 158-159,167,169-170,
    179, 181,186,253
Bloom, Myron pp.5,15,40,44,
    68,85,120,122-124,194,
    253,258
Boehner    p. 62
Boen, Jonathan pp.100,116,
    131,137,151,156

# Brass Ensemble Index

# Woodwind Ensemble Index

# Mixed Ensemble Index

ABOUT THE COMPILER

MICHAEL HERNON, Associate Professor of Music at the University of Tennessee at Martin, is a specialist in Medieval and Renaissance music and French horn pedagogy and literature.